Neoliberalising Old Age

Governments are encouraging later-life working and state pension ages are being raised. There is also a growing debate on intergenerational equity and on ageism/age discrimination. John Macnicol, one of Europe's leading academic analysts of old age and ageing, examines the effect of neoliberalism on the recent ageing and social policy agenda in the UK and the USA. He argues that the demographic and economic impulses behind recent policy changes are in fact less important than the effect of neoliberalism as an ideology, which has caused certain key problems to be defined in a particular way. The book outlines past theories of old age and examines pensions reform, the debate on life expectancy gains, the causes of retirement, the idea of intergenerational equity, the current debate on ageism/age discrimination and the likely human consequences of raising state pension ages.

JOHN MACNICOL is Visiting Professor in Social Policy at the London School of Economics and Political Science. He has published extensively on social policy, particularly the history of social policy. His previous books include *Age Discrimination: An Historical and Contemporary Analysis* (Cambridge University Press, 2006), *Paying for the Old: Old Age and Social Welfare Provision* (editor, 2000) and *The Politics of Retirement in Britain, 1878–1948* (Cambridge University Press, 1998).

Neoliberalising Old Age

John Macnicol

CAMBRIDGE
UNIVERSITY PRESS

CAMBRIDGE
UNIVERSITY PRESS

University Printing House, Cambridge CB2 8BS, United Kingdom

Cambridge University Press is part of the University of Cambridge.

It furthers the University's mission by disseminating knowledge in the pursuit of education, learning and research at the highest international levels of excellence.

www.cambridge.org
Information on this title: www.cambridge.org/9781107535541

© John Macnicol 2015

First published 2015

Printed in the United Kingdom by Clays, St Ives plc

A catalogue record for this publication is available from the British Library

Library of Congress Cataloguing in Publication data
Macnicol, John.
Neoliberalising old age / by John Macnicol.
    pages   cm
Includes bibliographical references and index.
ISBN 978-1-107-11518-7 (hardback) – ISBN 978-1-107-53554-1 (paperback)
1. Aging – Government policy.   2. Ageism.   3. Older people – Social conditions.
4. Older people – Services for.   I. Title.
HQ1061.M236   2015
305.260973 – dc23   2015014699

ISBN 978-1-107-11518-7 Hardback
ISBN 978-1-107-53554-1 Paperback

Contents

Figures

Tables

Acknowledgements

This book merges together several research themes that I have been investigating in recent years – in particular, ageing and social policy and neoliberalism/neoconservatism as an ideology, with regard to both the UK and the USA. It builds upon my previous researches into the history of retirement and the analytical complexities of age discrimination, while also drawing upon past work on neoconservatism and the 'underclass' debate in the USA. Both projects were initially supported by two different Leverhulme Fellowships, and I can only apologise to the Leverhulme Trust for the fact that the published results, while voluminous, have been rather slow to materialise in print. However, that is simply the way some researchers work.

Writing a single-authored book is never easy, involving countless hours of isolation and self-doubt; yet this is always more than balanced by exhilaration and the inspirational company of fellow-researchers. My first debt of gratitude is to the Department of Social Policy at the London School of Economics for continuing my status as a Visiting Professor, involving some teaching of its exceptional students and a most stimulating research environment. I would like to thank successive Heads of Departments (Anne West, Ali McGuire, Tim Newburn and David Lewis) for all their support. On an individual level, Mike Murphy has provided me with excellent advice and very friendly encouragement, while being a wise, restraining influence on matters demographic. David Piachaud's vast stock of knowledge on social policy and his exceptional generosity of spirit in discussing issues were much appreciated. We co-operated happily on the research and writing of a report on intergenerational equity commissioned by the Equality and Human Rights Commission, which revived my interest in that fascinating topic. A debt of gratitude is owed to the past and present Social Policy Departmental Managers at LSE, John Wilkes and Damian Roberts, for many acts of practical help. Among fellow-researchers in the Department of Social Policy I would especially like to thank Gail Wilson, Christine Canazza, Sean Boyle, Philip Noden and Robyn Rowe. Three LSE students provided me with much-needed help in the final stages: Jack Cunliffe performed electronic cosmetic surgery, expertly tidying up tables and reformatting the text; Liwan Huang and Alex Talbot rescued me when it came to the collation of the bibliography and checking of all the footnotes.

Many fellow-academics in the UK and around the world gave me help at various stages of this book, among whom I should especially like to thank Lars Andersson, Chris Ball, Andrew Blaikie, Elisabet Cedersund, Eileen Crimmins, Harry Hendrick, Rob Hudson, Steven Lukes, John Mattausch, Chris Phillipson, Debora Price, David Sinclair, David Smith, John Stone, Jonathan Wadsworth and the two anonymous readers for Cambridge University Press. I should also like to thank George Lawson, Maxine Offredy and Jamie Whittington for being wonderfully supportive friends. A particular debt of gratitude is owed to Sara Rix, for her kind encouragement and invaluable advice, drawn from a remarkable knowledge of all things gerontological in the USA. It goes without saying that all the above individuals bear no responsibility for any errors in this book. Aspects of my research were presented as seminar and conference papers in recent years, the most important of which were: the International Sociological Association Forum on Sociology, Barcelona, September 2008; the British Society for Gerontology Annual Conference, Bristol, September 2009; the International Sociological Association World Congress, Gothenburg, July 2010; the European University Institute, Florence, May 2011; the Social Policy Association Annual Conference, July 2012; the Gerontological Society of America Annual Scientific Meeting, San Diego, November 2012. I should like to thank the participants at these and other events for their very helpful comments. Finally, I would like to thank my editor at Cambridge University Press on this and my previous book, John Haslam, for all his wise guidance.

1   The changing meanings of old age

This book explores an issue central to the study of age and ageing: Do we wish to preserve old age as a discrete stage of life, to be protected by welfare policies specifically targeting 'the old'? Should old age be accorded a privileged status? This may recognise the needs of a particular age group with regard to health, income and social care. But by doing so, we support the inaccurate and possibly offensive definition of 'old age' as the stage of life beyond age 65 – a demarcation line that has no biological or cognitive significance, since human beings age at very different rates. Defining old age in this way may ghettoise and marginalise one group of people in society, encouraging prejudice against them via policies that 'single out, stigmatise and isolate the aged from the rest of society',[1] in a way that can be seen as subtly ageist. On the other hand, should we dispense with age as a categorisation and work towards an 'age-irrelevant', 'age-neutral' or 'ageless' society – one in which individuals will be judged by the content of their character, rather than their chronological age? Is the concept of old age an outmoded relic from the past?

In the pages that follow, the answer will broadly be that the latter course is fraught with dangers for older people and has emerged in the context of wider attacks on the welfare rights of all marginalised people in society that are themselves a product of the new economic and political agendas that began to take root in the 1970s and are now in full bloom in the United Kingdom (UK) and United States of America (USA).[2] The term 'neoliberalisation of old age' will be used to describe this process. Neoliberalism as an ideology will be subject to a forensic and critical analysis, particularly regarding its effect on welfare states. In addition, the current old age agenda will be placed in its historical context. In particular, an approximate threefold periodisation of postwar policy developments will be strongly implicit. The first period, lasting from 1945 to the OPEC-led

---

[1] Carroll Estes, *The Aging Enterprise* (1979), p. 2.
[2] This book is mainly about the UK, but some comparisons are drawn with the USA (especially in Chapters 4, 5 and 6).

oil price hike of 1973, was a period in which old age was generally viewed in western societies as a stage of life to be protected and the right to retirement remained sacrosanct. From 1973 to the early 1990s – the second period – there were increasing attacks from the political right on state provision for old age – particularly pensions, but also retirement itself. Finally, from the early 1990s to the present – driven by the growth of low-paid, part-time, casualised jobs – there has been an emerging consensus that the available supply of labour should be maximised, that therefore the trend to early retirement should be reversed, that state pension ages should be raised and that older people should be forced to work in paid employment until aged in their late sixties and early seventies.

The central thesis of this book is therefore that the old age agenda is being redefined and transformed. A 'back to the future' scenario is emerging, involving a return to pre-twentieth-century conceptualisations of old age as a marginal social category, applying only to the oldest-old and associated with extreme infirmity. This new agenda has been driven both by structural economic changes and by the neoliberal political revolution: the complex interaction between structure and agency will be a recurring theme of this book. Subsequent chapters will examine the ways in which aspects of the ageing debate have been framed in accordance with neoliberal principles and certain solutions have been presented as natural or inevitable, with particular regard to demographic pressures, pensions reform, the raising of state pension ages, retirement, intergenerational equity, ageism/age discrimination, and all related issues.

Since the 1970s, and particularly since the early 1990s – driven by the rise in the employment rates of many jobless groups[3] that lasted until 2008 – there has been increasing pressure to redefine old age almost out of existence in the name of agelessness, to remove the protective walls that have hitherto shielded older people and, in the process, to attack their welfare rights. The most obvious expression of this has been the pressure to raise state pension ages and force people to work later in life, but this is only a part of a wider onslaught against welfare states. An intriguing contradiction explored in this book is that this is occurring alongside the rediscovery of ageism, accompanied by policies purporting to counter it and other discriminations. Paradoxically, therefore, some rights are being enhanced in order that others can be diminished.

On many levels, the social agendas of twenty-first-century western societies are becoming like those of the nineteenth century: widening income

---

[3] The conventional unemployed, lone parents and older people. The exception were those on disability benefits.

inequality and the growth of a plutocratic super-rich whose activities are beyond political control; the effective political disenfranchisement of a substantial section of the population who do not actively support the neoliberal project (as opposed to passively accepting it); an increasing polarisation in labour markets between a well-remunerated, high-skills core and a large hypercasualised, often part-time, low-paid periphery; a reversal of the epidemiological transition with the reappearance of epidemics; a return to a class-stratified, qualitatively differentiated education system (in which private or religious providers are playing an increasing part); a shrinking of income support systems down to something resembling the Poor Law; and the disappearance of twentieth-century welfarist categories like 'disability', 'unemployment', 'old age' and 'retirement'. Not for nothing did an eminent gerontologist warn some years ago of 'the end of gerontology', and *The Economist* magazine in 2009 triumphantly proclaim 'the end of retirement'.[4]

Ageing and old age

Generally speaking, gerontologists make a heuristic distinction between two separate entities: On the one hand, *ageing* is a long and complex process from birth to death, involving the interaction of an individual and their environment, with many variables involved. This newer 'life-course' approach is currently in vogue and it examines diversity, multiple identities and the many social divisions that define an individual's life-time experiences. It is also popular with those who oppose the rigidity of age-based categorisations, in that it views life as a continuous journey rather than a series of stages. This approach may be sociologically sophisticated but its practicality is questionable: can we really factor into our analysis age, gender, class, ethnicity, location, cultural identity and so on, and track an individual's progress through life, taking all such variables into account? On the other hand, the concept of *old age* is much less problematic, since it scrutinises one discrete, chronological period – most often, age 65 and over (65+) – as the final phase of the lifecycle. This makes it simpler and more manageable, but in the process old age becomes marginalised and stigmatised. Such an approach is often criticised for being based on crude biomedical and welfarist perspectives. A major problem is that many gerontologists want to have it both ways –

---

[4] Bernice L. Neugarten, 'The End of Gerontology?' in Dail A. Neugarten (ed.), *The Meanings of Age: Selected Papers of Bernice L. Neugarten* (1996), pp. 402–403; 'The End of Retirement', *The Economist*, 27 June–3 July 2009.

to preserve age-based social protections while rejecting age targeting as inherently ageist.

Ageing and old age have long fascinated social scientists, medical researchers and lay people, for a number of obvious reasons. First, the ageing process affects us all, and we are acutely aware of it. It is central to much popular culture, and is deeply ingrained in our patterns of thought. Age is also a powerful social division, and must be factored in alongside class, gender and 'race'/ethnicity in any complete social investigation. The greatest feminisation of poverty and welfare benefit reliance is in old age, even if most ire is directed at younger claimants with greater labour market relevance. Age is a determinant of particular social outcomes, such as crime levels (though the precise causal mechanisms can be complex). Many other examples exist – age norms and age-appropriate behaviours, stages of human development, age tensions at the micro-level of the family, age stratifications in childhood, the age patterning of social phenomena, age-targeted social policies, ageism and age discrimination in employment, or the complex hierarchies of age and seniority that characterise the social world. Age stratifications, age norms and age-appropriate behaviours are powerful. They are internalised by all of us, and influence our social outlook: we all live by what Bernice Neugarten called 'social clocks' that determine the 'right' time to perform certain social functions (for example, marriage, commencement of a career, parenthood and so on).[5] Finally, old age and death pose enormous spiritual challenges.[6]

Old age is also a major reason for the existence of modern welfare states, which are essentially welfare states for old people: in the UK, retirement pensions consume roughly 40 per cent of total social security spending, and social security can amount to between a quarter and a third of total public expenditure. (By contrast, all out-of-work benefits cost a little over 10 per cent of total social security spending.) The transition to retirement involves, on average, a step down to half of a household's pre-retirement income and a widening of inequalities. Those of gender are perhaps the most striking: women outnumber men in the pensioner population by almost two-to-one (in 2011, 7,430,000 women as against 4,646,000 men) and therefore all discussions of income support in retirement are really discussions about the poverty of older women. Of those aged 65+ who live alone, 70 per cent are women.[7] In 2012/13 the average gross income for a single male pensioner was £350 per week whereas for

---

[5] Bernice L. Neugarten, Joan W. Moore and John C. Lowe, 'Age Norms, Age Constraints, and Adult Socialisation', and Bernice L. Neugarten, 'Age Distinctions and Their Social Functions', in Neugarten, *The Meanings of Age*, pp. 24–25.

[6] Thomas R. Cole, *The Journey of Life: A Cultural History of Aging in America* (1992).

[7] Age UK, *Later Life in the United Kingdom* (2014), p. 3.

a single woman it was £298 per week. Single male pensioners received on average £120 from an occupational and/or private pension; by contrast, the equivalent figure for women was only £73.[8]

Good income support in retirement is vitally important. State pensions are thus highly political, involving choices about what kind of society we wish to create, how much national income we are willing to redistribute to those past conventional working age, how much we value old age and so on. Pensioners are arguably the most economically vulnerable group in modern societies, since their ability to lift themselves out of poverty is very limited indeed. Retirement tends to be a one-way street: the labour market presents very few offerings to retirees who might wish to return to work, and there is little or no chance of adding to any existing stock of savings. In short, there are many 'underpensioned' people who suffer in old age the consequences of contingencies earlier in life that were beyond their control and often originate at the time of their birth. Those particularly at risk are women, part-time workers, the low-paid, the self-employed, disabled people, employees of small firms and ethnic minorities. This can be seen very clearly if one looks at the level and distribution of incomes in retired households (see Table 1.1).

From Table 1.1, a number of interesting conclusions can be drawn. First, there is a sharp step-down on retirement, and a heavy reliance on state benefits (especially by the poorest 60 per cent of pensioner households, for whom such benefits on average constitute about three-quarters of total household income). The amount yielded by private or occupational pensions is very low for every quintile other than the wealthiest: that this should be the case after many decades of their existence shows that such private schemes cannot provide the answer to income maintenance in retirement. Yet the expansion of private provision has been a central governmental aim for the past thirty years. Another salient point is that income from wages and salaries is very much skewed towards the top two quintiles, indicating that the higher social classes are more able to continue working after state pension ages ('retired' in this context means the head of the household being above state pension age). Again, income from both investments and private/occupational pensions is also markedly higher for the top two quintiles. Those with the highest incomes and holdings of wealth are most likely to continue working, indicating that accumulated wealth and private pension provision do not play a major part in incentivising retirement (to be explored further in Chapter 5).

---

[8] Department for Work and Pensions, *The Pensioners' Incomes Series. United Kingdom, 2012/13* (2014), p. 29.

Table 1.1 *Average incomes, taxes and benefits by quintile groups of retired households, £ per annum, 2012/13*

	Bottom	2nd	3rd	4th	Top	All households
Original income						
Wages and salaries	113	120	254	1,053	1,539	616
Self-employment income	35	82	52	51	142	72
Private pensions, annuities	1,758	3,274	4,955	9,665	23,552	8,641
Investment income	244	244	451	1,033	5,493	1,493
Other income	43	52	80	109	258	82
Total	2,194	3,771	5,792	11,912	30,984	10,931
Direct benefits in cash						
State pension	6,758	8,081	8,737	9,498	9,166	8,448
Other benefits	1,370	2,481	3,270	3,175	1,871	2,433
Total cash benefits	8,130	10,562	12,008	12,675	11,034	10,882
Gross income	10,324	14,332	17,800	24,586	42,019	21,812
Total direct taxes	1,044	1,117	1,427	2,678	6,676	2,588
Disposable income	9,280	13,216	16,373	21,908	35,343	19,224
Equivalised disposable income	11,274	16,002	19,471	24,778	41,538	22,612
Total indirect taxes	2,863	2,744	3,425	4,352	6,224	3,922
Post-tax income	6,417	10,472	12,948	17,556	29,119	15,302
Benefits in kind	5,600	5,739	6,178	6,330	5,822	5,934
Final income	12,017	16,211	19,126	23,886	34,942	21,237
Cash benefits as a percentage of gross income	79%	74%	67%	52%	26%	50%
State Pension as a percentage of cash benefits	83%	77%	73%	75%	83%	78%

Source: Office for National Statistics, *The Effects of Taxes and Benefits on Household Income, 2012/13* (2014), table 18A (figures may not add due to rounding).

In old age, the unexpected occurs: individuals may confidently plan for their retirement, but a sudden serious illness can destroy those plans. The health and social care costs associated with old age (and infancy) are also considerable: 80 per cent of an individual's lifetime health care costs are consumed during their first six years and their last three. It follows, therefore, that a major attack on welfare states, such as is occurring now, will focus on retired people. In the past thirty years, there have been increasing calls for the state to withdraw from pension provision in favour of the private sector, for state pension ages to be raised and for working lives to be extended.[9] One major political problem is that it is difficult to cut benefits to retired people because they have always been seen as a highly deserving group: they have paid for their state pensions throughout their working lives, they have generally contributed to the future by raising children, they on average suffer higher levels of poverty, ill-health and disability and they are most often retired involuntarily. Neoliberalising old age thus presents unique challenges: 'a significant change in attitudes to retirement is needed to extend working lives' is one laconic comment.[10] As Kirk Mann has observed, the attack on benefits for older people has therefore been couched in paradoxical language: population ageing is presented as an enormous problem, driving all before it, yet is also said to be a great 'success story' and a cause for celebration.[11] (After all, it would be tasteless to present the modest gains in longevity that have occurred recently as unwelcome.) Exotic metaphors are used, such as the 'ticking timebomb' of demographic change, which do not bear close scrutiny: for example, nobody using such apocalyptic language ever explains just what will happen when this alleged timebomb explodes. There is an intriguing juxtaposition of triumph and disaster. Yet in the final analysis the right to retirement is being undermined. A typical example is the statement by Nicholas Barr:

The great triumph of the twentieth century is that people are living longer lives and healthier lives. This is great good news. It means that many more people reach retirement age and that people live longer in retirement. But it also means that pensions cost more. The problem, however, is not that people are living too long, but that they are retiring too soon.[12]

Likewise, more coercive, stricter labour market activation is presented as providing new 'opportunities', removing 'barriers' to working, bestowing greater 'inclusion' and even achieving upward social mobility. As will be argued in Chapter 7, in recent years UK governments have hijacked the language of liberationist advocacy groups and turned it round to justify an erosion of the welfare rights of those very same groups. Hence the social model of disability has been used to withdraw benefits from disabled people, the language of feminism has been used to apply greater conditionality and activation to lone mothers on benefits and anti-ageism has been used to justify the raising of state pension ages. Anyone who has read policy documents emanating from UK governments over the past

[9] Well analysed in: Kirk Mann, *Approaching Retirement: Social Divisions, Welfare and Exclusion* (2001); Kirk Mann, 'Activation, Retirement Planning and Restraining the "Third Age"', *Social Policy and Society*, 6, 3, July 2007, pp. 279–292.

[10] Scottish Widows UK Ninth Annual Pensions Report, *Retirement Savings Across the Nation* (2013), p. 5.

[11] Mann, 'Activation', pp. 280–282.

[12] Nicholas Barr, 'Retirement Age – a Good News Story' (2010), blogs.lse.ac.uk

fifteen years will be aware of the linguistic contradictions that have to be negotiated and decoded.

In attempting to capture the elusive meanings of age, sociologists often distinguish between different kinds of 'time' or 'age'. These can be quickly summarised. *Chronological* age is calendar time, involving an interaction between *biographical time* (an individual's life-history) and *historical time* (the historical context in which individuals age, with different cohort and generational experiences). *Social* age refers to socially ascribed identity, status differentiation by age and so on, by age-graded laws, age norms, age expectations, rights and obligations. *Physiological* or *biological* age covers the varying changes in physical and cognitive functions – functional ability, muscle tone and strength, bone density, organ reserve, intellectual ability and so on – over the lifecourse. Finally, *psychological* age encompasses the subjective assessment by an individual of their own age.

Several generations of social scientists have attempted to construct overarching theories of ageing and society.[13] Activity theory was influential in the 1950s and argued, perhaps rather unsurprisingly, that old people should stay active as part of the process of adjustment to old age, nurturing supportive relationships. Disengagement theory was dominant in the 1960s. Based upon interviews with retirees in Kansas, it suggested that older people gradually disengage from active social roles, reducing their interactions with others; as part of this disengagement process, older men discard the role of worker.[14] Modernisation theory saw old age emerging as a discrete category with the development of advanced industrial societies, the growth of welfare state categorisations, the bureaucratisation of society, the spread of information retrieval systems and so on. It was partly in reaction to a perceived complacency and functionalism in such theories that 'critical gerontology' emerged in the 1970s in the USA (boosted in part by the civil rights movement and the reappearance of grey power). Age divisions were viewed as embedded in capitalist inequalities, reinforced by other divisions; old people were seen as economically and culturally marginalised by being deprived of work and other status-enhancing roles. It was from this broad critique that structured dependency theory emerged in the UK in the 1980s, also viewing age as a major cause of economic inequality under capitalism.[15]

---

[13] There are many sources outlining these theories. For a very useful recent summary, see Chris Phillipson, *Ageing* (2013), ch. 3.

[14] Elaine Cumming and William E. Henry, *Growing Old: The Process of Disengagement* (1961).

[15] Peter Townsend, 'The Structured Dependency of the Elderly: A Creation of Social Policy in the Twentieth Century', *Ageing and Society*, 1, 1, March 1981, pp. 5–8; Alan

Structured dependency was much misunderstood by its critics – some-times wilfully so. It merely suggested the obvious: that the transition to retirement deprives an individual of their ability to sell their labour and forces them to become dependent on the state for much of their income; their circumstances in retirement will reflect pre-retirement structured inequalities.[16] Opponents of structured dependency theory accused it of presenting an unduly pessimistic view of old age (emphasising poverty, disability and ill-health) in which old people were seen as a homoge-nous group, powerless to resist their fate. However, exactly the opposite was the case: structured dependency was a call to grey activism, and it emphasised the many divisions in retirement. Older people carried into retirement inequalities 'created and legitimated at an earlier phase of the life cycle, particularly though not exclusively through the labour market'.[17] The most striking of these inequalities were economic, as the distribution of pensioner household incomes cited earlier convincingly demonstrates.

By the 1990s, however, a new theoretical perspective had emerged – one with striking relevance for this study, in that its emergence par-alleled structural changes in western economies. Postmodern theories and lifecourse approaches viewed ageing as a continuous journey across the lifecourse, rather than a series of 'stages' (as implied by the older, rather deterministic, lifecycle model), with an extended middle age or mature identity being carried far into what had been old age. In late modernity, consumption was an increasingly important source of iden-tity; self-actualisation through lifestyle choice was manifested in patterns of consumption. Identities could be 'adopted and discarded over time, not as a consequence of any sense of progression or development, but at the caprice of the wearer... One can, at least in theory, hit the fast-forward and rewind buttons of life in order to cast the ageing process into oblivion.' Ageing had become 'a matter of consumer choice and contingent identities', and could be recycled repeatedly.[18] The 'Third Age' was presented as a time of activity, enjoyment and good health. Far from being characterised by bodily and cognitive decline, ageing was more negotiable: the ageing body was no longer determined by lifecycle

Walker, 'Towards a Political Economy of Old Age', *Ageing and Society*, 1, 1, March 1981, pp. 73–94.

[16] John Macnicol, 'Old Age and Structured Dependency', in Michael Bury and John Macnicol (eds.), *Aspects of Ageing: Essays on Social Policy and Old Age* (1990), ch. 3.

[17] Alan Walker, 'The Politics of Ageing in Britain', in Chris Phillipson, Miriam Bernard and Patricia Strang (eds.), *Dependency and Interdependency in Old Age: Theoretical Per-spectives and Policy Alternatives* (1986), p. 37.

[18] Simon Biggs, *The Mature Imagination: Dynamics of Identity in Midlife and Beyond* (1999), pp. 59, 61.

stages. Implicitly, this perspective also held up the ideal of agelessness: if the old markers of ageing were disappearing, in the conditions of late modernity, then the concept of 'old age' itself should be challenged. Grey activism should be directed at recognition rather than redistribution.

It is important not to over-simplify this postmodern turn in the sociology of old age, which was complex and contentious – and arguably has a long history.[19] It was not necessarily any more accurate than what had gone before, in that it tended to present old people as homogenous and undifferentiated (whereas inequalities *increase* after the transition to retirement). One problem was that it gained traction in academic sociology precisely because so many sociologists choose to operate at the level of generality; they are therefore over-willing to accept broad theoretical overviews, rather than wrestle with complex and often contradictory empirical evidence. The inconvenient fact is that this consumption-rich postmodern old age only applies to an elite of wealthy retirees – possibly only the top 5 per cent. Again, the notion that identities could be endlessly reinvented and that medical technologies could reshape the ageing body as part of this was far-fetched. In its defence, the idea of the postmodern lifecourse was perhaps more a description of an emerging minority trend than of a universal experience. For the purpose of this study, it only need be noted that the new postmodern turn spread through gerontology and influenced all working within it.

This new perspective had the potential to be liberating, by rejecting the metaphors of decay and decrepitude that had – to an extent – characterised older models of old age, and by fashioning a new positive mythology in which the status of old people could be enhanced by integrating them into society. However, this is not what happened. Against a background of increasing neoliberal hostility towards welfare states, this new analytical turn became the sociological basis for attacks on old people and a withdrawal of their welfare rights on the grounds that they were no longer in poverty. The change is summed up well by Robert Binstock's observation that, in the 1980s and 1990s, there occurred a conceptual transition from 'compassionate ageism', portraying old people as 'poor, frail, dependent, objects of discrimination, and above all "deserving"', to a much more hostile, neoliberal-influenced set of stereotypes depicting old people as 'prosperous, hedonistic, politically powerful, and selfish'.[20]

---

[19] For a good summary, see Carroll Estes, Simon Biggs and Chris Phillipson, *Social Theory, Social Policy and Ageing* (2003), ch. 3. On the history of postmodernity in general, see David Lyon, *Postmodernity* (1994).

[20] Robert H. Binstock, 'From Compassionate Ageism to Intergenerational Conflict?', *The Gerontologist*, 50, 5, 2010, pp. 575–576. See also, Thomas R. Cole, 'Generational Equity in America: A Cultural Historian's Perspective', *Social Science and Medicine*, 29, 3, 1989, pp. 377–378.

Neoliberalism and postmodernism embraced each other with unseemly eagerness – most strikingly, in the work of Anthony Giddens. However, it turned out to be the union of a shark with its prey. A sociologically elegant mythology of the prosperous pensioner was constructed in the face of empirical evidence that showed exactly the opposite to be the case. In the UK, the economic status of retirees had improved in absolute terms between the 1950s and the 1980s: in households where the head was aged 65+, real per capita expenditure had risen by at least 40 per cent between 1959 and 1981. However, one authoritative verdict was that this was probably lower than the rise experienced by the rest of the population.[21] The basic state pension had risen in relative terms since 1974, reaching 20 per cent of male average earnings in the late 1970s. But then the Thatcher-instigated decline set in and it fell from 1980, to 15 per cent by the early 1990s. Had nothing been done, it would have fallen to 6 per cent by 2040.[22] The proportion of pensioners receiving occupational pensions increased from 41 per cent in 1979 to 55 per cent in 1989. However, membership of occupational schemes has been in slow decline from the late 1960s to today, with the contraction of public sector employment, from 12,200,000 in 1967 to 8,200,000 in 2011.[23] Income inequality among pensioners was widening in the 1980s (reflecting an overall rise in income inequality), and in 1982/3 some 5,700,000 pensioners out of a total of 9,100,000 lived at or below the 140 per cent Supplementary Benefit level (then an accepted measure of relative income poverty).[24] To be sure, in the 1980s a smaller proportion of pensioners were on officially defined relative low incomes than working-aged families – but this was mainly because unemployment had pulled more working-aged people down the relative income scale, thereby displacing pensioners.[25] The overall picture was somewhat mixed – there had been both gains and losses in the relative position of retirees – but the empirical evidence clearly showed that there was substantial pensioner poverty.

In the face of these convincing statistics, the neoliberal attacks in the 1980s used assertion and anecdote rather than evidence. The shift of attitude within government in the early 1980s was replicated at a populist level by obedient commentators in the media, politics

[21] Mark Abrams, 'Changes in the Life-Styles of the Elderly, 1959–1982', in Central Statistical Office, *Social Trends 14: 1984 Edition* (1983), pp. 11–16.

[22] Paul Johnson, *The Pensions Dilemma* (1994), p. 5. By the late 1990s, those receiving the basic state pension had lost about £1,000 per annum as a result.

[23] Office for National Statistics, *Pension Trends. Chapter 7: Private Pension Scheme Membership, 2013 Edition* (2013), p. 3.

[24] Department of Health and Social Security, *Social Security Statistics, 1986* (1986), p. 271.

[25] Department of Health and Social Security, *Reform of Social Security, Vol. I*, Cmnd. 9517 (1985), p. 13.

and academic research. It was alleged that retirees were living at a high standard:

Anyone who meets pensioners regularly must be impressed by the relative prosperity which many of them enjoy, in contrast to the usual picture of the poor. Protected by an index-linked state pension, often benefiting from generous occupational pension schemes, living in homes whose soaring value makes them capital rich – and with the incalculable advantage of ample spare time – they frequently enjoy a standard of living better than they had during their working lives. Quite simply, the over-60s are our *nouveaux riches*.[26]

Politicians repeated the message that 'It is simply no longer true that being a pensioner tends to mean being badly off. . . For most it is a time to look forward to with confidence. The modern pensioner has a great deal to be envied.'[27] This was replicated at an academic level, though often via highly general assertions – for example, that their 'improved economic status' now gave older people 'the option of a fairly comfortable retirement which they may prefer to continued employment in unattractive work'.[28] As will be shown later in this book, other examples have gained popular, uncritical acceptance – that 'people are living longer', that retirement is largely voluntary or that working later in life makes one healthier.

Deconstructing neoliberalism

Neoliberalism is both an ideology *and* a stage of capitalism. Were it merely the former, the political left in the UK and the USA would have found it easier to oppose, and it would not have been espoused, in varying forms, by notionally different political parties. Its revival is therefore rooted in the profound changes that have taken place in western economies since the early 1970s (discussed later). Many of its adherents like to present its rise in purely human agency terms, as their collective victory in the battle of ideas, transforming the thinking of intellectual elites[29] – an approach that led Susan George to call them 'the Gramscian right'.[30] This explanatory narrative partly reflects the self-congratulatory, self-referential element

---

[26] Graham Paterson, 'The Caring for the Old that Leaves Me Cold', *Sunday Telegraph*, 10 Jan. 1988.

[27] John Moore, quoted in Phil Mullan, *The Imaginary Time Bomb: Why an Ageing Population is Not a Social Problem* (2000), p. 139.

[28] Paul Johnson, 'The Structured Dependency of the Elderly: A Critical Note', in Margot Jefferys (ed.), *Growing Old in the Twentieth Century* (1989), p. 71.

[29] A striking (and well-researched) example is Richard Cockett, *Thinking the Unthinkable: Think Tanks and the Economic Counter-Revolution, 1931–1983* (London, 1994).

[30] Susan George, 'How to Win the War of Ideas: Lessons from the Gramscian Right', *Dissent*, 44, 3, Summer 1997, pp. 47–53.

in neoliberalism; it also partly attests to the fact that this ideological revolution was a concerted campaign, funded by vast corporate donations channelled through neoconservative think-tanks and seemingly impartial bodies like the USA's National Bureau of Economic Research (NBER). But the explanatory narrative mainly arises from neoliberalism's own model of social change as a cultural process operating at the level of ideas. In this study, however, it will be emphasised that the rise of neoliberalism has been historically determined.

It is instructive to pause briefly and examine the case of the NBER in furthering the neoliberal cause. The NBER is a private, self-appointed body that passes itself off as an ideologically neutral, purely academic professional association. Its website declares that it is 'a nonpartisan research organisation dedicated to promoting a greater understanding of how the economy works', and that it is 'committed to undertaking and disseminating unbiased economic research in a scientific manner, and without policy recommendations'.[31] However, in practice the NBER is dedicated to the propagation of exclusively free market economics and has sponsored an enormous number of publications to that end. As will be seen throughout this book, it offers an exclusively supply-side, behavioural explanation for retirement, with labour market demand rarely mentioned. In 1983 the NBER received almost half of its funding from leading companies on the Forbes 500 list.[32] It has been bankrolled by right-wing foundations: according to the website SourceWatch, the John M. Olin Foundation, the Lynde and Harry Bradley Foundation, the Scaife Foundation and the Smith Richardson Foundation together donated nearly $10,000,000 to it between 1985 and 2001.[33] In mid-2013 the NBER had net assets of $101,723,584[34] – a magnificent treasure-chest that enables it to influence the hearts and minds of global opinion-formers. It now exerts something of an ideological stranglehold on the economics profession in the USA: sponsorship by the NBER is a sure method of career advancement. Its 'objective' analysis of the causes of retirement needs to be placed in that context. The UK's Department for Work and Pensions (DWP) are of course eager to accept the NBER's supply-side line on retirement: for example, a recent key policy document, *Fuller Working Lives* (2014), asserts that 'research has shown that the financial incentives or disincentives to carry on in work play a large part in explaining overall patterns of

---

[31] National Bureau of Economic Research, 'About the NBER', 2014, www.nber.org
[32] Mark Blyth, *Great Transformations: Economic Ideas and Institutional Change in the Twentieth Century* (2002), p. 158.
[33] 'National Bureau of Economic Research' (2010), www.sourcewatch.org
[34] NBER, 'About the NBER'.

retirement' and then quotes one NBER edited volume as the only source for this 'research'.[35]

Like all political ideologies, neoliberalism is complex, multi-faceted and fragmented, reflecting its structural and ideological origins. It has also experienced uneven geographical development and different hybridised forms. Many analytical problems derive from neoliberalism's ability to penetrate the social democratic parties of the industrialised world and shift their ideological focus to the right (as in the way it has colonised the UK Labour Party). Here only a brief outline description can be given: readers wanting more should look elsewhere,[36] and a more detailed account of its application to old age will be given in the pages that follow.

Neoliberalism has become a modern generic term for free market, libertarian ideas ostensibly supporting a minimalist state, the primacy of the deregulated market, the desirability of private provision of goods and services, the sanctity of individual liberty and so on. It is a political tradition that has a long history, going back to thinkers such as Bernard de Mandeville, Thomas Hobbes and Adam Smith[37] – although some would argue that in its modern incarnation it is a betrayal of those ideas, selecting only those aspects that favour a global elite and ignoring those that pose a radical challenge to *all* vested interests and private, unaccountable monopolies. In the nineteenth century, it was most closely associated with the 'Manchester school' of laissez-faire, free market economics. During the 1930s recession, economists like Friedrich Hayek, Ludwig von Mises, William Hutt and Lionel Robbins urged deflationary policies – essentially, cuts in money wages and public expenditure retrenchment – to lower the selling price of domestically produced goods on world markets and thus stimulate an economic revival. The policy of the UK Treasury in the 1930s was in fact based upon a moderate, politically acceptable version of this. During the Keynesian 'postwar consensus' period from 1945 to the early 1970s, economic liberalism was on the defensive and represented by small and seemingly insignificant bodies like the Mont Pelerin Society and the Institute of Economic Affairs (later joined by the Adam Smith Institute). However, the structural

---

[35] Department for Work and Pensions, *Fuller Working Lives – Background Evidence* (2014), p. 43. The NBER work cited is Jonathan Gruber and David Wise (eds.), *Social Security and Retirement Around the World* (1999).

[36] Among the best general accounts are: David Harvey, *A Brief History of Neoliberalism* (2005); Colin Crouch, *The Strange Non-Death of Neoliberalism* (2011); Damien Cahill, Lindy Edwards and Frank Stilwell (eds.), *Neoliberalism: Beyond the Free Market* (2012).

[37] As has often been pointed out, Adam Smith's *The Theory of Moral Sentiments* (1759) needs to be excluded from this categorisation.

economic changes of the 1970s and after created the ideal context for its revival.

In matters of social policy, neoliberalism is by and large opposed to state welfare, believing that true welfare is best delivered through family, friends, neighbours, charities and private for-profit agencies. Its most striking tenet is that welfare benefits (other than via safety nets for the really needy) tend to worsen the very problems they purport to solve: rewarding idleness and dependency encourages rational economic men and women to choose them. In the tension between liberty and equality, the claims of the former must always win out: equality can never be attained, and any attempt by the state to mitigate 'natural', market-driven inequalities will only be counter-productive.

Neoliberalism begins with what it sees as immutable laws of human nature (for example, that we are all Hobbesian beings in competition), and then proceeds to social prescriptions based upon these laws.[38] What often puzzles critics is that its empirical basis can be weak – evidence is often semi-anecdotal, in the form of little vignettes[39] – but neoliberalism's approach is to reorder the evidence to fit these seemingly naturalistic laws. The lack of an evidential base is also a function of neoliberalism's economistic nature: as argued here, it has been driven by the emergence of a new kind of capitalism, rather than by rational argument, and serves the interests of that new capitalism and the global elite who run it. Evidence is thus superfluous to its advancement. The most cogent historical examples of market liberal opposition to state welfare are to be found in the famous 1834 Report of the Poor Law Commission (also much criticised for its weak evidential base) and in the ideology of the Charity Organisation Society (dealt with in the following chapter). Libertarian economic radicalism has always had an uneasy relationship with traditional, 'dispositional' conservatism, and this relationship remains one of the ideological tensions within the UK Conservative Party to this day. Arguably, neoliberalism is also distinct from American neoconservatism. The latter tends to espouse social conservatism (in the private spheres, notably the family and religion) and a strong foreign policy (anti-communist, when it applied). In the USA, neoconservatives tended to express grudging support for the New Deal but opposition to the welfare expansion of the 1960s. By contrast, neoliberalism is more libertarian in matters of personal morality and less tolerant of all social policies.

---

[38] The unresolvable problem, which affects Hobbes's 'state of nature', is that human behaviour can never be observed in the abstract, decontextualised from its social environment.

[39] This was a feature of Charles Murray's *Losing Ground: American Social Policy, 1950–1980* (1984).

However, the boundaries between different ideological positions are porous, and any categorisation of different strands of conservatism cannot be hard-and-fast.

The structural drivers behind the neoliberal revival have been the post-1960s flows of private capital from declining heavy industry to the new service sectors, particularly financial services (the financialisation process), and the compositional labour force changes that have resulted from this. These new service jobs have tended to be more insecure, casualised, low paid, part-time and feminised: there is therefore greater labour turnover compared with job-for-life fordist capitalism. As a consequence, it is essential for the state to fashion new, stricter modes of work-discipline to direct people into such jobs, and this has been achieved by attaching greater conditionality and obligation to the receipt of welfare benefits – mainly, by compulsory activation policies. At the same time, deindustrialisation has created enormous social problems in the form of 'hidden unemployment', spatially concentrated in areas that have now become socially blighted. There have emerged 'underclass', 'troubled families', 'benefit dependency' and other personal deficiency discourses to explain these social problems in behavioural terms.

The neoliberal revolution has also been directed at the dominance of a global economic elite who are adept at using the power of the state and multinational corporations to further their own interests. This elite's power has been consolidated by the widening income and wealth inequalities within western nations and on a global scale. In this sense, the neoliberal revolution represents what Frances Fox Piven and Richard Cloward in 1982 called a 'new class war'.[40] As Gerard Dumenil and Dominique Levy put it, neoliberalism is 'a class phenomenon, in which upper classes have removed all limits to their power and income with disastrous consequences both for popular classes and even for the upper classes of the countries of the centre themselves, whose economies stagnate and become unmanageable'.[41] In this respect, neoliberalism often appears to be little more than a strategy for redistributing income and wealth upwards to the exclusive global elite. Globalisation has made it extremely difficult for democratic institutions to exert control over this elite. In any case, those institutions tend to be suffused with neoliberal ideology, and therefore compliant. Members of this global elite have thus been very successful at minimising their income tax liabilities at an individual and a corporate level: their payment of income tax has almost become a matter

---

[40] Frances Fox Piven and Richard A. Cloward, *The New Class War: Reagan's Attack on the Welfare State and its Consequences* (1982).

[41] Gerard Dumenil and Dominique Levy, 'The Crisis of Neoliberalism as a Stepwise Process: From the Great Contraction to the Crisis of Sovereign Debts', in Cahill *et al.*, *Neoliberalism*, p. 32.

of choice. In essence, the post-1970s economic revolution has involved the emergence of finance capital as an all-powerful social and political force, with a global financial elite in control.[42] Consumer debt has been a means of stimulating economic growth – with near-catastrophic consequences in 2008–2009. The Achilles Heel of Keynesianism may be inflation, but that of economic liberalism is public and private debt.

In the neoliberal analysis of economic change, labour market demand is little mentioned. Indeed, the activities of employers and global movements of capital are ignored. Instead, the emphasis is on supply-side, behavioural factors pertaining to individuals – skills, education, motivation, attitude, culture.[43] On the face of it, the aim is to create a deregulated economy, in which workers are forced to accept any job, at any wage and under any conditions. There therefore needs to be great fluidity of labour supply. Retirement (both conventional and 'early') interferes with this, by reducing the pool of available workers. Pension provision, allegedly the main cause of retirement, must therefore be cut back and/or privatised. Indeed, all welfare benefits are seen as disincentivising work, forcing up taxes and raising wage costs. Establishing a true free market economy will, it is claimed, maximise economic growth to the benefit of all via the trickle-down of wealth and income. However, in practice thirty-five years of largely neoliberal economic policies have produced in the UK a more income-unequal society than at any time since the early 1930s. On other economic indicators – annual GDP growth, personal saving, real wages, child poverty, unemployment, upward social mobility, personal debt, the increasing number of citizens dependent on payday loans to fund essential expenditure such as food and rent, the rise of food banks and so on – the outcomes have been woeful. The only real successes have been the containment of inflation and the enrichment of a tiny elite at the top of society.[44] These dysfunctional trends are often regarded by social democrats as puzzling and aberrant – why should modern capitalism have developed in this way? – yet they are the result of a deliberate political strategy.

An interesting feature of neoliberalism – most relevant to this study – is its ability to make its central tenets appear naturalistic, commonsense and unquestionable (akin to Gramsci's notion of cultural hegemony).[45] Hence the UK has become, ideologically speaking, a virtual one-party

---

[42] Anne Daguerre, 'New Corporate Elites and the Erosion of the Keynesian Social Compact', *Work, Employment and Society*, 28, 2, Apr. 2014, pp. 323–334.

[43] As will be shown in Chapter 5, this is strikingly demonstrated in neoliberal explanations of retirement.

[44] Harvey, *A Brief History*, pp. 154–156.

[45] The whole question of how ideologies become hegemonic is famously discussed in Steven Lukes, *Power: A Radical View* (2005 edn.), esp. ch. 3.

state, with social debates confined within strict parameters and dissenting voices marginalised. It is a process that has been termed 'cognitive locking',[46] whereby only one definition of a social problem is presented and therefore only one solution is possible – as in the notion that there is a demography-driven 'pensions crisis', for which the only solution is to raise state pension ages.[47] One reason for this is that the advancement of neoliberal ideology has been slow and incremental – a right-wing version of the Trotskyite permanent revolution – and therefore difficult to oppose: every step appears small and insignificant, but the cumulative effect is massive. Two obvious examples from the current social policy agenda in the UK are the conversion of schools into academies (originally supposed to be driven by parental choice, but now imposed by governments) and the slow privatisation of service provision in the National Health Service.

Like all political ideologies, neoliberalism is riddled with contradictions. One is that an exclusively human agency, behavioural model of social change is offered – yet neoliberalism is highly economistic, in that its policy prescriptions are based upon what is best for capital accumulation. Another is that the free market, anti-statist rhetoric exists alongside a more powerful, regulatory and coercive state – manifest in workfare schemes for benefit claimants, greater electronic surveillance over citizens and a new punitive penology.[48] The free market is only ever a hypothetical abstraction: in practice what we observe as market forces are a product of political control by the state. Under neoliberalism, the privatised service providers are actually highly dependent on the state, via taxpayer subsidies. The new model of privatisation – in operation since the late 1980s – is one in which the taxpayer provides the funding and bears the risk, and private capital takes the profit: the provision of essential services to a nation's population (notably, health care and education) will yield guaranteed profits, with no risk. Such services can also be presented as free at the point of delivery, and therefore still seemingly state-run, under democratic control and universal. For example, private companies now take enormous amounts of UK taxpayers' money to advise on overseas aid (particularly if it involves privatisation): hence the private consultancy Adam Smith International received £37,000,000 in 2011 from the Department for International Development to promote free market projects in the Third World.[49] The most extreme example

---

[46] Blyth, *Great Transformations*, p. 170.
[47] Jo Grady, 'Trade Unions and the Pension Crisis: Defending Member Interests in a Neoliberal World', *Employee Relations*, 35, 3, 2013, pp. 294–308.
[48] Loic Wacquant, *Punishing the Poor: The Neoliberal Government of Social Insecurity* (2009).
[49] Andrew Gilligan, '"Poverty Barons" Who Make a Fortune from Taxpayer-Funded Aid Budget', *Telegraph*, 15 Sept. 2012, www.telegraph.co.uk

was, of course, the 'military Keynesianism' of the Iraq War, which created a profit bonanza for US companies. Choice and competition may be the beguiling watchwords, but choice is illusory: in practice, private providers run services as a monopoly or a cartel, with very little real competition, and choice severely restricted. In this way, private providers are effectively removed from democratic control. This loss of democratic accountability is particularly significant in the case of the privatised utilities, since reliable and affordable energy supplies are so vital to everyday life.

An intriguing feature of neoliberalism is its uneasy relationship with mass democracy. The latter tends to be viewed with suspicion, as merely elevating into positions of power a cadre of self-serving politicians who are shielded from the discipline of market forces. Hence Harris and Seldon commented in 1979 that 'In principle, the economic market-place provides a perfect form of democratic selection. It has been likened to a perpetual referendum in which customers vote every day with their money for the widest possible choice between the offerings of competing suppliers.'[50] The authors did acknowledge that theirs was a purist model and that practical problems with market provision can arise, which the state needs to solve. Nevertheless, economic liberalism prefers marketplace democracy to ballot-box democracy and displays profoundly anti-democratic tendencies. A strong state is needed 'to promote economic freedom and markets and to neutralise the pathologies of democracy', as Mitchell Dean puts it.[51] Some even argue that we now live in conditions of 'post-democracy', with disturbing implications for civil society.[52] Many citizens now feel politically dispossessed and voiceless, marginalised from the broadly neoliberal consensus represented by conventional party politics. Arguably, the way that ordinary citizens in Scotland were galvanised into street-level political activism by the independence referendum of September 2014 was a striking example of this, as is the rise of the United Kingdom Independence Party (UKIP).

The standard economic liberal analysis of the 1930s depression in the UK is that money wages were too high, and this made British industry globally uncompetitive, in that the selling prices of its goods were also too high on world markets. Hence for Lionel Robbins, the 'rigidity of wages' in the UK was 'a by-product of unemployment insurance'.[53] The solution was wage cuts, but governments were allegedly too timid

---

[50] Ralph Harris and Arthur Seldon, *Over-Ruled on Welfare* (1979), p. 65.
[51] Mitchell Dean, 'Free Economy, Strong State', in Cahill *et al.*, *Neoliberalism*, p. 78.
[52] Colin Crouch, *Post-Democracy* (2004).
[53] Lionel Robbins, *The Great Depression* (1934), pp. 60–61.

to impose these, fearing the opposition of trades unions and the political repercussions of equivalent cuts in unemployment benefit. The need to pander to democracy thus prevented the economically correct solutions being enforced. Keynesian demand-side policies, which were said to have been applied from the Second World War onwards, were accused of being a fatal compromise with democracy, setting up inflationary tendencies that manifested themselves in the 1970s. Democracy thus prevented market forces from operating successfully. In a recession, the neoliberal solution is to cut welfare benefits, or make claiming them more difficult, so that wages can also fall. Production costs will then also fall, leading to greater competitiveness and, accordingly, economic growth. It is worth bearing this in mind when contemplating what has happened to welfare states recently.

In general, pure neoliberalism tends to view categories like 'old age', 'disability', 'unemployment' and even 'poverty' as mischievous welfarist constructs that encourage a false notion of rights. The only rights that individuals possess in a capitalist economy, it is argued, are over their private property and their ability to sell their labour at the market rate, regardless of their age, gender, ethnic background, disability status and so on. If, for example, they have disabilities, they must lower their earnings expectations in order to gain employment. The problem is, argues Martin Feldstein, that 'law and custom prevent firms from lowering wages to the levels at which it would pay to hire handicapped individuals'.[54] In similar vein, Richard Epstein suggests that, 'like everyone else, the disabled should be allowed to sell their labour at whatever price, and whatever terms, they see fit'.[55] The unguarded remarks made by Lord Freud, minister for welfare reform, in October 2014, to the effect that disabled people are not worth the National Minimum Wage and that some should be paid only £2 per hour, were entirely consistent with this central neoliberal principle.[56] When applied to older people, this prescription implies that old age should be defined down to a residual category, and that older people should work as late in life as possible. Retirement should be self-funded and privatised: citizens should only retire when they can afford to do so,[57] sustained by savings accrued during a working life and

[54] Martin Feldstein, 'The Economics of the New Unemployment', *The Public Interest*, 33, Fall 1973, p. 25.
[55] Richard Epstein, *Forbidden Grounds: The Case Against Employment Discrimination Laws* (1992), p. 484.
[56] Nigel Morris, 'Lord Freud: Tory Welfare Minister Apologises after Saying Disabled People are "Not Worth" the Minimum Wage', *Independent*, 15 Oct. 2014, www.independent.co.uk
[57] Foresight (Ageing Population Panel), *The Age Shift – Priorities for Action* (2000), p. 22.

by financial products purchased from private providers.[58] The role of the state would be limited to a residual, means-tested social assistance system akin to the nineteenth century Poor Law. One obvious way of effecting this is to raise state pension ages.

Conclusion

Since the 1970s, neoliberalism – a product of the complex interrelationship between structural and ideological factors – has exerted a growing influence on social and economic policy, particularly in the UK and the USA (two countries at the heart of the neoliberal revolution). Its emergence has been slow and incremental, with every stage of development justified by propositions that have been made to appear inevitable and naturalistic. A central tenet of neoliberalism is that old age should not be a specially protected stage of life and that the privileged status hitherto accorded to it in welfare states can no longer be justified. Older people should therefore be forced to work later in life (whether or not there are jobs for them) or become equal competitors in an enlarged reserve army of unemployed labour, and state pension support should be withdrawn. The justifying arguments have been many and various, ranging from the exotic sociological theories of postmodern ageing and the liberationist arguments of anti-ageism to hard-nosed economic imperatives that growth can only be achieved by expanding labour supply and a crude demographic determinism that presents old people as a major fiscal burden. Future chapters will consider these justifications, and elaborate on them.

[58] Debora Price and Lynne Livsey, 'Financing Later Life: Pensions, Care, Housing Equity and the New Politics of Old Age', in Gabia Ramia, Kevin Farnsworth and Zoe Irving (eds.), *Social Policy Review 25. Analysis and Debate in Social Policy, 2013* (2013), p. 67.

2   Old age in the past

The status of old age as a protected stage of life was associated with the long period of industrial capitalism from the 1880s to the 1970s. Often termed 'organised' or 'fordist' capitalism, it is said to have been characterised by fulltime, job-for-life, blue-collar male industrial employment and low employment rates of married women. This is broadly correct, although it must be remembered that within this time-span there were long periods of recession, mass unemployment and job insecurity. In many ways, fordist capitalism was really only successful from 1945 to 1975. However, in general the period from the 1880s to the 1970s was one in which retirement (both mandatory and culturally sanctioned) was used to dispense with the services of employees who were deemed – by the use of a simple age proxy – to be 'past their best' in terms of individual productivity. State pensions supported the 'worn-out' older worker, albeit at a very low standard of living. Retirement slowly spread down the age structure as there occurred the gradual shrinkage of those sectors that employed older workers.

In preindustrial times, old age was less well defined. In the absence of accurate birth recording, age categorisations depended upon the external, visible signs of ageing – wrinkled skin, grey hair, the menopause, grandparenthood, infirmity and so on. The question of whether old people were better treated and more respected in the past is one that has long intrigued social historians, and cannot be gone into here. What we can be sure of is that then, as now, old age occupied a cultural space that was ambiguous and dualistic, comprising respect and veneration on the one hand but hostility, fear and resentment on the other. Much interesting work has been done on ageing in non-industrial societies as a proxy for the preindustrial past.[1] Essentially, in the rural and early industrial economy of c. 1750–1880 in the UK, the status of old people was overwhelmingly

---

[1] For example, Nancy Foner, 'When the Contract Fails: Care for the Elderly in Nonindustrial Cultures', in Vern L. Bengtson and W. Andrew Achenbaum (eds.), *The Changing Contract Across Generations* (1993).

influenced by the fact that their labour – like that of married women and children – was needed in a highly labour-intensive production process.

In the mid-nineteenth century, with nearly four out of every five men aged 65+ still in employment (in contrast to only one in eight today), the association between 'retirement' and 'old age' did not exist as it does now. Instead, joblessness at older ages was more caused by inability to work through infirmity and was frequently the last stage of a long winding-down process whereby men moved to progressively lighter tasks as they aged, their incomes diminishing in the process. The Poor Law, which significantly juxtaposed the categories 'aged' and 'infirm', tended to supplement these falling earnings by outdoor relief. In the words of E. H. Hunt, such relief payments were 'disability supplements intended to off-set the diminishing market value of men no longer able to earn their keep but not yet sufficiently feeble to warrant full support'.[2] In a way, this was analogous to today's in-work benefits, though it is important to remember that even the aged were objects of highly deterrent Poor Law policies.

However, over the course of the nineteenth century women, children and old people were gradually shaken out of a labour market that was becoming more masculinist, factory-based and technologically innovative. For example, by the early 1900s fewer than one in ten married women were in paid employment, and children were obliged to attend school until the age of 11. The period from the 1880s to the 1970s can be seen as the classic era of job-for-life, male industrial employment, during which retirement spread down the age structure and the average age of permanent labour market exit slowly fell. There were powerful economic reasons for retirement. It contributed significantly to economic efficiency by ridding industry of workers who were deemed 'past their best', and did so in a cheap, convenient and socially acceptable way (avoiding all the expense, complexity and controversy of individual performance appraisal). State pensions were needed to facilitate this, and to counter the increasingly visible plight of the 'worn-out' older worker for whom a more competitive and technologically based labour market had no use. By the second decade of the twentieth century, most political conservatives therefore accepted, albeit sometimes rather grudgingly, that retirement was an inevitability. Indeed, it had become a social right. Although the prime causal forces were economic, the right to retirement became embedded in popular consciousness.

In the late nineteenth century, most enlightened conservatives (notably, Joseph Chamberlain) appreciated the need for some kind of

[2] E. H. Hunt, 'Paupers and Pensioners: Past and Present', *Ageing and Society*, 9, 4, Dec. 1989, p. 415.

state pension scheme: for them, the main point at issue was expense – specifically, whether a state scheme could be funded on the contributory principle – and much of their opposition derived from fears of the long-term fiscal effects of a non-contributory, tax-funded scheme (which, it was believed, would inevitably grow in cost as a result of democratic pressure). Their aim was to establish a contributory pension scheme that would be based upon citizens saving their 'own' money on an individualistic basis, with little risk-pooling or redistribution. The dilemma was that a contributory insurance scheme would do nothing for the 'bad risks' (women not in the labour market, the low-paid, the unemployed and irregularly employed) who most needed good income support in old age. If fully funded, it would also take decades to mature. Fully-funded schemes would therefore confer no immediate political kudos on those politicians who advocated them. However, all non-contributory, tax-funded schemes would be highly redistributive from rich to poor, from men to women and from the working-aged to the retired, and by the early 1900s the tax-funded 'endowment of old age' had become one of several radical socialist demands. The 1908 Old Age Pensions Act was therefore accepted reluctantly by conservatives as a *fait accompli*, but they were determined to contain the cost of this new social reform that had the potential to be highly expensive and redistributive.[3]

The neoclassical view of old age

However, in the late nineteenth century there was one section of political opinion that vigorously opposed state old age pensions and offered a conceptualisation of old age that was remarkably similar to that of today's neoliberals: it is therefore worth exploring. This rearguard action against 'the endowment of old age' by the state was led by the Charity Organisation Society (COS). Founded in London in 1869, the COS aimed to co-ordinate and control all private charities. These would then dispense relief only to the 'deserving' poor; the 'undeserving' would be dealt with by a stricter Poor Law run by Boards of Guardians sympathetic to COS principles and, if possible, based solely on workhouses with all outdoor relief abolished. The COS always regretted that the 1834 reform of the Poor Law had allowed outdoor relief to continue.

The COS's aim was to create an independent, self-sustaining working class deeply imbued with capitalist values, and to this end it viewed Poor Law relief as corrupting, eroding the social virtues of thrift, hard work

---

[3] For a summary, see John Macnicol, 'Introduction', in Macnicol (ed.), *Paying for the Old: Old Age and Social Welfare Provision, Vol. I: The 19th-century Origins* (2000), pp. vii–xxv.

and intergenerational family responsibility. The primary source of welfare should therefore be the intact working-class family, with a woman as its linchpin. Helen Bosanquet (a leading figure in the COS and a thoughtful social commentator) surveyed the institutions available to working-class people to permit them to save for their old age (which they could do, she maintained, if only they were thrifty enough), but concluded that the most important such institution was 'the natural and legal provision made through the family'. The best form of investment was 'a man's investment in his own family': reciprocity and obligation would encourage grateful children to support their aged parents. She eloquently wrote, in praise of intergenerational solidarity at the micro-level of the family:

Through the welding power of the family life the three generations form one homogenous whole with identical interests; nowhere is there any sharp break dividing us from the past and future. Our welfare was one with that of parents and grandparents, and is one with that of children and grandchildren; the 'family fortunes' knit all generations together, and make it impossible for us to disregard, whether in private or public action, the welfare of those who come after us.[4]

A secondary source of welfare should be the neighbourliness of small communities, and it is interesting that the COS's own private relief scheme for destitute old people attempted to reinforce this.

Like today's neoliberals, the COS tended to see all economic problems as attitudinal rather than structural. The great social evil to be overcome was not poverty (an artificial construct since all that mattered was how one managed on a low income) but pauperism (in today's parlance, welfare dependency). Pauperism was essentially seen as a degraded mentality rather than an economic problem: 'the spirit of dependence has to be exorcised', wrote Thomas Mackay.[5]

In that regard, the COS felt vindicated by the slow reduction in the pauperism rate that had taken place since the Poor Law reform of 1834, and believed that this could continue (providing that socialism did not gain ground, and cause the working class to rely on the state). Proposals for extensions of state welfare were viewed with the deepest hostility. The COS therefore regarded the agitation for state old age pensions that appeared in the 1890s with growing alarm. It staunchly opposed all suggested schemes, both voluntary and compulsory, though its hostility did diminish somewhat in the 1900s. It is instructive to examine the reasons for the COS's opposition, for they bear uncanny parallels with today's debate.

[4] Helen Bosanquet, *The Strength of the People: A Study in Social Economics* (1902), pp. 239–241, 182–183.
[5] Thomas Mackay, *Methods of Social Reform* (1896), p. 10.

The COS's first point was that the campaign for old age pensions did not emanate from the poor themselves: it was a middle-class movement,[6] led by a liberal elite, which then attracted support from a growing band of politicians (in the new era of electoral populism after the 1884 Reform Act) eager to seek votes by making reckless promises of increasingly expensive schemes. As Sir Edward Brabrook put it, 'candidates of all parties have vied with each other in promises of what they will do in this direction if returned to Parliament'.[7] The great danger in any state pension scheme was that it would create 'a new sort of pauperism',[8] with citizens increasingly looking to the state for help. Independence, thrift and self-reliance – those vital building blocks for any free society – would be undermined. For example, the knowledge that a state pension awaited one at the age of 65 would discourage saving. Another very interesting argument was that there was nothing significant about the age of 65. Why should it be 'the age at which a man is entitled to become partially dependent on the rates and taxes'? There was no social, fiscal or biological justification for choosing age 65 as 'the estate of life to which subsidy should be given'. Besides, old age was not as great as other social evils.[9] While pauperism in old age was excessive, it was not as great a problem as reformers like Charles Booth claimed. Nearly half of it had commenced before the age of 65 and was therefore *not* caused by old age as such.[10] It had originated in improvident habits acquired early in life: as Thomas Mackay put it,

Pauperism is not a question of poverty, but rather of habit and character. Time after time, those who observe these matters closely have seen two men starting life in exactly the same conditions, even among the very poorest class of agricultural labourers. One man will maintain his independence, and bring up his family respectably, and the other will laugh at his responsibilities, and end his days a pauper.[11]

The COS's analysis was not, however, wholly fatalistic and deterministic, since it believed that the redemptive power of its social work could change character and lead to the acquisition of social virtue.

For the COS, evidence showed that those who saved for their old age (for example, by joining a friendly society, and then paying a weekly

6 Bosanquet, *The Strength*, pp. 244–245.
7 Sir Edward Brabrook, 'Old-Age Pensions', in J. St. Loe Strachey (ed.), *The Manufacture of Paupers: A Protest and a Policy* (1907), p. 46.
8 *Ibid.*, p. 51.
9 Thomas Mackay, 'Old Age Pensions and the State', *Charity Organisation Review*, 121, Feb. 1895, pp. 40, 44.
10 C. S. Loch, 'Pauperism and Old-Age Pensions', in Bernard Bosanquet (ed.), *Aspects of the Social Problem* (1895), p. 154.
11 Mackay, *Methods*, pp. 197–198.

sickness benefit contribution at a level most working men could afford, it was alleged) tended not to become paupers after the age of 65.[12] In the long run, the best solution to old age pauperism was therefore to remoralise the non-old, and the most desirable form of social provision for old age – from the point of view of the individual and of society at large – was self-reliance, thrift and voluntary saving. Old age pauperism would decrease in the future, since social and working conditions would continue to improve as they had done over the course of the nineteenth century.[13] A final point is that, like so many neoliberals today, the COS viewed generous occupational pensions for the wealthy as entirely different in principle: they were a form of deferred pay, and therefore uncorrupting.[14]

It is important not to simplify and essentialise the COS's ideology, which was complex and intriguing, but it is clear that its proposed harsh welfare regime was directed at expanding labour supply and driving down the unit cost of labour in the conditions of the nineteenth-century urban labour market, with its large casualised sector and high job insecurity. The abolition of all outdoor relief was seen as a means to this end, since it would force the unemployed to take any job at any wage. Intriguingly, one of the COS's explicit objections to state pensions on the lines of Booth's scheme was that they would restrict the supply of labour: such pensions 'would tend to impair that mobility of labour which seems to be one of the most promising remedies for the evil of unemployment'.[15]

In the final analysis, the COS's ideology was embedded in an economic past. Its opposition to state pensions was backward-looking, in that it did not appreciate the need for retirement as a facilitator of economic modernisation and more rational workforce management in the new era of job-for-life industrial employment that was to pertain for most of the twentieth century. However, its time was to come again.

One nation in old age

Old age pensions provided by the state had been very controversial in the period from the 1880s to the 1908 Old Age Pensions Act. However, by the 1920s the economic value of retirement as an instrument of labour control was well appreciated by most political conservatives. This became even more important in the inter-war recession. High levels of

---

[12] *Ibid.*, pp. 41–42; Thomas Mackay, 'National Pensions', *Charity Organisation Review*, 8, 88, April 1892, p. 131.
[13] Bosanquet, *The Strength*, pp. 234–235.
[14] Oral evidence by Octavia Hill, *Royal Commission of the Aged Poor*, 1895, C-7684-II, vol. III, *Minutes of Evidence*, qs. 10472, 10549–52.
[15] Brabrook, 'Old-Age Pensions', p. 52.

unemployment created an urgent need for industrial restructuring and established an early exit agenda that dominated discussions of pensions and retirement in the period 1922–1939. Under the Conservative government of 1924–1929 there was a significant reform of state pensions, undertaken for economic as well as political reasons. The 1925 contributory state pension scheme of Neville Chamberlain (Minister of Health) was partly designed 'to make it worthwhile for the old men to come out of industry' (thereby assisting workforce downsizing and industrial streamlining), partly to outflank the Labour Party and partly to achieve a permanent and irreversible shift in funding to the more conservative basis of contributory insurance.[16] Those who now see the pay-as-you-go system of funding as little more than a deceitful and unsustainable 'Ponzi scheme' fail to appreciate the fiscally conservative motives behind its introduction: it was a safe alternative to highly redistributive tax-funded pensions. In addition, a large pay-as-you-go element is politically very attractive, since it enables benefits to be paid out relatively quickly after the scheme's introduction: a true funded pension scheme only matures after the first 16-year-old to join it finally reaches age 65.

At no point did Neville Chamberlain oppose state pensions in principle. Indeed, he daringly lowered the eligibility age to 65 for all those qualified under National Health Insurance to receive the new pension (initially, only 40 per cent of the 65–69 age group). The state pension age had been fixed at 70 for both men and women under the 1908 Old Age Pensions Act, largely for reasons of economy. Most late-nineteenth-century campaigners, such as Charles Booth, had advocated 65 as the eligibility age. This had emerged as the generally agreed age in public discussion, even though it had no biological or cognitive significance: as Barbara Shenfield aptly put it in 1957, it was an age 'which medically speaking has been pulled out of a hat'.[17] Lowering the age to 65, together with an improvement in the level of the pension, had been a major item on the agenda of the labour movement.[18] Chamberlain's actions thus left the labour movement in some disarray.

Reducing the state pension age even further to 60 was still a political issue, and in the 1930s mass unemployment engendered much discussion in liberal-left circles of a higher pension at age 60 conditional on

[16] Neville Chamberlain to Duncan C. Fraser, 20 May 1924, National Archives TNA PIN 1/4.
[17] B. E. Shenfield, *Social Policies for Old Age: A Review of Social Provision for Old Age in Great Britain* (1957), p. 103.
[18] The level of the state old age pension had been set at 5s0d (25p) per week under the 1908 Act, then raised to 10s0d (50p) in 1919. Many in the labour movement sought £1 per week.

retirement as a way of encouraging labour force exit and redistributing jobs to the young unemployed. Labour supply was to be contracted, in contrast to what has been the strategy of the last twenty years. In 1940, the women's eligibility age was lowered to 60, as a short-termist strategy for heading off political pressure for an across-the-board rise in the state pension. Curiously, the 1942 Beveridge Report did not recommend restoring the women's age to 65, even though Beveridge viewed pensioners with some ill-concealed hostility.[19]

Beveridge appeared to have established 60 and 65 as the state pension ages for women and men respectively. However, in the 1950s there was a small but growing lobby of free market opinion – precursors of today's neoliberals – arguing that state pension ages should be raised. Expenditure on pensions was seen as dysfunctional: it did not invest in youthful human capital and instead diverted resources to a non-working, unproductive section of the population who were mere passive consumers of wealth rather than producers of it. (The economic value of consumption as a stimulus to aggregate demand was ignored, as was the work performed by retirees in the informal economy.) Thus the 1949 Report of the Royal Commission on Population warned that changes in the numbers and proportion of people over working age were of special importance for overall economic welfare, not just in old age pension costs but in 'the excess of the consumption by the old over their production'.[20] Interestingly, the report expressed foreboding at the projected rise in the proportion of the UK population aged 65+ and hinted strongly that state pension ages might have to rise in the future.[21]

Another critical view was that, since state pension funding was pay-as-you-go, it was taxation in all but name and there was no fund to be invested: the level of aggregate savings was diminished and the process of capital accumulation was thereby inhibited. The most cogent expression of this view was to be found in the report of the 1954 Phillips Committee *On the Economic and Financial Problems of the Provision for Old Age*. In a section explicitly entitled 'Pensions and Capital Accumulation' it warned that the National Insurance scheme was heading for a deficit that would have to be met out of taxation 'so that it will actively impede the very process of capital accumulation on which, implicitly, it rests'. Accordingly, the report urged the government of the day to raise minimum state pension ages 'ultimately' – after a transitional period – to 68 (men) and 63 (women), though it did acknowledge that this would involve additional

---

[19] John Macnicol, *The Politics of Retirement in Britain 1878–1948* (1998), chs. 15 and 16.
[20] *Report of the Royal Commission on Population*, Cmd. 7695 (1949), p. 113.
[21] *Ibid.*, pp. 112–117.

expenditure on unemployment and sickness benefits and might not on its own result in higher employment rates. It also mentioned the desirability of equalising men's and women's eligibility ages at the higher figure.[22]

It is important to remember that today's debate about state pension ages has a long history, and derives from much more than concerns about a future ageing population or the burden of taxation that appear to have arisen relatively suddenly. By and large, the view on the political right has always been that state pension ages should be raised – or that state pensions should be little more than a residual, means-tested system of income support for only the very poorest retirees, the majority of provision being supplied by the private sector. This will, they hope, expand the supply of labour (thereby holding down wages) and contain tax levels. The free movement of capital will therefore be facilitated and economic growth will be maximised. By contrast, the left has defended existing ages, or (at times) sought to lower them – with the aim of tightening up the labour market, reducing recorded unemployment and increasing the bargaining power of workers, while redistributing income to the old. The TUC, for example, had sought a state pension age of 60 as far back as 1925. What has happened in the last twenty years is that the former view has slowly prevailed, and has become part of the dominant political orthodoxy.

The troubled recent history of the debate on state pension ages can be quickly summarised. The overall economic confidence of the 1950s and 1960s had led to a widespread acceptance in policy debates of old age as a stage of life to be protected, and for state pension ages to remain unchanged. Politically and economically, the 1950s were conducive to consensus politics. The Conservative Party had been weakened by its participation in coalition politics since 1931, and had allowed its internal policy-making machinery to atrophy during its long hegemony between 1931 and 1945. The Conservative Research Department was revived under Lord Woolton after 1945 and produced important reformist ideas to appeal to the middle ground of the electorate, the results of which were electorally evident in the 1950s. Labour actually won more total votes in 1951 (48.8 per cent of the electorate, as against the Conservatives' 47.9 per cent) but lost the general election. Thereafter, two further general election victories for the Conservatives were followed by a very narrow defeat in 1964. Clearly, full employment made one-nation conservatism appealing to the electorate. On the economic front, Keynesian demand management appeared to have delivered the magic triumvirate of

---

[22] *Report of the Committee on the Economic and Financial Problems of the Provision for Old Age*, Cmd. 9333, 1954, pp. 34, 49–51.

peacetime full employment, low inflation and reasonably consistent economic growth (despite some fluctuations). It seemed that the Second World War had permanently revived the UK's manufacturing base, providing a stable foundation for continued growth. In this optimistic economic context, the emphasis in policy was on retaining older workers in the workplace. A large number of enquiries, both official and unofficial, were conducted into the possibility of extending working lives. Essentially, by the end of the 1950s these studies had shown that most older workers were indeed remaining in work for as long as possible (given their health, and the availability of jobs). Two-thirds of men were working on past the state pension age anyway, and it would take a 'major change' in labour market behaviour to achieve an overall 1 per cent increase in the total workforce.[23]

Strikingly, both main political parties in the UK at this time rejected suggestions that state pension ages should be raised, and seem to have been very sensitive to old age as a political issue. Any extension of working lives was to be achieved by persuasion rather than compulsion. As the 1951 general election manifesto of the Conservative Party stated, 'the care and comfort of the elderly is a sacred trust. Some of them prefer to remain at work and there must be encouragement for them to do so.' Hence although concern was expressed at the 1953 Conservative Party conference that 'the economic burden on the State of caring for compulsorily retired workers will become intolerable by 1960', the suggested answer was encouragement by making continued employment economically more attractive to older workers. Likewise, the 1955 Conservative general election manifesto promised no raising of state pension ages. By the late 1950s, both Conservative and Labour general election manifestos were focusing more on improvement of the state pension, against a background of Labour's *National Superannuation* scheme of 1957.[24]

Reading the social policy literature of the 1950s and 1960s reveals clearly this broad political consensus that old age and retirement should remain a specially protected stage of life. One apposite example will suffice – the short and succinct book *The Welfare State* (1964), written by Peter Goldman, Head of the Conservative Research Department and the personification of liberal, one-nation conservatism. Goldman had had a promising career as a prospective MP until he stood as a Conservative

---

[23] *Report of the Committee on the Economic and Financial Problems,* pp. 24, 49, 50–51.
[24] F. W. S. Craig, *British General Election Manifestos 1900–1974* (1975), pp. 172, 199, 224; Craig, *Conservative and Labour Party Conference Decisions 1945–1981* (1982), p. 98. On National Superannuation, see Hugh Pemberton, 'Politics and Pensions in Post-war Britain', in Hugh Pemberton, Pat Thane and Noel Whiteside (eds.), *Britain's Pensions Crisis: History and Policy* (2006), pp. 49–51.

candidate in the famous 1962 Orpington by-election (which the Liberals won in spectacular fashion). In *The Welfare State* he devoted a chapter to old age, in which he outlined the policy options available. Many individuals found enforced retirement to be an unpleasant shock, and there were 'sound economic as well as social reasons' for encouraging extensions of the working life; however, he recognised that there was 'no enormous reservoir of employable male labour over the age of 65'. Four policy options could be considered – raising state pension ages, employment quotas for older workers, enabling greater transferability of occupational pension schemes and the promotion of part-time working and phased retirement – but all of these had practical and political disadvantages. In an observation highly relevant to today, Goldman warned that raising state pension ages when there were no jobs to be filled might only result in more expenditure on unemployment and sickness benefits. What is striking about Goldman's position is his hostility to any erosion of the existing welfare rights of older people, and his desire to preserve retirement as a free choice.[25] It was an attitude embedded in the industrial culture that then pertained: retirement was integral to fordist capitalism.

It is difficult to conceive of this now, but for a time – in the early 1960s – economic optimism was so great that there briefly emerged a consensus that working lives would shorten, retirement would be taken at progressively earlier ages and there would be abundant leisure for all. A playful old age would slowly extend down the age structure, funded by the limitless economic growth that would accompany the technological revolution. It seemed to be fulfilment of Keynes's prediction in 1930 that eventually the working week would consist of only fifteen hours.[26]

In the late 1970s, there was a debate on the possibility of equalising the men's and the women's ages.[27] This was in part impelled by wider discussions of gender equality and in part an anticipation of the new state pension scheme introduced by the 1975 Social Security Pensions Act (which particularly changed the pension entitlement of women). Four principal options were discussed: equalisation between men and women at age 60; the same at age 65; provision for flexible retirement somewhere between ages 60 and 70; and a revenue-neutral point between ages 60 and 65 (63 being the most discussed – for example, it was favoured

---

[25] Peter Goldman, *The Welfare State* (1964), pp. 46–55.

[26] J. M. Keynes, 'Economic Possibilities for Our Grandchildren' (1930), in Keynes, *Essays in Persuasion* (1931). The idea of a shorter working week survives today – for example, as suggested by the New Economics Foundation.

[27] See, for example, Department of Health and Social Security, *A Happier Old Age: A Discussion Document on Elderly People in Our Society* (1978), ch. 3.

by the National Association of Pension Funds).[28] The many pros and cons were considered, including the transitional problems. Interestingly, several cautionary points were made (apart from the cost of equalising both ages at 60 or 63): that fairness would require an equivalent reduction in National Insurance contributions; that the necessary jobs did not exist; that there would be rises in expenditure on other benefits; and that this would be a betrayal of implicit promises made to existing pensioners, violating their rights under the contributory principle.[29] Interestingly, these objections seem to have vanished from today's public debate.

Very quickly, however, western economies began to run into trouble and by the early 1980s, as neoliberalism took hold, a different attitude towards old age in the welfare state was emerging – in many ways a resurgence of the nineteenth-century neoclassical views of the COS. Initially, the labour movement reacted to rising unemployment by reviving its 1930s policies of encouraging early exit and redistributing jobs to the younger unemployed. It therefore still supported a lowered state pension age: in 1976 and 1981, the Labour Party annual conferences passed motions in favour of lowering the eligibility age to 60, with a state pension of 'not less than one half average gross earnings for a married couple and one third average earnings for a single person [1976] . . . the object being to combat the growing problem of adult and school leaver unemployment and the advancement of new technology [1981]'.[30] However, the political climate was rapidly changing on both sides of the Atlantic, and the attacks on state pension provision intensified. In 1983, the Reagan administration passed legislation amending the Social Security Act so that there would be gradual increases in eligibility ages – to 66 between 2000 and 2009, and 67 between 2017 and 2027. A year later, a debate on intergenerational equity took off in the USA. Identical developments were taking place in the UK. In 1980 the Thatcher government recalibrated the formula for annual rises in the state pension, such that henceforth it was linked only to prices, rather than either wages or prices – whichever rose higher. Interestingly, the National Insurance contributions that in part paid for the state pension remained pegged to earnings. In a statement of breathtaking unrealism, the Chancellor of the Exchequer responsible, Sir Geoffrey Howe, retrospectively justified this cut by arguing that 'the great majority of pensioners have meanwhile enjoyed large increases in that part of their income that comes from private savings'.[31] The result,

[28] National Association of Pension Funds, *Towards Equality in Retirement Ages* (1977), p. 12.
[29] Equal Opportunities Commission, *Equalising the Pension Age* (1978).
[30] Craig, *Conservative and Labour Party Conference Decisions*, pp. 435–436.
[31] Geoffrey Howe, *Conflict of Loyalty* (1995), p. 135.

as mentioned in the previous chapter, was a slow but steady fall in the relative value of the state pension, bequeathing to the 1997 Labour government the unenviable task of pension reform. It is no exaggeration to say that this has been the most radical and profound change in state pension policy in the postwar period, the deleterious effects of which will be felt for years to come as successive governments grapple with the problem of restoring the state pension's historic relative value. In 1982 the cabinet considered a paper by the Central Policy Review Staff (commissioned by Mrs Thatcher and Sir Geoffrey Howe) outlining drastic cuts in the whole welfare state.[32] Four years later, the Conservative government considerably reduced the scale of the State Earnings-Related Pension Scheme (SERPS) (later introducing incentives for people to contract out of it and into private pension schemes). Finally, in 1989 the Thatcher government contemplated raising the state pension age, arguing that this was necessary because of improved health and longevity, a diminishing supply of younger workers in the future and a corresponding numerical increase in older people.[33] By the 1990s and 2000s, there were increasing demands from those on the political right that the state pension age should be raised to 68 or even 70,[34] generally accompanied by dire warnings of the demographic changes that lay in store.

Economic transitions

These changes in the old age agenda can only be properly understood if the economic background is briefly sketched in. It is often stated that Mrs Thatcher's aim was to 'roll back the state', but this is meaningless without any explanation for the economic rationality behind this aim.

From 1945 to 1973, western economies enjoyed a long boom, fuelled by cheap oil and a neocolonial relationship with the Third World, which kept the price of raw materials low. Expensive global transportation also meant that nation-state economies could remain self-contained and relatively impervious to international competition. In retrospect, the period 1945–1973 can be seen as a relative economic golden age for the industrialised nations, during which the world economy was characterised by sustained growth, and both price and exchange rate stability. To be sure, there were some warning signs before then – for example, the mild recession of the late 1950s and the first appearance of unemployment

---

[32] Alan Travis, 'Margaret Thatcher's Role in Plan to Dismantle Welfare State Revealed', *Guardian*, 28 Dec. 2012, www.theguardian.com

[33] David Hughes, 'Thatcher's Work-to-70 Plan for the Old', *Sunday Times*, 29 Jan. 1989.

[34] For example, Alan Pickering, *Pensions Policy: How Government Can Get Us Saving Again* (2004), p. 1.

blackspots in the mid-1960s – but the year 1973 rightly stands as an economic watershed.

All of this began to change from the early 1970s onwards.[35] The immediate impetus was, of course, the 1973 oil price shock. Following the Yom Kippur War, the Organisation of the Petroleum Exporting Countries (OPEC) decided to raise the price of oil and end their subservient relationship with the industrialised western superpowers. Having been less than $2 a barrel before 1973, the price of oil quickly quadrupled and reached $34 by mid-1979. The rapid rise in the price of oil was traumatic, sending shock waves through developed economies, fuelling rampant inflation and triggering a massive economic restructuring, with private capital moving out of heavy manufacturing and into new service-based sectors. One such service sector was welfare services – health care, education, private pensions, insurance against risk and so on – and henceforth they became products to be privatised, then bought and sold across the world.

The effect on industrialised labour markets was dramatic. In the UK, between 1981 and 2006, the proportion of all jobs that were in manufacturing fell from 31 per cent to 17 per cent (for men) and 18 per cent to 6 per cent (women). By contrast, over the same period jobs in banking, finance and insurance rose from 11 per cent to 21 per cent of all jobs (men) and from 12 per cent to 19 per cent of all jobs (women).[36] The inherent weaknesses of western economies had been evident for some time: in the UK, for example, unemployment had been rising since the mid-1960s and areas of deindustrialisation were beginning to develop. The events after the 1970s essentially speeded up a restructuring that was incipient.

The social, economic, political and cultural changes inaugurated by this restructuring were interconnected in highly complex ways, with a blurring of cause and effect. (For example, did low birth rates in the 1970s enable more women to enter the labour market, or did women's increasing labour force participation, in response to the growth of part-time jobs, cause birth rates to fall?) As with all economic analyses, one cannot ultimately 'explain' precisely why western economies changed so dramatically at this point in history. Again, the social and economic traumas of the 1970s – in America, inflation, a rise in the poverty rate, stagnating real wages, rising unemployment and economic inactivity, post-Watergate/post-Vietnam pessimism – eroded those grand narratives of progress that had dominated postwar political culture.

---

[35] B. W. E. Alford, *Britain in the World Economy Since 1880* (1996), p. 245.
[36] Office for National Statistics, *Social Trends No. 37 2007 edition* (2007), p. 48.

The process of explanation may therefore be very challenging, but there is no difficulty in identifying the key social changes. For the purposes of this study, we need only consider several interrelated labour market developments, which fashioned a prescriptive ideology that all adults of working age should support themselves through paid employment and that the state should enforce this by stricter modes of discipline (activation, conditionality, sanctions, benefit withdrawal and so on): an increase in women's employment, instituting a move from the male breadwinner model to the adult breadwinner model; the growth of part-time, low-paid, insecure service jobs, which contributed to widening income inequality and tended to be non-unionised, thereby weakening the power of organised labour; a relative (and sometimes absolute) fall or stagnation in wages; the search by large corporations for higher profits, involving increasing global competition, downsizing, outsourcing of production to new overseas workforces and a downward pressure on wages; and, as a consequence of this restructuring and technological innovation, a decline in the employment rates of older men (only partly offset by a slight rise since the early 1990s). Such jobless older men were, of course, geographically concentrated in areas of chronic deindustrialisation and became the core of the long-term unemployed. Between 1971 and 1994 the economic activity rates of men aged 55–59 fell from 95 per cent to 76 per cent. For men aged 60–64, the 1971 level of 86 per cent had fallen to 51 per cent by 1994. By 2013, the rates had risen – but only slightly – to 81 per cent for men aged 55–59 and 59 per cent for men aged 60–64.

The new economic order that emerged after 1973 was one that puzzled many economic analysts and led to a discrediting of Keynesian economics.[37] Keynesianism demand management had seemingly delivered steady, non-inflationary, full-employment economic growth in the 1950s and most of the 1960s. Yet in the 1970s Keynesianism appeared to have failed: unemployment and inflation both rose and economic growth was sluggish – the phenomenon of 'stagflation'. Having been only 5.0 per cent in January 1970, UK inflation rose rapidly to 26.9 per cent in August 1975; it then fell, but rose again with the second spike in commodity prices, to 21.9 per cent in May 1980. Likewise, unemployment rose steadily in the 1970s and early 1980s, peaking at over 3,000,000 in the autumn of 1982 (14.0 per cent of the labour force). It was against this economic background that monetarism re-emerged (first introduced by a Labour government in 1976) and claimed to offer the answer: the key

---

[37] This was paralleled by an interesting debate among economic historians about whether, at an ideological level, the 'Keynesian revolution' had actually occurred – or whether structural economic changes were the cause.

to price stability was control of the money supply, and once the money supply was restricted, high unemployment would act as a deflationary device by reducing aggregate demand. The flow of investment away from declining sectors of the economy and into new ones would be facilitated. (This radical cure for the economy was only made possible by North Sea oil revenues, which funded unemployment benefits for some and tax cuts for the rich – unlike the case of Norway, where oil revenues were wisely invested for the future benefit of all the nation.) The new economic landscape proved fertile ground for the re-emergence of neoliberalism.

The re-emergence of neoliberalism

Economic liberalism had lain somewhat dormant in the twenty-five years after the Second World War – the Butskellite 'postwar consensus' was a broadly social democratic one – but in the 1970s neoclassical ideas began to resurface, and henceforth they exerted a growing influence on welfare states in general and the old age agenda in particular. In the USA the big corporations had been relatively tolerant towards the cost of federal Social Security up to the 1970s, but the economic and social transformations of that decade caused them to change their position.[38] Welfare states were accused of exerting a damaging fiscal drag on western economies and discouraging working at a time when a rapid transformation of those economies was needed. State support in old age was seen as encouraging retirement and restricting labour supply. All of this led to a growing hostility towards the British and American welfare states. It is often thought that the 'crisis of Social Security' in the USA is a relatively recent phenomenon, yet it was under attack as far back as the 1970s by those who sought to privatise it.

There can be no better illustration of this new political trend than the career of Martin Feldstein, Professor of Economics at Harvard, neoconservative stalwart, NBER President for some three decades and guru of US supply-side economics. In the 1970s, Feldstein was arguing that the USA's system of unemployment benefit had increased the rate and duration of unemployment,[39] and that Social Security for retirees had been a major contributory cause of rising retirement rates, as well as reducing the level of aggregate saving and therefore the rate of capital

---

[38] John Myles, 'Postwar Capitalism and the Extension of Social Security into a Retirement Wage', in Margaret Weir, Ann Shola Orloff and Theda Skocpol (eds.), *The Politics of Social Policy in the United States* (1988), pp. 274–275.

[39] Feldstein, 'Economics of the New Unemployment', p. 38.

accumulation.[40] (This was against a background of a generally slowing rate of capital accumulation in the US economy at large.) By the mid-1980s, Feldstein was confidently declaring that 'now there is widespread agreement that the conditions of unemployment, retirement, a low level of accumulated assets, and very high medical bills are in part the result of rational choices by the individuals affected'.[41] The logical solution was to cut back and privatise Social Security – a cause which Feldstein has strongly supported since the 1970s.[42]

Given that retired people absorb such a large proportion of welfare state spending, it is not surprising that a new old age agenda began to appear at this time, based upon the broader neoliberal critique of what had gone wrong in western economies. Chapter 5 will explore the issue of male early retirement in more detail: it is sufficient to note here that, by the 1980s, it was clear that the economic activity rates of older men were falling. Initially, this was encouraged by governments (both tacitly and explicitly) as a means of streamlining workforces – for example, by the UK's 1977–1988 Job Release Scheme to encourage early retirement, or by the decision to massage the official unemployment figures by moving older men onto long-term sickness and disability benefits and, in effect, permanent unemployment. These have often been viewed retrospectively as 'causes', whereas they were in fact the policy consequences of rising unemployment among older men.

However, as western economies slowly restructured and recovered from the early 1990s, and most employment rates rose, governments began to look for ways of forcing the forgotten army of jobless older men back to work. The economic recovery of the 1990s involved an expansion of low-grade, poorly remunerated insecure jobs (often part-time) and it was against this background that early retirement became increasingly problematised (and age discrimination in employment rediscovered). By the 1990s there were increasing concerns that male early retirement would inexorably spread down the age structure, creating a growing dependent population aged 50+ that would be very expensive to support. The explanation offered for the historical spread of retirement was a supply-side, behavioural, rational choice one – that it had been caused by state pensions and higher levels of savings. Other claims increasingly

[40] Martin Feldstein, 'Social Security, Induced Retirement, and Aggregate Capital Accumulation', *Journal of Political Economy*, 82, 5, 1974, pp. 905–926; Feldstein, 'Toward a Reform of Social Security', *The Public Interest*, 40, Summer 1975, pp. 83, 85.
[41] Martin Feldstein, 'The Social Security Explosion', *The Public Interest*, 81, Fall 1985, p. 95.
[42] Martin Feldstein, 'Facing the Social Security Crisis', *The Public Interest*, 47, Spring 1977, pp. 88–100; Feldstein (ed.), *Privatizing Social Security* (1998).

made from the 1980s onwards were that there had been a substantial misallocation of resources between the old and the young, and that this intergenerational inequity needed to be rebalanced.[43] As shown in the previous chapter, many commentators claimed that older people actually enjoyed good health and financial security, that they were well integrated into society and that their poverty rates were exaggerated.[44] Pension schemes were said to be the product of 'vote-catching policies' promised by irresponsible politicians, and the pay-as-you-go aspect of their funding was said to be unsustainable with a future ageing population.[45] The similarities with the COS's views a hundred years earlier are striking.

Perhaps the most interesting overall critique was the claim that welfare benefits were impeding labour supply at a time of economic restructuring when it was vital that displaced workers should quickly move to new jobs, regardless of remuneration levels or working conditions. Male early retirement was a major obstacle to fluidity of labour. One solution increasingly posited was that older people should remain in work later in life, thus enlarging the number of competing job-seekers, holding down wages, increasing economic growth and reducing pension expenditure. As the US neoconservative think-tank, the Hudson Institute, suggested in 1997, three strategies were henceforth needed – expanding the pool of available workers, increasing labour force participation and promoting upward labour mobility: 'All three sets of remedies begin with the premise that an aging America needs to increase its supply of highly skilled workers willing to enter or remain in the labour force.'[46] In the decades after the 1970s, the strategy of achieving sustained, non-inflationary economic growth by expanding labour supply and thereby containing wage demands gradually became the new economic orthodoxy.[47]

To an extent, the control of inflation had always been a central political aim for western political leaders. Runaway inflation was politically and economically disastrous: for the immediate postwar generation of politicians, memories of Weimar Germany were still strong. In addition, price stability was always a very sensitive issue within the British Conservative Party (in government, 1951–1964, 1970–1974 and 1979–1997), dividing the left and right wings of the Party. On a famous occasion in

---

[43] These issues are fully explored in later chapters.

[44] See, for example, Stephen Crystal, *America's Old Age Crisis: Public Policy and the Two Worlds of Aging* (1982), esp. pp. 14–18.

[45] Norman Barry, 'Pensions and Policy-Making in Great Britain', in Alan Peacock and Norman Barry, *The Political Economy of Pension Provision* (1986), pp. 11–12.

[46] Richard W. Judy and Carol D'Amico, *Workforce 2020: Work and Workers in the 21st Century* (1997), pp. 7–8.

[47] Harvey, *A Brief History*, pp. 22–26.

January 1958, the Chancellor of the Exchequer, Peter Thorneycroft, and two of his lieutenants, Nigel Birch and Enoch Powell, resigned from their ministerial posts because of plans to increase public expenditure (despite the fact that the Treasury's overall strategy in the 1950s was vigilantly deflationary). The Prime Minister, Harold Macmillan, was thereafter viewed by the free market, right-wing of the Party as a quasi-socialist, since he had seemingly boosted inflation by a vote-catching rise in government spending. Control of inflation was also vital to the new economic order, in which finance capital was replacing industrial capital as a consequence of the shift in the UK's economic base from manufacturing to service industries, including financial services: low inflation creates a stable, predictable world in which finance capital can flourish. Whether this obsession with price stability is to the benefit of everyone is a moot point: it may greatly help the financial services industry and the global elite, but it has detrimental side effects for others. Indeed, some view the construction of an 'inflationary crisis' at this time as a class strategy, since inflation is most damaging to those at the top of society – the business elite of creditors who have capital to invest – rather than those in debt at the bottom of society, for whom moderate inflation, successfully contained, can actually be quite beneficial.[48]

Reducing inflation and then successfully containing it has therefore been at the core of macro-economic policy for the last four decades. As early as February 1974, the Conservative general election manifesto declared that 'the gravest threat to our national well-being has been the menace of unrestrained inflation',[49] and soon after taking office in 1979 – in her famous 'The Lady's Not for Turning' speech to the 1980 Conservative Party conference – Mrs Thatcher identified reducing inflation as 'our prime economic objective... No policy which puts at risk the defeat of inflation – however great its short-term attraction – can be right.' Somewhat disingenuously, Mrs Thatcher denied that this was a new strategy, born of monetarism, and argued that it was for the common good. For example, inflation punished savers, and raised unemployment: countries that had lower rates of inflation also had lower levels of unemployment.[50] (Clearly she had forgotten the 1930s in the UK, when mass unemployment was accompanied by deflation.)

However, it is clear that a new economic era had begun. 'The government's overall priority is to reduce and contain inflation', began the 1981

[48] Blyth, *Great Transformations*, pp. 147–151, 286. For a brief but entertaining discussion, see Ha-Joon Chang, *23 Things They Don't Tell You about Capitalism* (2010), pp. 51–61.

[49] Craig, *British General Election Manifestos*, pp. 377–378.

[50] Margaret Thatcher, 'Speech to Conservative Party Conference' (1980), www.margarretthatcher.org

governmental white paper *Growing Older* (the rest of which was a fairly innocuous survey of provision for retirement).[51] The importance of this new strategy was eloquently expressed in his memoirs by Sir Geoffrey Howe, Mrs Thatcher's first Chancellor of the Exchequer and economic liberal. Restrictions on the money supply were essential if price stability was to return: while Prime Minister, Mrs Thatcher, had the Retail Price Index figure 'engraved on her heart – indeed, re-engraved, from month to month'. The new economic orthodoxy, writes Howe, was that 'success against inflation was a crucial component of a return to long-run economic growth and stability, particularly in the UK'. Accordingly, Howe, in his 1980 budget speech, declared that 'restraint of the growth of money and credit is, then, essential and it needs to be maintained over a considerable period of time in order to defeat inflation'.[52] So important was this strategy that – controversially – the brief peak in unemployment in the early 1990s was seen by the Chancellor of the Exchequer, Norman Lamont, as a price 'well worth paying' to reduce inflation.[53]

By the 1990s and 2000s expanding labour supply and controlling inflation were written into all UK macro-economic policies and became part of the overall economic strategy of the European Union (for example, the 2000 Lisbon Treaty set a target employment rate of 70 per cent for member states). Under New Labour, it seemed to be delivering sustained economic growth and contributed greatly to the heady optimism of the 1997–2008 period. Hence in July 2007 Prime Minister Gordon Brown reiterated the promise that, in order to maintain economic stability, 'we will get to grips with inflation, we always have done in the last 10 years'; somewhat unfortunately, in the light of subsequent events, he predicted that 'the economy will continue to grow this year, next year and the year after'.[54] Even more strikingly, in one of his last media interviews as Prime Minister (on 8 April 2010, one month before the general election), Gordon Brown repeatedly emphasised that the control of inflation had been New Labour's greatest achievement, creating the conditions for stable economic growth. The post-2008 recession, he argued, had been caused by international forces outside New Labour's control and not by domestic economic policies.[55] In order to understand why the control of inflation had become absolutely central to New Labour's macro-economic policies, the next chapter will examine the crucial

[51] Department of Health and Social Security, *Growing Older*, Cmnd. 8173 (1981), p. iii.
[52] Howe, *Conflict*, pp. 130, 161, 163.
[53] Norman Lamont, *In Office* (1999), p. 90.
[54] Graeme Wearden, 'Brown Vows to Keep Inflation Under Control', *Guardian*, 6 July 2007, www.theguardian.com
[55] BBC Today Programme, 8 Apr. 2010, www.bbc.co.uk

transformation in social democratic thinking that occurred in the 1990s. It was a transformation that was to have a profound effect on the politics of old age.

Conclusion: back to the future

In the twenty-first century we seem to be moving backwards to a nineteenth-century conceptualisation of 'old age' whereby the term is ceasing to apply to citizens aged in their mid-sixties and above and will henceforth be only applicable to the 'oldest old'. The parallels with the Charity Organisation Society are striking. Its views were also derived from both firm ideological convictions and a labour market segmented into a small skilled core and a large periphery of casualised workers, which required that labour supply be maximised and work-discipline strongly enforced. Since the economic turmoils of the 1970s, the strategy of restraining inflation and enlarging labour markets has been central to macro-economic policy; older people are seen as having a vital role to play in this strategy. This has had a transformative effect on the concept of old age. It has been the core driver of change, with other factors (notably demographic concerns) mixed in as secondary justifications.

3   Pensions reform, from the 1990s onwards

The period 1979–1992 was traumatic for the Labour Party in the UK, involving the loss of four general elections, the hegemony of Thatcherism and bitter internal divisions within the political left. Under the leadership of Neil Kinnock, the Party moved more to the centre ground in an attempt to become electable and capture the hearts and minds of those floating voters who are the key to winning general elections. By the early 1990s, many in the Labour Party felt that it had failed to understand the material aspirations of the skilled working class and lower middle class, the rise of consumer culture, the effects of globalisation and the increase in home ownership. It is also the case that the Party was having to survive in a world of growing corporate power and associated media hostility,[1] as well as the erosion of its electoral base with the decline of heavy industry and attendant changes in the UK's occupational structure.

The centre-left accordingly began to fashion a social democratic version of the new neoclassical orthodoxy, as part of a broader macroeconomic strategy of creating non-inflationary economic growth without the boom and bust of previous decades. Moving jobless people off benefits and into work would expand labour supply and contain wages, since more workers would be competing for jobs; the inflationary tendencies that had previously accompanied economic booms would be held in check. From a Keynesian perspective, more people in work would also boost aggregate demand by raising purchasing power. Economic growth would then be stimulated, and an economic virtuous circle would be created. The centre-left's view of the Thatcher experiment was that it had cynically and cruelly used mass unemployment and deindustrialisation as a means of achieving several aims: the rapid restructuring of British industry from manufacturing to service jobs, also assisting the growth of finance capital; the destruction of trades union power specifically, and working-class culture generally; and a deflating of the economy, since mass unemployment reduced aggregate demand. The result

---

[1] Very clearly demonstrated during the 1992 general election campaign.

was a growth of long-term unemployment (often presented as male early retirement or work-disability), widening inequality, a sharp rise in child poverty, more insecure employment and whole areas of the UK blighted by deindustrialisation.

This critique was given added urgency by the recession of 1989–1992, when inflation rose and unemployment briefly reached 3,000,000. As the UK economy slowly recovered from 1994 onwards there was a growing political movement for state intervention to help unemployed people find jobs. This moral critique of the Thatcher/Major indifference to the personal tragedy of long-term unemployment was to become a powerful emotive weapon in the 1997 general election campaign. It also enabled New Labour, under Tony Blair, to fashion an ideological strategy that essentially took credit for what was happening anyway and which was experienced by nearly all advanced industrial societies. The collapse of communism in Eastern Europe seemed to undermine Marxism as a viable analysis, and ushered in the prospect of a global capitalism with massive new markets, giving unprecedented power to transnational corporations and further weakening organised labour. A final ingredient was Labour's unexpected defeat in the 1992 general election (up to the last minute, polls had predicted a Labour win). This also caused it to move ideologically to the right in an attempt to capture the electoral 'middle ground'. Labour's failure was all the more galling since Americans in the same year voted in a Democratic President, Bill Clinton, with moderate centre-left views. All in all, the early 1990s was a time of great change for the social democratic left in the UK.

The Borrie report

A cardinal principle of the new realism was that Labour had to work within the existing constraints of globalisation and the powerful multinationals. The solution was to fashion new supply-side policies to reskill, re-educate and, if necessary, remotivate the long-term unemployed and help them back into work. This would be the central function of the 'social investment state'. Mild coercion was to be accompanied by policies to enhance 'social justice' – a concept that was only vaguely defined. The new political position was one that went 'beyond left and right' and represented a creative adaptation to the new global economic forces.

It was against this background that in late 1992 the new Labour leader, John Smith, established a Commission on Social Justice chaired by Sir Gordon Borrie to find a way forward for the social democratic left. Membership of the Borrie Commission on Social Justice consisted of those on the moderate left, and its recommendations represented an acceptance of the new capitalism that had emerged since the 1970s, characterised by more insecure labour markets, demographic pressures, changes in family and gender roles, economic uncertainty and so on. Above all else, a future Labour government would have to work within the existing constraints of global economic forces and not attempt to redistribute economic power away from the big corporations. As Peter Townsend critically commented, of the Borrie Commission members, 'Without saying as much, they appear to have been governed by the belief that to win the next election the Labour Party must bow to the pressures of the international market, reduce long-standing aspirations to social equality and withdraw from the most costly commitments to the welfare state.'[2]

The Borrie report of 1994 (published after John Smith's untimely death) approached the sensitive issue of stimulating labour market demand with some caution. Demand management was increasingly 'an international, rather than a national, issue', but UK governments could do something through investment rather than consumption-led booms (which had proved harmful and inflationary in the past).[3] Employment growth could be created by supply-side policies that would move jobless people into economic activity. Borrie established the rather simplistic and historically inaccurate narrative – one that has become a new orthodoxy – that in the past the welfare state had been too 'passive', unconditionally providing cash benefits for the unemployed on the assumption that a future economic upswing would restore full employment.[4] Instead, the social security system should be 'a springboard for economic opportunity' via 'active' labour market policies to move people off benefits and into work. 'The quickest route out of poverty' was 'a good job at a fair wage'; 'employability' was now more important than job security, and the long-term unemployed should be reintegrated back into the labour market. More intensive labour market activation was to be accompanied by 'real choices across the life-cycle in the balance of employment, family, education, leisure and retirement'[5] – something of a contradiction. Significantly, 'the maintenance of low inflation' was one of several

---

[2] Peter Townsend, 'Persuasion and Conformity: An Assessment of the Borrie Report on Social Justice', *New Left Review*, 213, Sept.–Oct. 1995, p. 137. For another interesting critique, see Chris Pierson, 'The Welfare State: From Beveridge to Borrie', in Helen Fawcett and Rodney Lowe (eds.), *Welfare Policy in Britain: The Road from 1945* (1999), pp. 208–224.

[3] Commission on Social Justice, *Social Justice: Strategies for National Renewal: The Report of the Commission on Social Justice* (1994), pp. 162–164.

[4] *Ibid.*, p. 20. The labelling of the past welfare state as 'passive' completely ignored all the powerful sanctions that had existed to force unemployed people off benefits – for example, the wage stop and the four-week rule.

[5] *Ibid.*, p. 21.

key aims. There was mention of job creation through public investment, but the preferred option was via 'concerted attempts to match employee aspirations with employment through guidance, training and counselling' and enhancing employability (it was not envisaged that there would be any supply–demand mismatches).[6] A reformed welfare state would help citizens negotiate the new risks and uncertainties over a lifecourse, but ultimately what mattered was personal responsibility at an individual level.

Old age and retirement did not figure strongly in Borrie: most of its concerns were with the working-aged, who were seen as potential economic contributors. It highlighted the fall in the relative value of the basic state pension, but did not suggest an across-the-board increase; instead a new means-tested pension guarantee should be introduced for the poorest pensioners, with the state pension age being set at 65 for both men and women. Overall, however, its espousal of an anti-inflationary, labour supply strategy for economic growth was likely to pave the way for a raising of state pension ages as a way of forcing older people to work later in life via more intensive activation.

Richard Layard and activation

In the 1990s, the moderate social democratic left in the UK was much influenced by Richard Layard, a Professor of Economics at the London School of Economics and a leading authority on unemployment. Layard presented an economically complex and seductively elegant version of the new economic consensus represented by the Borrie report.

Layard considered in detail the problem of long-term unemployment, which he judged to be economically dysfunctional, socially wasteful and personally tragic for those affected. Since the 1960s, there had been fluctuations in the level of unemployment, but a growing core problem was that of long-term joblessness. It was in part a result of the UK's deindustrialisation, and therefore quite localised, but it had been exacerbated by government policies (notably, the encouragement of early retirement and a shifting of people from unemployment benefits onto disability benefits). Hence the proportion of unemployed who had been out of work for more than twelve months rose from 18 per cent in 1960 to 38 per cent in 1991.[7] The UK was not alone. The problem of the older male 'discouraged worker' was one experienced by many industrialised economies at this time.

---

[6] *Ibid.*, pp. 105, 173, 175–176.
[7] Richard Layard and John Philpott, *Stopping Unemployment* (1991), p. 6.

Layard recognised that the major impulse behind currency inflation had been the rise in commodity prices in 1973–1974 and 1979–1980,[8] but boom-and-bust cycles had contributed too. An overheating of the economy would be accompanied by falling unemployment and rising inflation; this would in time necessitate deflationary measures, resulting in falling inflation but rising unemployment and economic stagnation. The question was how the UK could break out of this endless cycle of boom and bust.

A crucial element in Layard's analysis was his contention that the historic inflation/unemployment trade-off (which had frustrated nearly every postwar government) only applied to the *short-term* unemployed.[9] Long-term unemployment had little effect on inflation: its growth in the recent past had not restrained inflation as much as it should have.[10] Layard therefore concluded that reintegrating the long-term unemployed back into the labour market would *not* be inflationary. There was simply no need to maintain a large reserve army of labour.

Central to Layard's analysis was his contention that there was no such thing as a 'lump of labour' or 'lump of output' (that is, a fixed number of jobs in the economy at any one time). Moving unemployed people off benefits and into work (with higher incomes) would stimulate aggregate demand, boosting economic growth and increasing the total number of jobs without inflationary pressures being created.[11] More workers competing for jobs would contain wages, and the wage-price spiral would not occur. It was, in essence, a redesigned Keynesian labour supply strategy – a 'new supply-side agenda for the left'.

In the 1990s, Layard's remedies seemed a beguilingly attractive alternative to neoliberal deflationary policies. They would achieve several complementary aims – the reduction of unemployment, the control of inflation, steady economic growth and an attack on the human tragedy of long-term unemployment. However, they did present several serious problems, which were glossed over in the heady optimism of the New Labour years. First, it was not self-evident that the 'lump of labour' was a fallacy: when the trend to part-time employment since the 1950s was

---

[8] Richard Layard, Stephen Nickell and Richard Jackman, *The Unemployment Crisis* (1995 edn.), p. 7.

[9] Richard Layard, *How to Reduce Unemployment by Changing National Insurance and Providing a Job-Guarantee* (1985), p. 9.

[10] Richard Layard and Stephen Nickell, 'Unemployment in Britain', in C. R. Bean, P. R. G. Layard and S. J. Nickell (eds.), *The Rise in Unemployment* (1986), p. 123.

[11] Richard Layard, *What Labour Can Do* (1997), pp. 62–63. The idea that the lump of labour is a 'fallacy' has a long history in economic thought, and received its most famous expression in Paul Samuelson, *Economics: An Introductory Analysis* (1958 edn.), pp. 551–552.

taken into account, there appeared to be no net growth of fulltime equivalent jobs proportionate to population growth.[12] All that had happened was that available work had been sliced up more thinly, and distributed to a larger number of workers. An internal contradiction was that, if increasing labour supply was not to have inflationary effects, there *had* to be a lump of labour, since wages would only be held down if more workers competed for a finite number of jobs. Pushing more workless people into the low-paid, insecure jobs that formed the basis of the economic recovery of 1992–2008 had the effect of decreasing the number of benefit poor, but increasing the number of working poor. This was reflected in the growth of the proportion of children in poverty who lived in a household where at least one parent worked, which rose from 42 per cent in 1997 to 66 per cent in 2013. Indeed, the UK's economic recovery after 2008 was also based upon a growth of low-paid jobs, such that, by late 2014, there were concerns that revenue from income tax was falling because fewer and fewer earned enough to qualify for it.[13] A striking feature of economic growth in the last twenty years has been that it has become harder to 'work your way out of poverty'. Again, only once the short-term unemployed had found jobs would the long-term do so – and, as Layard acknowledged, re-employing the short-term unemployed would be inflationary. Finally, Layard's theories appeared vindicated when a version of them was operationalised by New Labour after 1997 because employment growth was taking place anyway. (The fact that this growth in the UK was fuelled by consumer debt and inflated house prices was insufficiently appreciated.)

Layard's prescriptions were highly relevant to the changing conceptualisation of old age, for two reasons. First, he enthusiastically advocated labour market activation policies, even going so far as to suggest a 'job guarantee' for the long-term unemployed.[14] These were to be balanced by greater conditionality and a stricter test of willingness to work. Layard took the neoclassical, behavioural view that the benefit:wages replacement ratio had become too generous since the 1960s and sanctions against benefit claimants had been unwisely relaxed.[15] One group

---

[12] John Macnicol, *Age Discrimination: An Historical and Contemporary Analysis* (2006), pp. 96–101.

[13] 'Income Tax Revenue Could be Lower than Expected, Finance Watchdog Says', *Guardian*, 13 Oct. 2014, www.theguardian.com

[14] Layard, *How to Reduce Unemployment*, p. 11; Richard Layard, *How to Beat Unemployment* (1986), pp. 97–98.

[15] Richard Layard, Stephen Nickell and Richard Jackman, *Unemployment, Macroeconomic Performance and the Labour Market* (1991), pp. 472–473; Layard and Philpott, *Stopping Unemployment*, pp. 16–17; Layard, *More Jobs, Less Inflation: The Case for a Counter-Inflation Tax* (1982), p. 42.

to whom activation should be applied was the early retired and possibly even the conventional (age 65+) retired. A second interlinked point is that Layard resoundingly criticised past policies of encouraging early retirement. Far from redistributing jobs to the younger unemployed, early retirement merely reduced labour supply, increased long-term unemployment, boosted inflation, inhibited economic growth and actually made a country poorer: those countries (such as Japan) that had higher levels of later-life working did not have higher levels of overall unemployment.[16] Early retirement merely reduced overall employment and impoverished a nation. Clearly, if the lump of labour was a fallacy then more jobs could be created for the early retired without any adverse effects on younger job-seekers. Layard's reasoning was elegant, but he offered no estimates of how many new jobs would be needed, or exactly where they would come from.

Anthony Giddens, welfare states and old age

Anthony Giddens was a second major intellectual architect of Third Way ideology in the 1990s. He represents most clearly the social democratic version of the convergence of the sociological and political redefinition of old age that was taking place under neoliberalism's influence, just as Richard Layard represents the changes in economic thinking.

As one of the UK's leading and most prolific sociologists, Giddens personified a wider move in British sociology away from historical materialism and class analysis and towards an emphasis on self-identity through consumption, lifestyle, culture, gender and so on – in other words, an analysis that downplayed economic factors. Giddens argued that radically new social forces – in particular, globalisation and the collapse of communism – had significantly changed the social and political agenda. These were supplemented by other complementary forces – the emergence of a digitalised knowledge economy (enabling information to spread more widely across the developed world), a disillusionment with metanarratives of historical progress (notably, Marxism), rising levels of consumerism and lifestyle politics and the emergence of sectional interest groups based upon a new politics of identity (feminism, gay liberation, anti-racism, disability rights, anti-ageism).

Western democracies had no choice but to accept the inevitability of these new, all-powerful global economic forces, and adjust to them. These

---

[16] Layard *et al.*, *Unemployment, Macroeconomic Performance*, pp. 502–506; Layard *et al.*, *Unemployment Crisis* (1994), p. 107; Layard, *What Labour Can Do*, p. 75.

forces had 'limited the capability of national governments to manage economic life and provide an ever-expanding range of social benefits'.[17] Giddens rejected the view of some commentators (notably, Paul Hirst) that globalisation was not necessarily new (world trade having been proportionately larger in the 1890s), or that its effects were being exaggerated in order to make it appear omnipotent (for example, many of the new service jobs, being essentially interpersonal, one-to-one jobs, could not be exported to the Far East).

For Giddens, the new Third Way was intended to be a creative and positive response by centre-left 'progressives' to the profound and interconnected socio-economic changes that had taken place since the 1970s – economic, demographic, family-formation, cultural, social and relational. His espousal of the concept of 'structuration' was an attempt to reconcile the potentially antagonistic concepts of structure and agency. It was skilfully (and, some might say, opportunistically) applied to globalisation's effect on welfare states. The new structural constraints of the global economy were enormously powerful, but could be shaped somewhat by individual and collective agency. For example, the closure of a factory might be a consequence of outsourcing in the name of corporate profits, but the resultant jobless workforce should possess the resilience and personal responsibility to look for new work and the state should help them by active labour market policies and retraining programmes that would be integral to a reformed welfare state. Repeatedly, Giddens claimed that the Third Way was not a capitulation to neoliberalism,[18] but many critics argued that, for all their superficial persuasiveness and sociological elegance, Giddens's views were, in the final analysis, an apologia for global capitalism. He tended to view global corporations as all-powerful, and presented a vision of the world as an enormous capitalist market, in which such corporations could roam freely, unhindered by nation-state governments. 'The masters of the economy, and the other "excluded at the top", can sleep in peace: they have found their Pangloss', was one acerbic comment.[19]

Giddens's views were complex, and articulated in many publications; they have also aroused a vast amount of comment and criticism,[20] so it is important not to simplify and essentialise them. A major interpretative difficulty is that his style was discursive, positing ideas speculatively on

[17] Anthony Giddens, *The Third Way and Its Critics* (2000), p. 2.   [18] *Ibid.*, p. 163.

[19] Pierre Bourdieu and Loic Wacquant, 'NewLiberalSpeak: Notes on the New Planetary Vulgate', *Radical Philosophy*, 105, Jan.–Feb. 2001, p. 5.

[20] For example, Will Atkinson, 'Anthony Giddens as Adversary of Class Analysis', *Sociology*, 41, 3, June 2007, pp. 533–549.

the basis of flimsy evidence. Two examples will suffice: 'Welfare dependency is probably in some part a real phenomenon, not just an invention of neo-liberalism' was an intriguingly worded statement, unsupported by any longitudinal evidence of welfare benefit claim duration. (The juxtaposition of 'probably' and 'in some part' was puzzling.) Second, Giddens's bold claim that 80 per cent of illnesses were lifestyle-related, and therefore preventable, would have surprised many working in health research; again, no evidence was offered.[21]

Giddens envisaged a redesigned welfare state that would meet the new challenges of globalisation. In an analysis very similar to those of Borrie and others, he argued that the structural constraints imposed by the new, all-powerful global economic forces could be mitigated by a new 'social investment state', with active labour market policies designed to propel jobless individuals back into work replacing the allegedly 'passive' welfare state of the past. Economic growth would thus be boosted, by a raising of aggregate demand and reductions in social security expenditure. Giddens's threefold prescription for macro-economic policy rested on neoclassical economic orthodoxy: 'keep inflation low, limit government borrowing and use active supply-side measures to foster growth and high levels of employment'.[22]

Giddens was propagating his ideas at a time of widening income and wealth inequality, yet he remained relatively untroubled by this trend, arguing that it was no longer the job of the welfare state to redistribute income and wealth and reduce inequalities of outcome. Instead, promoting social inclusion was the answer – a 'dynamic, life-chances approach to equality, placing the prime stress upon equality of opportunity'.[23] This was couched in the language of 'rights and responsibilities': equality of opportunity would be balanced by the obligation to move off benefits and take any job.

On old age and retirement, Giddens had much to say. The notion of the lifecycle, with its discrete stages, was said to be a relic of a bygone fordist era – an era of male job-for-life blue-collar capitalism, with a working life terminated by enforced retirement. In late modernity, an individual's progress through the lifecourse was more fluid and uncertain: there was a disembedding from the traditional structures and constraints of time and space[24] – notably, age stages. The old, accepted markers of time, such as long marriages and lifecycle stages, had given way to a greater fluidity that

---

[21] Anthony Giddens, *In Defence of Sociology: Essays, Interpretations and Rejoinders* (1996), pp. 236, 255.
[22] Giddens, *Third Way and Its Critics*, p. 73.   [23] *Ibid.*, p. 86.
[24] Anthony Giddens, *Modernity and Self-Identity* (1991), p. 2.

individuals had to negotiate by reflexive processes in order to meet the challenges of new risks. These new risks presented hazards and dangers – for example, of an ecological catastrophe – but also opportunities: this was particularly true of the lifecourse, which could be renegotiated. Old age was a risk to be insured against. Accordingly, retirement itself, as one of the previous 'stages', had become deinstitutionalised and had lost its old meaning. Middle age was now said to extend from midlife to extreme old age. Retirement was a 'ghetto', from which old people should be 'liberated'. This 'ghetto' was in effect a form of welfare dependency.[25] In all of this, the assumption was that individuals had considerable control over their own lives.

The 'problem' of an ageing population could be ameliorated by reforming the whole idea of retirement and viewing older people 'as a resource, rather than a problem'.[26] Recognising the impact of the new individualism 'might mean abolishing involuntary retirement, plus other innovations'.[27] Giddens did not explain how involuntary retirement could be abolished, other than by outlawing a fixed retirement age (presumably, age 60/65). Given that, when Giddens was writing, six out of ten men had retired before the age of 65, the effect would only have been limited. In 'other innovations' he even suggested the abolition of state pensions underpinned by 'a statutory right to work' for old people, but did not elaborate.[28]

For Giddens, categories like 'pensioner' were therefore constructs of the old, allegedly passive, discredited welfare states and should be abandoned. He was particularly robust when it came to 'the expectation that older people have to be cared for by the state', which resulted in 'a culture of dependency as noxious as any other'.[29] This somewhat brutal verdict was dressed up in the beguiling language of self-actualisation and opportunity, representing that intriguing mix of celebration and authoritarianism that characterises neoliberal discourses on ageing:

Ageing used to be more passive than it is now: the ageing body was simply something to be accepted. In the more active, reflexive society, ageing has become much more of an open process, on a physical as well as a psychic level. Becoming older presents at least as many opportunities as problems, both for individuals and for the wider social community.[30]

Much of what Giddens said about retirement was couched in a grandiose, apocalyptic style – yet it was empirically weak, in that it was unsupported

[25] Anthony Giddens, *The Third Way: The Renewal of Social Democracy* (1998), p. 120.
[26] *Ibid.*   [27] Giddens, *In Defence of Sociology*, p. 244.
[28] Giddens, *Third Way and Its Critics*, p. 40.   [29] *Ibid.*
[30] Giddens, *The Third Way*, p. 119.

by any specific evidence. He never explained exactly what was meant by the deinstitutionalisation of retirement, nor what was qualitatively new in it: for example, did individuals now have greater control over the exact timing of their retirement? As will be discussed in Chapter 5, there had always been a spread of retirement ages – most notably, by social class – and a complex mixture of voluntary and involuntary causes, with the latter predominating. All that had changed was that the average age of permanent labour market exit had fluctuated – falling from the early 1970s, then rising briefly in the late 1980s before falling again, then slowly rising from the early 1990s with an improving economy. Again, a quick glance at the income distribution statistics for pensioner households (see Chapter 1) showed that a consumption-rich self-actualisation could only be enjoyed by the top 20 per cent of pensioners (at best). Nor did Giddens explain precisely where the jobs would come from if mandatory retirement ages and state pensions were abolished. What exactly was meant by old age becoming 'a much more diverse and actively shaped process than it used to be', or 'more open and negotiable'?[31]

We can see, therefore, that by the time New Labour was swept to power in the May 1997 general election, several different tributaries of influence – the long-standing neoclassical strategy of expanding labour supply, the growing power of the global financial services industry, the social democratic critique of high unemployment, a swing away from neo-Marxist political economy approaches in academic social science and the post-1992 rising employment rates – had converged together to fashion a new centre-left 'progressive' agenda that was profoundly influenced by neoliberalism.

Pensions reform

As was outlined in Chapter 1, state pensions are both a major item of government expenditure and a vital basic income for many people (particularly women, who tend to be poorer in old age than men). They are also an economic necessity, in that they support a section of the population historically marginalised from the workforce in the name of economic efficiency or as carers. The labour market presents very few offerings to retirees who might wish to return to work, and there is little or no chance of adding to any existing stock of savings. As such, pensions are highly political, involving hard choices about what proportion of national income should be redistributed to a group who are, in the conventional sense, economically inactive. Expenditure on pensions has often been

---

[31] Giddens, *Third Way and Its Critics*, pp. 39–40.

viewed with hostility in certain quarters as 'dead' expenditure, since it does not invest in future generations. Added to this is the fact that there are difficult technical problems inherent in all state pension systems: for example, a selective system that targets the poorest pensioners is efficient, but the necessary means-testing penalises thrift and saving; in a contributory scheme, benefits tend to be restricted to what the poorest can afford in contributions; and private pension provision has yielded such low benefits historically that it offers no realistic basis for any future system (as shown in Chapter 1, the average income from private/occupational pensions and annuities in the UK is only £8,641 per household).

Pension systems are notoriously complex and forbidding. This complexity derives to some extent from the inherent technical problems – funding mechanisms, eligibility criteria, risk equalisation and so on – which baffle all except those who work fulltime in the financial services industry; in addition, there are many future unknowns such as life expectancy projections, labour market participation rates and performance of the economy or the stock market. Adding to this inherent complexity is the problem of many vested interests, each with its own agenda. The private pensions industry has always sought to shape state pensions policy in Britain, and successive governments have been over-willing to listen to it – to the extent that increasing the business of the financial services industry has frequently seemed a more important aim than delivering good state pensions.[32] Indeed, the two issues are inter-linked: so arcane and forbidding are the mysteries of pension funding that the debate has been dominated by this small group of experts. On the face of it, the prevailing governmental perspective at the moment is one of libertarian paternalism, derived from neoliberalism's model of social change and attempting to 'nudge' citizens into making particular pension choices between these complex options, with a bias towards encouraging private provision – regardless of that sector's historic under-performance.

The inherent technical problems of pensions have given rise to a particular mode of depoliticised, technocratic analysis in which administrative factors are over-emphasised: the extraordinary complexity of the UK system, and the failure of successive governments to reform it, are often attributed to piecemeal growth and the fact that each additional, incremental pension reform has been grafted onto existing structures – the end result being an increasingly complex, multi-layered system with different

---

[32] Stephen M. Nesbitt, *British Pensions Policy Making in the 1980s: The Rise and Fall of a Policy Community* (1995). For an interesting exploration of the political power of pension funds, see Robin Blackburn, *Banking on Death* (2002).

elements locked in, making it near-impossible to reform. This process is often conceptualised as 'path dependency'. However, path dependency cannot explain many things – such as why the UK has the sixth-richest economy in the industrialised world, yet has one of the worst basic state pension schemes, in terms of replacement rates.[33] All in all, the complex system of state support to retirees that has emerged in the UK since the early twentieth century is less the result of accumulated administrative factors than of political choices about redistribution.

The convoluted and rather troubled postwar history of the state pension in the UK can be summarised quickly. Ostensibly, Beveridge had been charged with the task of merging and universalising the 1908 non-contributory and 1925 contributory pension schemes into one system, funded by National Insurance contributions and taxation on a 'pay-as-you-go' basis. In his 1942 report, Beveridge had controversially argued that pensioners should not immediately share in the principle of subsistence benefits applied to other groups of claimants. On the commencement of the new social security scheme, pensioners were to receive a benefit some 45 per cent below the level of unemployment and sickness benefits. Only after a period of twenty years would full 'subsistence' be attained. However, his parsimony was strongly opposed by Ernest Bevin, Minister of Labour in the wartime coalition government, and Beveridge's 'golden staircase' transition to full subsistence pensions was abandoned. The new state pension scheme was implemented by the 1946 National Insurance Act, with pensions at the same monetary level as other benefits.[34]

The shift to complete contributory funding kept the pension level contained, as the Treasury had long desired – ostensibly on the principle that flat-rate contributions had to be set at a level that the low-paid could afford. This placed an upper limit on the monetary value of flat-rate benefits – as, indeed, it was designed to do. Accordingly, there had to be massive supplementation by the National Assistance Board: in 1951, people over state pension age made up 969,000 out of the 1,462,000 total National Assistance claimants (or nearly two-thirds). Beveridge had by no means succeeded in simplifying matters. The UK still had a multi-tiered, complex archaeological structure of state pension provision that few citizens understood: at the bottom, a tax-funded, means-tested system of social assistance for the very poorest and operated by the National

---

[33] If path dependency is, as its advocates claim, a useful explanatory concept, then it must apply to *all* these different national systems: it cannot, therefore, explain the peculiarities of one of those systems.

[34] Macnicol, *Politics of Retirement*, chs. 13–16.

Assistance Board; above that, an inadequate contributory pension that failed to combat pensioner poverty on its own; and, at the top, private and occupational pensions for a wealthy minority – though generally offering benefits that only topped up the state pension. Postwar pensions policy had not prevented a 'two nations' of rich and poor in retirement.[35]

By the end of the 1950s, some form of earnings-related addition to the state pension was being discussed by both the Conservative and Labour Parties. Labour's plan for *National Superannuation* (1957) was matched by the Conservative government in its introduction of earnings-related supplements in 1961. The private sector was favourably treated, with occupational schemes being allowed to contract out. State pensions continued to be a major unresolved political issue in the 1960s and 1970s. The 1975 Social Security Act introduced the State Earnings-Related Pension Scheme (SERPS) (again, with contracting out), and the system of annual uprating by either average earnings or prices (whichever was higher). The mid-1970s probably represent the high-point of government generosity on state pensions, reflecting Barbara Castle's determination to improve the scheme. However, as already noted, SERPS was drastically cut back (and nearly abolished) by the Thatcher government in 1986, following the 1985 white paper on *The Reform of Social Security*. The policy of the Conservative governments in the 1980s became increasingly hostile to the state pension scheme and dedicated to replacing it wherever possible by an expanded private and occupational pensions sector and 'a new partnership' with the private sector. The intention was 'to retain the basic national insurance pension as a foundation on which additional provision can be built, but to move to a position in which that additional pension provision derives from contributions by employers and employees to occupational and personal pension schemes rather than from SERPS'.[36]

As noted in Chapter 2, most significant of all was that government's decision to uprate the basic state pension only in line with prices, which handed a slowly growing pensions crisis to its successors. By 1993, Michael Portillo (Chief Secretary to the Treasury) was admitting that the basic state pension would be worth only 'a nugatory amount' in the coming century because earnings growth was so outstripping price growth.[37] By 2012/13 the shortfall was in the region of £38 per week when the full basic state pension was £107 per week – a loss per pensioner of nearly

---

[35] Richard M. Titmuss, 'Pension Systems and Population Change', in Titmuss, *Essays on 'The Welfare State'* (1958), pp. 56–74.

[36] Department of Health and Social Security, *Reform of Social Security*, pp. 24–25. For a useful account of the 1980s, see Nesbitt, *British Pensions Policy Making*.

[37] Quoted in A. B. Atkinson, *State Pensions for Today and Tomorrow* (1994), p. 9.

£2,000 a year. If there was any rationale to this policy, it was to destroy the state pension over time, in the hope that the private sector would fill the gap and increase its business – with only the very poorest pensioners receiving means-tested income support. This was clearly emerging as the neoliberal strategy in the 1990s: for example, the World Bank saw the 'public pillar' of old age support, via state pension schemes in its member states, as having only 'the limited object of alleviating old age poverty'; such schemes should be 'modest in size, to allow ample room for other pillars, and pay-as-you-go'; above all, this pillar of state provision should have an 'unambiguous and limited objective'.[38] It was clear that the World Bank saw old age as a time of life that could offer great financial opportunity for private providers.

At the time of New Labour's entry into government in 1997, there were several broad positions on state pension reform.[39] First was the 'back to Beveridge' strategy of reversing the cutbacks to SERPS that had taken place and restoring (over time) the link with average earnings.[40] At the 1996 Labour Party annual conference, the veteran Labour politician, Barbara Castle, attempted to persuade the Party's leadership to adopt this strategy, with no success. In the run-up to a general election, New Labour had controversially decided to reassure voters by not making any major additional public expenditure commitments. Its approach was basically to enlarge means-testing for the poorest pensioners and encourage more private savings and private pensions. A second, more cautious, approach was to halt the relative decline in the value of the state pension, add a means-tested 'top-up' for the poorest pensioners (as suggested by the 1994 Borrie report) but not restore the full value of SERPS.[41] A third strategy was to means-test and residualise the basic state pension by paying it to the poorest two-thirds of pensioners, and encourage private provision (as recommended in the report of the 'Retirement Income Inquiry', set up by the National Association of Pension Funds and the Institute for Fiscal Studies).[42] This would have resulted in a three-tier

---

[38] World Bank, *Averting the Old Age Crisis: Policies to Protect the Old and Promote Growth* (1994), p. 16.

[39] A very good brief discussion is: Barbara Waine, 'Paying for Pensions', in Helen Jones and Suzanne MacGregor (eds.), *Social Issues and Party Politics* (1998), ch. 10. For another succinct survey, from ten years later, see Debora Price, 'Towards a New Pension Settlement? Recent Pension Reform in the UK', in Tony Maltby, Patricia Kennett and Kirstein Rummery (eds.), *Social Policy Review 20: Analysis and Debate in Social Policy, 2008* (2008), ch. 3.

[40] Peter Townsend and Alan Walker, *The Future of Pensions: Revitalising National Insurance* (1995).

[41] As outlined in Labour Party, *Security in Retirement* (1996).

[42] The Retirement Income Inquiry, *Pensions: 2000 and Beyond, Vol. 1* (1996).

system: at the bottom, an 'assured pension' – means-tested, but distinct from income support; above this, a funded national scheme, replacing SERPS, which would have provided higher pensions based upon earnings-related contributions, and run by the private pensions industry (supervised by a government body); at the top would have been the wealthiest pensioners relying on private provision. Fourth was the suggestion of 'private pensions for all', advocated by the maverick Labour MP, Frank Field, the Dahrendorf Commission on Wealth Creation and Social Cohesion and the outgoing Conservative government just before the 1997 general election.[43] Fifth was the idea of a citizen's pension, on the lines of the 1908 Act's provisions – a tax-funded state pension paid equally to men and women in their own right, regardless of marital status, with the only qualifying condition being a certain length of residence (not entirely unproblematic). There would be no means-tests, but those who still received high incomes past state pension age could be subject to 'claw back' by income tax. Despite appearing to be impossibly utopian, this scheme eventually won the support of quite hard-headed realists like the National Association of Pension Funds and the Liberal Democrats.[44] Finally, there was the default strategy of doing nothing – allowing the basic state pension to decline in relative value, forcing more pensioners to rely on means-tested income support and hoping that the private pensions industry would expand. Underpinning this would be a raising of the state pension age for men and women to 67 and an end to final-salary schemes (as suggested by the Conservative MP, David Willetts).[45]

John Major's Conservative government actually began the process of raising state pension ages by the 1995 Pensions Act, which provided for a phasing-in between 2010 and 2020 of a state pension age of 65 for women. As mentioned in the previous chapter, the idea of a common retirement age between men and women, perhaps combined with financial incentives to claim the state pension as late as possible, had been discussed sporadically for some time.[46] The 1995 Act was in part a response to EU pressure for gender equalisation, but it also provided an opportunity to cut the cost of state pensions and marked the first concrete policy proposal enshrining the long-standing neoliberal aim of raising state pension ages. New Labour's approach, once in government, was to target the poorest pensioners, as the Borrie report had suggested,

---

[43] Frank Field and Matthew Owen, *Private Pensions for All: Squaring the Circle* (1993).

[44] National Association of Pension Funds, *Towards a Citizen's Pension* (2005); David Laws, Danny Alexander and Matthew Oakeshott, *Reforming UK Pensions: Liberal Democrat Proposals* (2005).

[45] David Willetts, *The Age of Entitlement* (1993).

[46] For example, Department of Health and Social Security, *Growing Older*, pp. 15–17.

first via the Minimum Income Guarantee and then Pension Credit (from late 2003). This approach was a relatively parsimonious focus on those pensioners in greatest need, but means-testing has never been popular with the financial services industry, since it can act as a deterrent to saving.[47]

By the time the Turner Commission was appointed in 2002 to provide a long-term solution to the whole postwar pensions problem, there was an even more complex, multi-layered system – means-tested Pension Credit, the basic state pension, the State Second Pension, Stakeholder Pensions and regulated private provision. New Labour made important long-term commitments to a restoration of the earnings link, a simplification of the State Second Pension and a reduction in the number of qualifying years to thirty. This last reform was desperately needed, given that, owing to their often-different contribution records (largely a result of caring duties) and other gendered inequalities over the lifecourse, only a minority of women reaching state pension age have been entitled to a full basic state pension: the proportion has slowly risen, but was still only 46 per cent in 2013, in contrast to 80 per cent in the case of men[48] – what Secretary of State Alan Johnson in 2004 called 'a national scandal'.[49] As Debora Price puts it, 'Women are much more likely than men to undertake care work and housework within the household, are more likely to work part-time and for low pay, are more likely to have interrupted histories of paid work, and are less likely to be in the paid workforce as they approach state pension age'.[50] The UK was paying a high price for having moved away from the 1908 state pension scheme, for despite it bestowing a more robust entitlement the contributory principle had failed to deliver adequate pensions to those who needed them most: the slow decline in the relative value of the basic state pension was resulting in an inexorable increase in means-testing, such that by 2005/6 nearly half of pensioner households were entitled to Pension Credit.

The DWP had decided on four policy options – poorer pensioners, higher taxes and/or National Insurance contributions, a raising of state pension ages and more saving. These had become entrenched as the only acceptable options – for example, they were very similar to those outlined by the World Bank for 'older economies with large public

[47] Price, 'Towards a New Pension Settlement?', p. 52.

[48] Becky Barrow, 'Only 46% of Women Get Full Basic State Pension', *Daily Mail*, 11 Dec. 2013, www.dailymail.co.uk

[49] Press Association, 'Women's Pensions "a National Scandal"', *Guardian*, 20 Oct. 2004, www.theguardian.com

[50] Debora Price, 'Closing the Gender Gap in Retirement Income: What Difference Will Recent UK Pension Reforms Make?', *Journal of Social Policy*, 36, 4, Oct. 2007, p. 562.

pillars', in *Averting the Old Age Crisis* (1994): 'raising the retirement age, eliminating rewards for early retirement and penalties for later retirement, downsizing benefit levels (in the frequent cases in which they are overgenerous to begin with) and making the benefit structure flatter (to emphasise the poverty reduction function), the tax rate lower, and the tax rate broader'.[51] In its first report, the Turner Commission firmly declared that 'there are no alternatives to these four choices'.[52] Of these four, the first two were ruled out, and therefore the Commission recommended the preordained favourite: pension ages were to be equalised at 66 by 2030, 67 by 2040 and 68 by 2050. In addition, saving for retirement through the private sector was to be encouraged by auto-enrolment into workplace pensions administered by the financial services industry. The group to be covered were the low-paid – those hitherto neglected by the private pensions industry and therefore no threat to its core business.[53] By incremental processes, raising state pension ages became a cardinal principle of pensions reform, accepted by all three main political parties with relatively little criticism. It has been presented as the unavoidable quid pro quo for restoring the earnings link – although, as this study argues, the longer term, overall strategy is to expand labour supply.

The reports of the Turner Commission expertly amassed a wealth of seemingly incontrovertible evidence to justify what were presented as policy inevitabilities. The Commission made effective (if somewhat one-sided) use of demographic projections: the number of people aged 65+ as a proportion of those aged 20–64 would rise from 27 per cent to 48 per cent by 2050, and, were no rise in state pension ages implemented, the proportion of GDP spent on state pensions, it was said, would rise from 6.1 per cent to 16.1 per cent.[54] The Commission repeatedly emphasised worsening crude dependency ratios in the future without setting this in the context of increasing GDP per worker and therefore the rising national wealth that could be spent on pensions.

A singular feature of the reports was their analysis of recent policy developments as a series of mistakes at the collective level – a human agency explanation par excellence: employers had neglected their company pensions; pension fund managers had ignored the evidence of increasing longevity until it was too late, and had been lulled into a 'fool's paradise' by a booming stock market; even the Government Actuary's Department in 1981 had supplied incorrect evidence for life expectancy

---

[51] World Bank, *Averting*, pp. 21–22.
[52] Pensions Commission, *Pensions: Challenges and Choices. The First Report of the Pensions Commission* (2004), p. 12.
[53] Price, 'Towards a New Pension Settlement?', p. 60.
[54] Pensions Commission, *First Report*, pp. 13–15.

gains at age 65. All in all, a collective mindset of 'irrational exuberance' had prevented the correct reformist steps being taken.[55] It was an analysis that ignored both the structural economic changes that now required higher labour market participation by older people and the post-Thatcherite political strategy of severely containing state pension provision.

Overall, the Turner Commission reports reflected the DWP's neoclassical position: despite the occasional mention of 'macroeconomic shocks', labour market demand was rarely mentioned and 'the retirement decision' was viewed as a result of choice and incentives. The assumption was that five policy drivers 'could' sustain the rise in older people's employment rates that had commenced in the early 1990s: continuation of 'sound macroeconomic policy'; the increasing shift from defined benefit to defined contribution pension provision; continued focus on Incapacity Benefit reform; active labour market policies to encourage search for work at all ages; and age discrimination legislation.[56] The first was relatively meaningless, and took credit for the rise in older people's employment rates that was occurring anyway across the industrialised world; the second, third and fourth implied a reduction of welfare rights; the fifth was the legitimating principle behind that reduction. There was little specific guidance on exactly where the required new jobs would come from: the hope was that improving health plus a continued rise in older people's employment rates would cause average ages of retirement to rise in line with rises in the state pension age.

It was against this background that the Conservative/LibDem coalition government announced in early 2013 that there would be introduced a new flat-rate, single-tier state pension of £144 per week (at 2014 prices), to commence in April 2016. This will replace all existing state pension provision, but only for those claiming after that date. The aim is to dispense with means-testing by setting the level of the new pension at the current level of Pension Credit. It is likely that this has been done to assist the private pensions industry, who will be in charge of auto-enrolment (much as the Conservatives' 1925 Act was in part designed to boost private provision by ending means-testing for most pensioners).[57] The new single-tier pension is emphatically not a citizen's pension, since eligibility will be by National Insurance contributions or credits. And although it will commence in April 2016, its provisions will only apply

---

[55] *Ibid.*, pp. 94, 114, 124.   [56] *Ibid.*, p. 38.
[57] Price and Livsey, 'Financing Later Life', p. 72; Deborah Mabbett, 'The Second Time as Tragedy? Welfare Reform under Thatcher and the Coalition', *Political Quarterly*, 84, 1, Jan.–Mar. 2013, p. 48.

to new claimants: the existing scheme will continue for decades until its last beneficiary dies off.

There has been much conjecture about who would be winners and who would be losers under the new single-tier pension, and how many anomalies will be created.[58] First, it represents no overall increase in funding: it is designed to be cost-neutral, and even to save money. The level of the new flat-rate pension is an improvement, but against that will be the loss of Additional Pension provision, and the fact that £144 is still well below the official poverty line for a single retiree (£178 per week before housing costs). Had the Thatcher government's cutting of the state pension not taken place, it would in any case have reached this monetary level by 2008. The number of minimum qualifying contributions or credits has been raised from 30 to 35. There is now in place the 'triple lock' formula for annual uprating of pensions – by whichever is the highest out of increases in average earnings, the Consumer Price Index or 2.5 per cent – but this could be an economy, since the higher Retail Price Increase has been abandoned. Much more will be needed to restore the basic state pension to the relative value it had in the late 1970s, let alone bring it up to the average for the industrialised societies that belong to the Organisation for Economic Co-operation and Development (OECD). Employers will no longer be able to contract out of paying full National Insurance contributions for those employees in defined benefit occupational schemes, which may well cause more of such schemes to close. All in all, this latest pensions reform reflects the climate of austerity into which it has been born. As one critical commentary puts it, 'Future pensioners will be asked to pay five years extra National Insurance contributions, get a state pension that is less than they could earn under the current system and be forced to work longer before they can draw it.'[59]

As has been emphasised earlier, state pensions are very expensive, and a major rise in their value would be a significant public expenditure commitment. In the present political climate, this is something that none of the three main UK political parties is prepared to support, despite a £29 billion surplus in the National Insurance Fund,[60] the theoretical possibility of increasing revenue by abolishing the upper earnings limit

---

[58] For a useful discussion, see Liam Foster, 'Towards a Fairer Pension System for Women? Assessing the Impact of Recent Pension Changes on Women', in Kevin Farnsworth, Zoe Irving and Menno Fenger (eds.), *Social Policy Review 26: Analysis and Debate in Social Policy, 2014* (2014).

[59] National Pensioners Convention Briefing, *Single Tier State Pension* (2013), p. 4.

[60] House of Commons Library, *National Insurance Contributions: An Introduction* (2014), p. 5.

for contributions and, of course, greatly widening income and wealth inequality that should make taxing the rich more possible. Office for National Statistics projections are that the cost of basic and state second pensions, winter fuel allowance and other benefits to pensioners was a grand total of £94 billion for 2012/13 and will rise to an anticipated £438 billion by 2062/3; however, as a proportion of GDP this is a rise of only 2.4 percentage points, from 6.0 per cent to 8.4 per cent.[61] As with all such fiscal projections, this was speculative given that nobody can know what total GDP will be in the 2060s. The number of people of state pension age is projected to rise by 31 per cent between mid-2012 and mid-2037, and then stabilise. (Both of these projections take account of the proposed new flat-rate pension and more rapid changes in state pension ages (see below).) Raising the state pension age by one year is calculated as saving about £13 billion.

The pace of reform was in part a product of the lack of political opposition in the House of Commons to this radical change, in contrast to outside it, and a process of ever-rising eligibility ages now seems to be in place. Very quickly, Lord Turner himself had joined in the demands for an even higher age, declaring that he now wished that he had been 'more ambitious' in his recommendations. Before becoming Prime Minister David Cameron likewise stated that the whole process would be accelerated.[62] Without attracting much comment, the Turner report had enunciated a radically new principle of state pension provision: that, on average, cohorts would only be entitled to a fixed period of time in state-supported retirement. In his Autumn Statement in December 2013, the Chancellor of the Exchequer, George Osborne, announced that plans were to be speeded up. Future state pension ages would be based upon changes in life expectancy, such that citizens should expect to spend 'up to' one-third of their adult life in retirement. The wording was puzzling, but was somewhat clarified when the government report *Fuller Working Lives* was published in June 2014: now it was stated that 'people should expect to spend only around one third of their adult life in receipt of a state pension'.[63] The use of the word 'only' was very significant: the eligibility criterion had shifted from age entitlement (which pertained for all the twentieth century) to cohort entitlement (as in the Turner report)

---

[61] Office for National Statistics, *Pension Trends. Chapter 5: State Pensions, 2013 Edition* (2013), pp. 20–21.

[62] Myra Butterworth, 'Plans to Raise State Pension Age Not Radical Enough, Says Lord Turner', *Telegraph*, 3 July 2009, www.telegraph.co.uk; 'Pension Age Could Rise to 68 Quicker Under Cameron', *Daily Mail*, 23 Sept. 2009, www.dailymail.co.uk

[63] DWP, *Fuller Working Lives – Background Evidence*, p. 12.

to individual entitlement – quite possibly a prelude to the state pension being privatised via individualised accounts, possible time-limiting of benefit receipt, a reduction of risk-pooling and a major erosion of the solidaristic principles that hitherto underpinned state pension provision. Paying out a state pension for only a fixed number of years would eliminate actuarial risk and make the pension a much more attractive prospect for privatisation.

This changed policy could result in a state pension age of 66 being established between 2018 and 2020, 67 between 2026 and 2028, 68 by the mid-2030s and even a suggested 69 by the late 2040s.[64] At this rate of increase, a child born today would not receive a state pension until age 77. By the second decade of the twenty-first century, UK pensioners were experiencing the consequences of the increasing neoliberalisation of the UK's political culture that had taken place since the 1970s.

Conclusion

The improvements made to the state pension by Barbara Castle in the mid-1970s represent the high-point of the conception of old age as a stage of life to be protected. From then on, old age and retirement began to be subjected to a series of ever-increasing attacks by the political right – attacks that were consistent with a broadly neoliberal tradition extending back at least to the nineteenth century Charity Organisation Society but which became increasingly relevant in the changing economic conditions after the 1980s. In the 1980s, the restructuring of the UK economy was predicated upon deflationary policies that required a large labour reserve: early retirement was a means to this end and was therefore encouraged. However, the economic recovery from the early 1990s onwards led to rising employment rates and an accelerated growth of low-paid, casualised, often part-time jobs. Expanding labour supply once again became central to macro-economic policy, and early retirement became problematised. This led to the 'rediscovery' of age discrimination in employment and moves to raise state pension ages, as well as proposals to extend compulsory activation policies to older jobless people. The explanatory narrative offered by neoliberalism emphasises demographic pressures as the main apolitical driver behind these changes, and therefore the next chapter will consider these pressures.

---

[64] Ian Pollock, 'Autumn Statement: Wait Longer for Your State Pension', BBC News, 5 Dec. 2013, www.bbc.co.uk

4   Demography as destiny?

Do we face an impending crisis of old age, brought about by demographic changes? Are these changes so monumental that a fundamental redefinition of retirement is needed? This chapter will examine the demographic drivers that seem to have changed the ageing and social policy agenda, considering in particular the extent to which there really is a 'crisis', whether this alleged crisis has arisen only very recently and whether urgent and radical action is justified.

Discourses on ageing and old age have always been permeated by demographic concerns. It is, of course, only right and proper that governments should plan for the future by making projections for likely changes in the size and age composition of future populations in order to anticipate future health, social security and social care costs, plus education and other age-based expenditure. The problem is that such projections are always replete with uncertainties, based as they are on alternative assumptions of future fertility behaviour and likely mortality trends. It is therefore difficult to predict the future: for example, few people in the late 1930s forecast the rise in fertility that was to commence in 1941, just as few in the late 1960s predicted the 'baby bust' that was soon to follow. As the Office for National Statistics candidly admitted in 1993, 'the one certainty of making projections is that, due to the inherent uncertainty of demographic behaviour, they will turn out to be wrong as a forecast of future demographic events or population structure'.[1]

In addition, population projections tend to become politicised, reflecting the vested interests associated with the funding of retirement, health care, housing and so on. They can also symbolise deep-seated fears of ageing, decrepitude and death on a personal and collective level. Many gerontologists maintain that concerns over future ageing populations are deeply irrational – the terms 'gerontophobia' and 'apocalyptic demography' are often used – deriving from these psychological phobias. They

---

[1] Quoted in Office for National Statistics, *Pension Trends. Chapter 2: Population Change* (2012), pp. 2–7.

also object to the demographic determinism that maintains that a population with a particular age structure must inevitably possess certain behavioural characteristics – for example, the assumption that the fact that there are in the UK now more pensioners than there are children aged under 16 must have a profound effect on collective behaviour. At the societal level, demographic concerns can be a metaphor for collective insecurities about economic decline, loss of global dominance, the waning of imperial power, racism, dysgenic trends and so on. This was certainly the case with the 'population panic' in the UK in the late 1930s, which was in part reflective of insecurities about the future of the British Empire and the drift to war with Germany.

Population ageing today tends to be debated in a manner less than wholly rational, with long-known demographic trends being presented as entirely novel, historically unprecedented and apocalyptic. It is undeniable that future population ageing presents challenges for industrialised societies, but numbers alone mean nothing. Crude dependency ratios relating to those aged 65+ as a proportion of those aged 15–64, or some other denominator, are therefore misleading. The key issues are: first, productivity at an individual and collective level; and, second, the willingness of a society to redistribute the fruits of that productivity to its retirees. What has happened in the last forty years is that neoliberalism as an ideology has profoundly affected – indeed, contaminated – the demographic debate, reinterpreting population trends in such a way as to engender pessimism and justify the raising of state pension ages and cutbacks in social policies for older people. Demographic alarmism has become, in Phil Mullan's words, 'a politically respectable way of legitimising the anti-welfarist cost-cutting mood'.[2]

'People are living longer'

It is against this background that the phrase 'people are living longer' has acquired totemic significance in the UK as a proposition that cannot be challenged. 'Everybody knows we are living longer. It is like an express train', was the confident declaration of Steve Webb (pensions minister) in September 2011.[3] In defiance of the actual evidence, Webb claimed that 'most 65-year-olds can expect to live until their late 80s'.[4] The

---

[2] Phil Mullan, *The Imaginary Time Bomb: Why An Ageing Population is Not a Social Problem* (2000), p. 93.

[3] 'Government Says State Pension Age is Rising Too Slowly', 11 Sept. 2011, www.bbc.co/news

[4] Philip Inman, 'Retirements to Spike in 2012 Due to Postwar Passions', *Guardian*, 21 Sept. 2010, www.theguardian.com

demographic inevitabilities were also emphasised by Danny Alexander, Chief Secretary to the Treasury: combining upbeat, celebratory rhetoric with stark warnings seemingly based upon unideological, naturalistic evidence, Alexander said that living longer was

a fact of life for the entire population . . . the plain fact of the matter is that people are living much longer now than they were even 20-odd years ago and that's a fantastic thing for society. But we have to ensure that it is affordable in the context of our pensions, and we're asking people through the state pension age to work longer.[5]

Likewise, a DWP spokesman warned that the timetable for raising the state pension age to 67 was too slow 'due to the staggering increases in life expectancy'.[6] Announcing a DWP press release a month earlier, which claimed that a baby born in 2011 was going to be eight times more likely to reach the age of 100 than one born in 1931, and a 20-year-old three times more likely, Webb implied that the justification for reforming public sector pensions and raising state pension ages was purely empirical: 'The dramatic speed at which life expectancy is changing means that we need to radically rethink our perceptions about later lives. We simply can't look at our grandparents' experience of retirement as a model for our own. We will live longer and we will have to save more.'[7] The word 'dramatic' – employed adjectivally or adverbially – has been greatly over-used by the DWP in the last decade. For example, the 2006 green paper, *A New Deal for Welfare*, referred to the 'dramatic and welcome increases in life expectancy' over the previous fifty years as a justification for raising state pension ages,[8] just as the Turner Commission made an opening declaration that 'life expectancy, both at birth and at 65, has increased dramatically and will continue to rise'.[9]

As was noted in Chapter 1, the contradictory justification is that population ageing is both a cause for celebration *and* a potential catastrophe that requires people to work later in life via 'a major cultural shift' on their part, assisted by legislation to combat age discrimination. Reflecting the influence of postmodern optimism, these new demographic realities

---

[5] James Chapman, '"People Are Living Longer So it's Time to Pay Up": Government Remains Defiant in Face of Strike Over Pension Reforms', *Daily Mail*, 18 June 2011, www.dailymail.co.uk

[6] Robert Winnett, 'State Pension Age to be Lifted to 67 a Decade Earlier Than Planned', *Telegraph*, 12 Sept. 2011, www.telegraph.co.uk

[7] Department for Work and Pensions, '20-year-olds Three Times More Likely to Reach 100 than their Grandparents', DWP Press Release, 4 August 2011, www.dwp.gov.uk

[8] Department for Work and Pensions, *A New Deal for Welfare: Empowering People to Work* (2006), Cm. 6730, p. 63.

[9] Pensions Commission, *First Report*, p. 2.

will require from citizens 'a shift in attitude and behaviour across society so that old age is no longer perceived as a time of dependency and exclusion'.[10] As ever, potentially coercive policies to force people to work later in life are presented in emollient, self-congratulatory terms, using the language of empowerment, and economic problems are redefined as cultural, attitudinal and behavioural.

The demographic background

What is the long-term demographic background to this renewed call to raise state pension ages? It can be sketched in quite briefly. Beginning in the 1870s, the British birth rate began to fall, reaching a low-point in 1933. There was a peak of births in the year 1920, when more babies were born than at any point in the twentieth century (as is often the case after a war). This large birth cohort did briefly swell the number of retirees in the mid-1980s, featuring to some extent in the Thatcherite attacks on old age provision. However, the fact that it was quickly followed by very small birth cohorts defused any demographic alarmism. The post-1870s fall in average family size was experienced by nearly all industrialised societies, had complex interrelated causes and was part of the long-run demographic transition process. Interestingly, it led to marked concerns about a future ageing, and possibly even declining, population. The peak of apocalyptic demography was probably the late 1930s: numerous dire predictions were made,[11] such as Sir William Beveridge's warning in 1937 that 'the people of these islands are heading for disappearance'.[12] However, this pessimism quickly evaporated with the rise in the birth rate that occurred from 1941 onwards.

The number of people aged 65+ in the UK was only some 700,000 in 1841 (equivalent to 4.5 per cent of the population). By 1901, this had risen to roughly 1,500,000, but overall population growth meant that this still represented only 5 per cent of the population. By 1981 those aged 65+ had increased to 8,500,000 people (15 per cent of the population). This proportionate trebling was not accompanied by any economic catastrophes attributable to population ageing. By 2012 those aged 65+ numbered 10,800,000 (nearly 17 per cent). Contrary to popular misconception, therefore, for the past three decades the UK has *not* had a significantly ageing population. Past birth rates are more important than

---

[10] Department for Work and Pensions, *Building a Society for All Ages*, Cm 7655 (2009), pp. 6, 7.

[11] For example, Enid Charles, *The Twilight of Parenthood* (1934). For an overall discussion, see Macnicol, *Politics of Retirement*, pp. 259–264.

[12] Press cutting from *Yorkshire Evening Post*, 11 Feb. 1937, Beveridge Papers XII 15.

mortality falls in determining the size and proportion of a population that is in old age, and therefore the more-or-less stable percentage during the period 1980 to 2010 was a function primarily of the small birth cohorts of 1915–1941 entering old age. However, with the large birth cohort baby boomers moving beyond the age of 65, plus the effects of immigration, this proportion is projected to rise to 22 per cent in 2031 and just over 24 per cent in 2060 – a proportionate rise of 50 per cent compared with now. According to one European Union estimate, the total UK population was 62,008,000 in 2010 and is projected to rise to 71,874,000 in 2035 and 78,925,000 in 2060.[13]

Looking back to the postwar period, it is important to remember that there was not a consistently large number of births during the baby boom period of 1941–1970 in the UK. The total number of births averaged 800,000 per annum between 1941 and 1981, and peaked at just over 1,000,000 in 1947 and 1964. There are therefore 'first wave' and 'second wave' boomers. In 1952 the number of UK births was only 793,000 – a mere 10 per cent above the average for the 'baby bust' 1930s and as low as in 1991. Hence the number of people in the UK celebrating their 65th birthday in 2010 was c. 640,000; it increased to c. 800,000 in 2012, but then *decreased* and will still only be c. 650,000 in 2017.

Births and deaths, UK

Other countries experienced slightly different patterns: In the USA, there was a rise from 1940 onwards, and a consistently high birth rate between 1950 and 1960, but then a steady decline in the 1960s; France experienced a rise between 1941 and 1947, and then a steady fall to the mid-1970s; Germany's postwar birth rate was high until the early 1960s, and then it declined.[14] Clearly, those UK citizens born in small cohort years (notably the early 1950s) would rightly feel aggrieved at being included with large cohorts – an obvious case of guilt by association.

It follows, therefore, that the core of the problem for the remainder of the twenty-first century in the UK is the ten-year birth cohort of second wave boomers born in the 1960s who will be pensioners from the mid-2020s to the 2050s. To this will be added the continuing effects of immigration (both new immigrants and the children of past ones): of the projected 10,900,000 increase in the UK population between 2010

---

[13] Eurostat news release, 'EU27 Population is Expected to Peak by around 2040', 8 June 2011, ec.europa.eu/eurostat

[14] Jane Falkingham, 'Who Are the Baby Boomers? A Demographic Profile', in Maria Evandrou (ed.), *Baby Boomers: Ageing in the 21st Century* (1997), pp. 18–21.

Millions

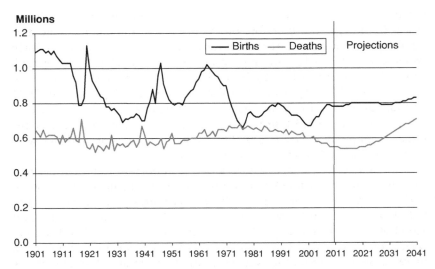

Figure 4.1 Births and deaths, UK.
Source: Jen Beaumont, 'Population', in Office for National Statistics, *Social Trends 41 2011 Edition* (2011), p. 4.

and 2035, 5,800,000 (or 53 per cent) will be attributable to natural increase, and 5,100,000 (47 per cent) to net migration inflow. Even then, 2,300,000 of this natural increase will be indirectly attributable to migration (that is, children born to first generation migrants).[15] The UK population pyramid for the final three decades of the twenty-first century will resemble the Empire State Building – straight sides with a triangular peak beginning at age 70.

In modern populations, there are two principal drivers of increasing numbers of old people: the size of past age cohorts, affected by past birth rates and immigration, and gains in life expectancy caused by falling mortality. The problem faced by the UK over the next thirty years is much more a function of the former than the latter. Unfortunately, that is not how the problem is presented in today's public debates. It is the latter that is blamed, and the impression left is that it is the 'dramatic' increases in life expectancy that are the cause. For example, *Fuller Working Lives* (2014) puts it, when discussing early retirement and its alleged harmful effects on the individual and the economy generally, 'demographic change and increasing life expectancy is making this problem more acute, and people will need to work longer to fund their retirement';

---

[15] Office for National Statistics, *Pension Trends. Chapter 2*, pp. 2–6.

the state pension age is being raised 'in response to the life expectancy challenges'.[16] This presents a much stronger case – after all, who could disagree that living longer is a good thing? Raising state pension ages thereby becomes an unfortunate necessity – the price to pay for maintaining the relative value of the state pension in the face of seemingly all-powerful and entirely welcome demographic pressures. By contrast, a justification based upon past cohort size or immigration is much less powerful and is easily undermined – for example, by the argument that the baby boomers have paid for their state pensions through past taxes and National Insurance contributions, or by the case of the smaller mid-1950s birth cohorts. In fact, the greater area of concern for fiscal policy in the future is the funding of social care, given that the number of those aged 80+ in the UK is set to double between now and 2037.

It is essential to make a distinction between life expectancy at birth and life expectancy at age 65 (for many years, the age at which most European state pension systems commenced). This is generally not done, and failure to make that distinction engenders exaggerated pessimism and fatalism about the demographic pressures. Hence it is frequently stated that, when state pensions were first paid at the age of 70 in 1909, life expectancy at birth was just under 50 years.[17] It is therefore only logical that state pension ages should now be raised. Another example is the technically inaccurate statement, made in 2010, that

After the Second World War, the state pension age was set at 65 for men, at a time when life expectancy for a man was 66.4 years and for a woman 72.5 years. By last year, life expectancy had risen to 77 years for a man and 82 years for a woman in England – but the pension age has remained the same.

By 2056, it was claimed, men and women in England would on average be living to 84 and 89 years respectively: hence state pension ages had to rise.[18]

However, it is life expectancy at age 65 that is crucial in regard to pension funding: if life expectancy at birth increases faster than life expectancy at age 65 (which in essence is what has been happening in the long run), then pension schemes benefit since there are more survivors of working age to pay in but they claim benefits for a relatively short time. If, on the other hand, gains in life expectancy at birth slow down (most

---

[16] Department for Work and Pensions, *Fuller Working Lives – A Framework for Action* (2014), p. 5; DWP, *Fuller Working Lives – Background Evidence*, p. 12.

[17] Mark Littlewood, 'Work on Into Your 70s. It Will be Good for You', *The Times*, 16 May 2013.

[18] James Chapman, 'Millions More to Wait Until 68 for Pension', *Daily Mail*, 19 July 2010, www.dailymail.co.uk

probably because mortality among the non-old can in practice fall little further) and life expectancy at age 65 continues to rise, then considerable problems are created for pension systems, since there will be little or no increase in National Insurance contributions and taxes to meet the increase in liabilities. The calculation is of course a complex one, and must be undertaken carefully: for example, the level of contribution receipts is dependent on many variables (such as employment rates in late middle age, or the size of the tax and contribution base).

Life expectancy at birth in the UK has in the long run increased more rapidly than life expectancy at age 65. The significant mortality gains have been among the non-old. Hence between 1841 and 2006, the gains in life expectancy at age 65 in England and Wales were only six additional years for men and eight additional years for women.[19] Historically, the great success has been in conquering death in youth and middle age such that now only 15 per cent of newborn males and 10 per cent of newborn females are projected to die before the age of 65. It is even claimed that a girl baby born today will have a one-in-three chance of living to 100 years of age and a boy baby a one-in-four chance.[20] The challenge henceforth is to extend life at later years, both quantitatively and qualitatively.

What has happened in the last thirty years?[21] Both life expectancy at birth and life expectancy at age 65 have been increasing recently – but one glance at the numbers shows that exaggerated claims are being made. For males, life expectancy at birth rose from 70.8 years in 1980/2 to 78.7 years in 2010/12; for females, the rise was from 76.8 years to 82.6 years over the same period. This represents increases for males of 7.9 years, and for women of 5.8 years. This is equivalent to a gain of 3.0 months per annum for males and 2.4 months per annum for females. If we convert total life expectancy at birth into months, we arrive at 944 months for males and 991 months for females. By this calculation, the current gain for males is only 0.3 per cent of a total life per annum and that for females 0.2 per cent per annum.

Gains in life expectancy at age 65 have also been relatively modest. Based upon 2010/12 mortality rates, at age 65 a UK male could expect to live another 18.2 years and a female another 20.7 years. Over the past thirty years, male life expectancy at age 65 has risen by 5.2 years and female by 3.8 years. That is equivalent to 2.0 months per annum (males) and 1.5 months per annum (females). Expressed as a percentage of the

---

[19] Christina Victor, *Ageing, Health and Care* (2010), p. 19.
[20] Office for National Statistics, *UK Interim Life Tables 1980–2 to 2008–10* (2011).
[21] Statistics in this and the following paragraph are from Office for National Statistics, *National Life Tables, United Kingdom, 2010–2012* (2014).

total months of expected life at age 65 (218 for men, 248 for women), it represents an annual average increase over the thirty years of only 0.9 per cent for males and 0.6 per cent for females. The phrase 'people are living longer' is therefore misleading: it is more accurate to say that more people are surviving to age 65 (these total numbers currently swelled by the exceptionally large first wave baby boom cohort) and, once there, are then living only slightly longer. By no means do these annual increases in life expectancy represent 'an express train'.

There is, of course, much debate about whether these modest longevity gains will continue. Life expectancy at age 65 in the USA has increased by less than in the UK over the past thirty years, and there was a temporary and brief concern in 2010 that it might have stalled.[22] Again, a crucial element is 'healthy' or 'disability-free' life expectancy. Here the evidence is less reassuring, since in the UK healthy life expectancy appears to be becoming a progressively smaller proportion of overall life expectancy.[23] Assertions that today's children may not live as long as their parents may be sensationalist in tone, but they do remind us that many respected demographers doubt that progress will be sustained and that, for a substantial minority, health status and mortality rates at later ages may actually decline. It is the subject of no little controversy.[24] Positive trends (such as smoking cessation, better diets and higher disposable incomes) may be offset by negative ones (rising obesity, widening income inequality, new epidemics and so on). The 'obesity timebomb', for example, may result in catastrophic levels of diabetes, heart disease, strokes and cancers: one projection is that 48 per cent of UK men could be obese by 2030, compared with 26 per cent in 2011.[25] In the UK population, levels of pre-diabetes (a high-risk state for developing diabetes and associated complications) have risen from 11.6 per cent in 2003 to 35.3 per cent in 2011.[26] On the other hand, levels of obesity may fall owing to greater public awareness of its detrimental consequences (though

[22] Elizabeth Lopatto, 'Life Expectancy in the US Drops for First Time Since 1993, Report Says', *Bloomberg*, 9 Dec. 2010, www.bloomberg.com.news

[23] Dame Carol Black, *Working for a Healthier Tomorrow* (2008), p. 30; Carol Jagger, Ruth Matthews and James Lindesay, 'Compression of Disability? Morbidity and Disability in Older People to 2030', in New Dynamics of Ageing, *Modelling Needs and Resources of Older People to 2030* (2010), pp. 6–7, www.lse.ac.uk/collections/MAP2030

[24] For opposing views, see S. Jay Olshansky *et al.*, 'A Potential Decline in Life Expectancy in the United States in the 21st Century', *New England Journal of Medicine*, 325, 11, 17 March 2005, pp. 1138–1145; Jim Oeppen and James W. Vaupel, 'Broken Limits to Life Expectancy', *Science*, 296, 10 May 2002, pp. 1029–1031.

[25] Peter Walker, 'Half of UK Men Could be Obese by 2030', *Guardian*, 26 Aug. 2011, www.theguardian.com

[26] Arch G. Mainous III *et al.*, 'Prevalence of Prediabetes in England from 2003 to 2011: Population-Based, Cross-Sectional Study', *BMJ Open*, 9 June 2014.

remedial action will have to be swift if it is to reverse the trend). Pro-
jecting into the future is inherently hazardous. One instance is cigarette
smoking: if its incidence has reached the lowest practicable level, the
benefits of its reduction will be a 'one-off' gain, confined to the so-called
'golden generations' (born just before or after the early 1930s), and there
will be no further gains.[27] Similarly, there may be no more blockbuster
drugs. A further problem is that progress may involve postponing death
for only a short time, during which time individuals may be sicker or
may die of something else ('substitute mortality'). Ultimately, the challenge will be to retard the cell deterioration that constitutes the biological
ageing process, and this may be many decades or even centuries away.[28]

Unlike the politicians, professional demographers are rightly wary
about predicting future trends. For example, when the respected International Longevity Centre in London assembled a group of experts
to discuss this question in 2008, the resulting report was noticeably
cautious about predicting the future, constantly emphasising the uncertainties that make predictions hazardous. It concluded: 'Ultimately, no
"right" answer is possible, and some subjective judgement will always be
involved . . . policymakers may wish to adopt a "prudent", more conservative approach by using a range of possible projections.'[29]

The whole debate about raising state pension ages becomes even
more complicated when one considers the pronounced regional and class
inequalities in life expectancy. In 2010/12 the highest male life expectancy
at birth in England and Wales (82.9 years) was in East Dorset, and the
lowest (74.0 years) in Blackpool – a difference of 8.9 years. For females,
the highest life expectancy at birth (86.6 years) was in Purbeck, and the
lowest (79.5 years) in Manchester – a difference of 7.1 years. For life
expectancy at age 65, the regional differences were 5.2 years for men and
5.1 years for women.[30] Within these broad areas are internal variations:
Kensington and Chelsea or Richmond upon Thames have experienced
more rapid improvements in longevity than has Tower Hamlets. Again,
there is currently a seven-year difference between the top and bottom
social classes in regard to life expectancy at birth, and a four-year one
at age 65.[31] The existence of these regional and class inequalities has

[27] Mike Murphy, 'The "Golden Generations" in Historical Context', *British Actuarial Journal*, 15, Supplement, 2009, pp. 151–184.

[28] For a useful summary, see Kenneth Howse, 'Review of Longevity Trends to 2025 and Beyond, Jan. 2009, *Beyond Current Horizons* (Department for Children, Schools and Families), www.beyondcurrenthorizonz.org.uk

[29] International Longevity Centre-UK, *Choosing Population Projections for Public Policy* (2009), pp. 8, 11.

[30] Office for National Statistics, *Life Expectancy at Birth and at Age 65 for Local Areas in England and Wales, 2010–12* (2013), pp. 9, 12.

[31] Victor, *Ageing, Health and Care*, p. 49.

given rise to the logical suggestion that state pension ages should vary by occupation and region. However impractical this might be, it does at least remind us that aggregate data are misleading and are an unfair justification for raising state pension ages.

Finally, the seemingly incontrovertible empirical case is often based upon speculative projections into the future, and then sensationalised by a largely uncritical press – as in the newspaper report headlined 'Today's Tots Could "Live to be 120"': this reported governmental claims that 'babies born today could eventually spend half of their lives in retirement', and quoted Iain Duncan Smith warning that 'in a country in which 11 million of us will live to be 100, we simply cannot go on paying the state pension at an age that was set early in the last century'.[32] It is of course only right and proper that governments should prepare for the future. However, one must bear in mind that all projections are to an extent political, and those related to demographic change have often turned out to be wrong. There are many future unknowns. As the Office for National Statistics admits, 'Population projections are uncertain and become increasingly so the further they are carried forward in time. They do not attempt to predict the impact that future government policies, changing economic circumstances or other factors might have on demographic behaviour.'[33]

A recent phenomenon?

A curious feature of the current debate is that gains in life expectancy at age 65 are presented as relatively recent and wholly unexpected. (As was shown in the previous chapter, this explanatory narrative was pushed strongly by the Pensions Commission.) A striking example was the comment by Patrick Grattan in 2006 that 'Another change in the past few years is that we have become aware of the increased speed in the growth of life expectancy. With the benefit of hindsight we were all (including the actuarial profession), sleep walking for a few decades. The Pensions Commission administered a reality check in its first report in October 2004.'[34] The implication is that the entire actuarial profession – a profession with a long and respected history – had been grossly negligent, collectively unaware that mortality rates at later ages were falling, and that pension fund managers foolishly allowed themselves to be lulled into a

[32] Matt Chorley, 'Today's Tots Could "Live to be 120"', *Independent*, 31 July 2011, www.independent.co.uk

[33] Office for National Statistics, '2011 Census', 7 Feb. 2014, www.ons.gov.uk

[34] Patrick Grattan, 'Ageing and Employment: Looking Back, Looking Forward', in Linda Bauld, Karen Clarke and Tony Maltby (eds.), *Social Policy Review 18: Analysis and Debate in Social Policy* (2006), p. 296.

false sense of security by a booming stock market in the 1990s. Suddenly and unexpectedly, it is alleged, a crisis arose and it became imperative to raise state pension ages.

To be sure, there may have operated something of a structural lag effect, whereby the implications of these changes filtered through slowly to the wider political and business community, thus encouraging employers to become complacent. However, overall this narrative is simplistic and unconvincing. It completely ignores the fact that in the 1990s employers plundered their pension funds and/or took 'contribution holidays' in order to boost their profits or achieve workforce downsizings[35] – part of the inexorable push by employers to reduce labour costs – and that falls in stock market values with the ending of the 'dot.com bubble' impacted very negatively on the whole private pensions industry. Another crucial factor was Chancellor Gordon Brown's 1997 'raid' on private/occupational pensions when he abolished the tax relief paid to pension funds and companies, thus saving an estimated £118billion for the Treasury between 1997 and 2014. This resulted in the closure of most defined benefit pension schemes and a fall in the number of workers covered by such schemes from 5,000,000 to 1,700,000. Before this happened in 1997, such pension funds were in surplus, and clearly able to cope with the demographic pressures.

The suspect nature of these demographically deterministic arguments can be demonstrated by casting an eye at the USA, where the whole 'compression of morbidity' debate (over what was happening to health status in old age, and the complex relationship between morbidity, disability and mortality) took off in the 1970s precisely because it was noticed that life expectancy at age 65 was increasing while health care utilisation rates among older Americans were also rising, pointing to the disturbing prospect of an increasingly infirm elderly population that was growing in size. In other words, all of this was known some four decades ago.

The American debate

For about two-thirds of the twentieth century the steady gains in life expectancy at birth in the USA greatly outstripped the gains in life expectancy at age 65, which were so small as to be virtually insignificant. From 1900 to 1950 in the USA, life expectancy at birth for males rose by 41 per cent, whereas at 65 it rose by only 13 per cent. For

---

[35] Jo Grady, 'From Beveridge to Turner: Laissez-faire to Neoliberalism', *Capital and Class*, 34, 2, 2010, p. 164.

Table 4.1 *Expectation of life in years, USA*

		1950	1960	1970	1980	1990	2000	2010
Males:	at birth	65.6	66.6	67.1	70.0	71.8	74.1	76.2
	at age 65	12.8	12.8	13.1	14.1	15.1	16.0	17.7
Females:	at birth	71.1	73.1	74.7	77.4	78.8	79.3	81.0
	at age 65	15.0	15.8	17.0	18.3	18.9	19.0	20.3

Source: National Center for Health Statistics, *Health, United States, 2012: With Special Feature on Emergency Care* (2013), p. 76.

females, the respective gains were 45 per cent and 26 per cent.[36] Hence the statistician Louis Dublin (who wrote prolifically on the demographics of old age) noted in 1928 that there had been gains in life expectancy at birth, 'but in the period of old age the improvement is almost entirely negligible'.[37] Again, the theory of the epidemiological transition, posited in 1971, presupposed that human longevity had more or less reached its natural limit.[38] Many demographers in the 1960s thus believed that no further gains at later ages could be made.[39]

However, mortality rates at later ages began to decline significantly from the 1960s onwards (slightly earlier for women than for men). The decline was relatively modest, but it was noticeable (see Table 4.1).

The precise causes of this – the balance between medical, lifestyle and environmental factors – have been much debated and cannot be discussed in detail here, but clearly factors such smoking cessation, reductions in coronary heart disease, and better treatment of chronic illness have been important. It is also interesting that the transition in western societies from blue-collar industrial to service employment worsened the job prospects of older men but seems to have improved their chances of survival at later ages: the two phenomena may be purely coincidental, or they may be interlinked.

In America from the late 1970s onwards, therefore, there developed a burgeoning debate over whether the noticeable gains in life expectancy at age 65 would be sustained and whether they would be accompanied

---

[36] Lois M. Verbrugge, 'Recent, Present, and Future Health of American Adults', *Annual Review of Public Health*, 10, 1989, p. 334.

[37] Louis I. Dublin, *Health and Wealth: A Survey of the Economics of World Health* (1928), p. 157.

[38] S. Jay Olshansky and A. Brian Ault, 'The Fourth Stage of the Epidemiologic Transition: The Age of Delayed Degenerative Diseases', *Milbank Quarterly*, 64, 3, 1986, p. 358.

[39] Kenneth G. Manton, 'The Dynamics of Population Aging: Demography and Policy Analysis', *Milbank Quarterly*, 69, 2, Spring 1991, p. 311.

by improvements in health. It could not necessarily be assumed that falling mortality would be accompanied by diminishing morbidity. The 'optimists' argued that health status at later ages would improve and life expectancy gains at later ages would slow up, being terminated by what James Fries called 'natural death' (that is, deaths increasingly clustering around the age of 85).[40] In the great trade-off between longevity and quality of life, this would limit the former but improve the latter, and would contain health and social care costs. The 'pessimists' argued that longevity would increase but disability-free life expectancy would not. As Ernest Gruenberg put it in 1977, in the previous four decades life-saving technology had outstripped health-preserving technology, 'and the net effect has been to worsen the people's health'.[41] Hence western societies would be burdened by growing numbers of infirm very old people leading poor-quality lives and requiring expensive care.

At this point in the debate (before the large baby boom cohorts began to approach old age), the focus was primarily on numbers being swelled by improved survival rather than birth cohort size. Therefore, initially the debate was over whether these early falls in later-age mortality would be maintained. In his classic 1980 article, Fries followed earlier demographers such as Leonard Hayflick in maintaining that there was a biological limit to human survival. Both the survival and the morbidity curves would become rectangularised. He mistakenly argued that the number of very old persons would not increase and he underestimated the longevity gains that were then taking place, describing those at age 75 as 'barely perceptible'.[42] By 2011, rising longevity in the USA had forced him to raise 'natural death' to over 90 years, and he now observed that 'the maximal attainable mean life expectancy appears to be greater than 90 years and is almost certainly less than 100'.[43] However, his notion of a stalling in longevity may well be proven correct in the long run. Others at the time were also uncertain over whether the gains in life expectancy at age 65 would be sustained. In the 1970s, the US Social Security Administration

---

[40] James F. Fries, 'Aging, Natural Death and the Compression of Morbidity', *New England Journal of Medicine*, 303, 3, 17 July 1980, pp. 130–135; James F. Fries, 'The Compression of Morbidity', *Milbank Memorial Fund Quarterly/Health and Society*, 61, 3, Summer 1983, pp. 397–419.

[41] Ernest M. Gruenberg, 'The Failures of Success', *Milbank Memorial Fund Quarterly/Health and Society*, 55, 1, 1977, p. 22. See also Morton S. Kramer, 'The Rising Pandemic of Mental Disorders and Associated Chronic Diseases and Disabilities', *Acta Psychiatrica Scandinavia*, 62, 1980 (Suppl. 283), pp. 382–397.

[42] Fries, 'Aging, Natural Death', p. 131.

[43] James F. Fries, Bonnie Bruce and Eliza Chakravarty, 'Compression of Morbidity 1980–2011: A Focused Review of Paradigms and Progress', *Journal of Aging Research*, 2011, p. 4.

had assumed they would not, but then revised its projections upwards in 1981.[44]

As the 1980s progressed there was increasing acknowledgement among informed commentators that life expectancy at age 65 was increasing, and that this seemed to be ushering in a new demographic era. In a seminal article in 1982, Kenneth Manton discussed the debate between the 'optimists' and the 'pessimists' and concluded that 'the evidence suggests that we have not exhausted the potential for life-expectancy changes due to control of chronic diseases'. In the future, he argued, these medical interventions might become even more effective, and there might develop techniques for slowing down the biological ageing process. Societies needed to be aware of the implications of these new demographic trends.[45] In 1985 Manton and Beth Soldo observed that the current ageing trends in the US population were 'historically unique' and hence were 'neither well understood nor documented'. Four key ones were: the rapid growth of the oldest old (aged 85+); increases in life expectancy at advanced ages; the predominance of females at advanced ages; and reductions in the age-specific mortality rates of certain major chronic degenerative diseases.[46] Likewise, Dorothy Rice and Jacob Feldman commented in 1983 that 'in the early 1970s an unanticipated decline in mortality rates for older men began' and in the following year Lois Verbrugge noted that the falls in mortality at all ages over the past decade amounted to 'an unanticipated phenomenon'.[47] In the mid-1990s, three leading demographers looked back at the declines in later-age mortality that had taken place over the previous twenty-five years, and called them 'quite remarkable'.[48] Awareness of these changes certainly entered into wider discussions of old age: for example, in 1987 Phillip Longman commented, regarding the previous twenty years, that 'the increase in the life expectancy of the elderly has been so dramatic in the last two decades that researchers are at a loss to explain it fully'.[49]

[44] Kenneth G. Manton, 'Changing Concepts of Morbidity and Mortality in the Elderly Population', *Milbank Memorial Fund Quarterly*, 60, 2, Spring 1982, pp. 230–231.

[45] *Ibid.*, pp. 183–244, 233 (quote).

[46] Kenneth G. Manton and Beth J. Soldo, 'Dynamics of Health Changes in the Oldest Old', *Milbank Memorial Fund Quarterly*, 63, 2, Spring 1985, pp. 206–207.

[47] Dorothy P. Rice and Jacob J. Feldman, 'Living Longer in the United States: Demographic Changes and Health Needs of the Elderly', *Milbank Memorial Fund Quarterly*, 61, 3, Summer 1983, p. 390; Lois M. Verbrugge, 'Longer Life But Worsening Health? Trends in Health and Mortality of Middle-aged and Older Persons', *Milbank Memorial Fund Quarterly*, 62, 3, Summer 1984, p. 475.

[48] Eileen M. Crimmins, Mark D. Hayward and Yasuhiko Saito, 'Changing Mortality and Morbidity Rates and the Health Status and Life Expectancy of the Older Population', *Demography*, 31, 1, February 1994, p. 159.

[49] Phillip Longman, *Born to Pay: The New Politics of Aging in America* (1987), p. 93.

This new demographic landscape was uncharted territory, presenting novel challenges and many uncertainties. One was how to reduce disability levels in old age (and, indeed, how to define and measure disability). Another was that, with the survival curve becoming increasingly rectangularised, there were decreasing gains to be had from reductions in mortality in childhood, youth and adulthood: the elimination of all deaths under the age of 50 in most advanced societies would only add about three years to life expectancy at birth. Taken together, these new challenges represented the old gerontological aim of not only adding years to life, but also life to years.

We can see, therefore, that by the 1980s American demographers, social scientists and government officials were well aware that life expectancy at age 65 was rising, and that this might continue. It is quite mistaken to present this as a recent phenomenon. However, there remains great doubt in the USA over how long these gains will continue, and whether they will be accompanied by improving health status such as to justify forcing US citizens to work later in life.

The UK debate

The compression of morbidity debate was of course taken up by UK demographers – though perhaps less vigorously – and followed a similar pattern. 'Expectation of life has changed very little for the elderly themselves' was Vera Carstairs's verdict in 1981, reflecting the prevailing view that no further gains in mortality at later ages could be made.[50] Yet only a few years later, the agenda had radically changed, and every gerontologist was having to discuss the implications of the mortality gains that were taking place in old age.[51] The American 'compression of morbidity' debate was also widely discussed.[52]

Was the UK Government Actuary's Department caught unawares? Again, a quick perusal of the evidence shows the answer to be an emphatic no. Mortality projections were revised in the 1980s, and thereafter there was full awareness of what was happening. To take but one example, in 1999 the Office for National Statistics published some 1996-based population projections. It turned its attention to recent longevity gains,

---

[50] Vera Carstairs, 'Our Elders', in R. F. A. Shegog (ed.), *The Impending Crisis of Old Age: A Challenge to Ingenuity* (1981), p. 33.

[51] Examples are: Christina R. Victor, *Health and Health Care in Later Life* (1991), pp. 50–53; Anthony M. Warnes, 'The Ageing of Populations', in Warnes (ed.), *Human Ageing and Later Life: Multidisciplinary Perspectives* (1989), pp. 60–61.

[52] See, for example, Mike Bury, 'Arguments About Ageing: Long Life and its Consequences', in Nicholas Wells and Charles Freer (eds.), *The Ageing Population: Burden or Challenge?* (1988), pp. 17–32.

Table 4.2 *Expectation of life at age 65 in the UK*

	1997	2001	2031
Males	16.1	16.6	18.0
Females	19.6	20.3	21.5

calculating that, in the 1980s and 1990s, life expectancy at birth for females had been increasing by about 2 years per decade, with that for males increasing a little faster. It concluded that 'If the present rates of increase in expectation of life continued throughout their lifetimes, then boys born now would, on average, live to age 92 and girls to age 95 with a large proportion surviving to be centenarians.' Regarding life expectancy at age 65, the ONS study offered the projections shown in Table 4.2 (based on death rates assumed for the remainder of each cohort's lifetime).[53]

This 1996-based projection assumed that life expectancy at age 65 would increase between 2001 and 2031 by 1.4 years for men and 1.2 years for women. On that basis, the projected expectations at age 65 for 2011 can be interpolated as 17.1 years for men and 20.7 years for women. These numbers were a slight underestimate for men (the actual figure for 2011 was 18.2 years) and exactly correct for women (20.7 years in 2011). Demographic concerns also figured in UK government publications in the 1980s Thatcher-inspired debate on cutting back state provision of old age: for example, *Growing Older* (1981) asserted that 'not only are more people living longer, but the average age of the older generation is rising' and the 1985 white paper, *Reform of Social Security*, warned of increasing numbers of pensioners and worsening crude dependency ratios.[54] In short, recent gains in life expectancy at age 65 – far from being 'dramatic', sudden and unexpected – were anticipated some three decades ago and there remains much uncertainty over whether they will continue.

Social and economic consequences

There has been much speculation over what might be the deleterious economic effects of an ageing population in the future, uncannily

[53] Office for National Statistics, *National Population Projections 1996-based* (1999), pp. 27, 32.
[54] Department of Health and Social Security, *Growing Older*, p. 1; *Reform of Social Security*, p. 15.

similar to the pessimism of the 1930s. These effects will allegedly include declining stock market values with fewer savers, reductions in aggregate demand and stagnant economic growth as workforces proportionately diminish.[55] The main seemingly powerful argument behind raising state pension ages is that the old age dependency ratio will worsen markedly, bringing increased pension, health and social care costs. The ratio of people aged 65+ divided by those aged 15–64 in the UK was 10 per cent in 1960, 25 per cent in 2010 and is projected to rise to 42 per cent in 2060. Will this inevitably create catastrophic problems?

The first point to note is that any worsening of the gerontic (old age) dependency ratio is being counterbalanced by a lessening of the child (neontic) dependency ratio. In 1971, 25.5 per cent of the UK population was aged 0–16 and 13.2 per cent aged 65+ – a combined dependency ratio of 38.7 per cent. By 2031, these proportions are projected to be 18.0 per cent and 22.3 per cent respectively, giving a combined neontic and gerontic dependency ratio of 40.3 per cent – an increase of only 1.6 percentage points.[56] Even then, one of the first lessons in gerontology is that demography is not destiny, and that numbers alone mean nothing. Crude age-based dependency ratios are misleading unless they are recalculated taking into account such factors as the total size of the labour force and participation by age and gender, adjusting for fulltime or part-time work.[57] Using the number of people of working age as the denominator is flawed; instead, the size of the workforce must be used. At just under 30,000,000, the UK's total labour force is now larger than it has been since modern records began in 1971 (although the massive growth of part-time jobs has offset this). An ingenious alternative has recently been constructed by two demographers: pointing out that there are more non-working 'dependants' of working age than there are older people not in work, Spijker and MacInnes have argued that if instead one defines 'dependants' as those with fewer than fifteen years to live (the point at which they become, on average, moderately expensive with regard to health and social care costs), and divide them by the number of people actually in work, then the 'dependency ratio' has fallen by one-third in the last forty years. They also point out that the proportion of the total population in work (48 per cent) is almost the same as it

[55] Well discussed in Greg O'Neill, 'The Baby Boom Age Wave: Population Success or Tsunami?' in Robert B. Hudson (ed.), *Boomer Bust? Economic and Political Issues of the Graying Society, Vol. I: Perspectives on the Boomers* (2009).

[56] Office for National Statistics, *Social Trends No. 41, 2011 Edition* (2011), p. 19.

[57] The best discussion of this is still Jane Falkingham, 'Dependency and Ageing in Britain: A Re-Examination of the Evidence', *Journal of Social Policy*, 18, 2, April 1989, pp. 211–233.

was sixty years ago (46 per cent).[58] Taking this one step further, it is a fair assumption that people only become, on average, very expensive (in terms of health and social care costs) in the last two years of their lives – and this is unaffected by how long they actually live: the last two years are merely postponed. There is also no correlation between dependency ratios and economic performance: the fact that there can be a labour force of record size during the current recession indicates that numbers alone mean very little. As will be shown in the following chapter, a higher proportion of UK men of all ages were in employment in 1931 (90.5 per cent) than in 1951 (87.5 per cent) – yet the former was a time of deep recession, and the latter of full-employment economic growth.[59] It is also worth considering the fact that the shortfall in older people's labour force participation is not that great: the employment rate for the 50–64 age group is currently 67 per cent – only six percentage points below the overall UK employment rate of 73 per cent (for the total 18–64 age group) and a lot higher than that for the 18–24 age group (only 56 per cent).[60]

Where the social and economic effects of future population ageing are concerned, two things really matter: first, productivity; second, redistribution. Regarding the first, it is how societies and economies adjust to demographic changes that is crucial, rather than the changes themselves. Fears of a more top-heavy population pyramid by the middle of this century are predicated upon the assumption that the steep-sided, triangular pyramid that pertained in the mid-nineteenth century is the desirable norm, and that anything else is aberrant. Yet for centuries before industrialisation and the demographic transition, the UK had a very youthful age structure and suffered many dysfunctional social consequences as a result. As is well known, youth correlates with high levels of crime, social disorder, violent and traumatic deaths, unemployment, extra-marital births and so on – and can therefore be just as expensive as an ageing population, although in different ways. At 22 per cent, the proportion of the UK population aged 65+ in 2031 – when the second wave baby boomers are well into retirement – will be little different to that currently experienced by Japan (24 per cent), Italy (21 per cent) and Germany (21 per cent). (Interestingly, Germany, while having this age distribution, was often held up as having the most successful economy in Europe.) To be sure, the Eastern European countries face

[58] Jeroen Spijker and John MacInnes, 'Population Ageing: The Timebomb That Isn't?', *British Medical Journal*, 347, f6598, 12 Nov. 2013, www.bmj.com
[59] Women's employment rates remained at c. 34 per cent in each year.
[60] Department for Work and Pensions, *Older Workers Statistical Information Booklet 2013* (2013), p. 15.

far greater problems in the future than does the UK, partly because of
out-migration. The projected proportions of people aged 65+ in these
countries in 2060 is 36 per cent in Latvia, 35 per cent in Poland and
35 per cent in Romania.[61]

When it comes to the output of a future workforce, the key factor is not
its total numbers so much as its productivity as measured by total and
per capita Gross Domestic Product (GDP). Greg O'Neill has pointed
out, in an elegant essay on this topic, that the US workforce is twice as
large as it was at the end of the Second World War yet total productivity is
eight times greater: individual productivity has on average quadrupled.[62]
Similarly, in the UK GDP per capita has virtually trebled in the fifty
years since 1962[63] and it is not unreasonable to surmise that this will
continue well into the future. In all advanced industrial economies over
the past hundred years the average working week has decreased, yet
per capita productivity has risen. Indeed, the whole history of economic
development over the last 200 years has been a story of smaller workforces
yielding higher productivity. In the future, per capita productivity may
increase so rapidly as to cause great human problems. A much more
disturbing prospect is that we might be on the verge of a dystopian
era in which electronic and other technology may drastically shrink the
number of jobs needed – including many white-collar, middle-class jobs.
Driverless trains and cars, airborne drones, three-dimensional printers,
supermarket self-checkouts – these are but a few examples of where
future technology may create more wealth with smaller workforces, and at
controversial human cost. The secret of economic growth is technology,
not numbers.

Taking this argument one logical step further – fewer younger workers
might actually have a beneficial effect on western economies, by forcing employers to innovate technologically rather than relying on labour-
intensive solutions. Fewer younger workers would also improve the bargaining power of labour and exert an upward pressure on wages (contrary
to what is happening now, and contrary to neoliberal economic strategies). The UK currently has nearly 3,400,000 working-age people without jobs – the 'hidden unemployed'[64] – so labour shortages cannot be
said to be a problem. Arguably, a major difficulty in modern economies is

[61] Eurostat news release, 'EU27 Population'.
[62] O'Neill, 'Baby Boom Age Wave', p. 15.
[63] Simon Rogers and Ami Sedghi, 'UK GDP since 1955', *Guardian*, 25 Oct. 2013,
www.theguardian.com
[64] Christina Beatty, Steve Fothergill and Tony Gore, *The Real Level of Unemployment 2012*
(2012). Adding in the 'under-employed' (those working part-time who wish fulltime
work), the total could be nearer 5,000,000.

that there are insufficient jobs for all who could work, and need to work. The most effective way to defuse the demographic timebomb is not to raise state pension ages but to have full employment. However, in today's political climate the only strategy on offer is the neoclassical assumption that more supply of labour will automatically create more demand for it.

How will an ageing population affect Gross Domestic Product (GDP)? There have been few serious attempts to estimate this – largely because predicting economic futures is so hazardous – but recently the DWP went to some lengths to publicise the allegedly beneficial macro-economic impact of extending working lives. A report, commissioned by the DWP from the National Institute of Economic and Social Research (NIESR), claimed that a one-year extension of working life all round would increase real GDP by about 1 per cent six years after its implementation, and raise the level of employment by about 1.6 per cent. This was, of course, relatively meaningless without a projection of the rise in total GDP that would take place by 2030. If there were no change in the state pension age, it was claimed, there would be some 3,000,000 fewer people of working age by 2030 (quite what effect this would have was not explained). Unsurprisingly, the NIESR report was awash with normative, supply-side assumptions about 'the retirement decision' as voluntary choice and said nothing on the crucial issue of where the jobs would come from or how much older people's savings would be eroded by their having to wait longer for the state pension.[65]

The futility of crude demographic determinism is revealed by the fact that, in 2008, many western economies were brought to the brink of melt-down by a near-catastrophic debt crisis – a crisis that has suddenly and radically changed the fiscal and political landscape, and has placed a massive new burden of public debt on the shoulders of future generations. The crisis is a pan-European one and by no means over. It was induced by the behaviour of a relatively small number of bankers, and not by an ageing population.

Conclusion

Today's hegemonic consensus is that rapidly rising life expectancy is creating an urgent and inevitable need to raise state pension ages – a need that is purely evidence-driven and uncontaminated by political ideology. However, seemingly naturalistic phenomena are always mediated through prevailing political cultures. All social issues are of course driven by

[65] Ray Barrell, Simon Kirby and Ali Orazgani, *The Macroeconomic Impact from Extending Working Lives* (2011).

empirical evidence, but the interpretations of that evidence can be many and varied. Undoubtedly, there are difficult demographic pressures to be faced by the UK over the next thirty years, but arguably these are more manageable and less threatening than other issues – climate change, the unresolved problem of consumer debt, inflated house prices, widening inequalities of income and wealth, creating jobs for all who need them and so on. The 'problem' of a future ageing population in the UK is more one of large birth cohorts reaching retirement, supplemented by the immigration of young adults and their subsequent children,[66] rather than of 'dramatic' increases in longevity. Members of these cohorts will have in theory paid for their state pensions through their National Insurance contributions, and the poorest of them will not survive to claim the pension, or will live only a short time on it. In the future, higher total and per capita productivity is likely to be achieved with smaller workforces; the question will then be whether there exists the political will to redistribute the fruits of this higher productivity to retired people.

[66] Future restrictions on immigration (which is becoming a politically controversial cause) would therefore moderate the ageing of the UK population.

5   Retirement

Why do people retire? The question may seem odd in the twenty-first century, when retirement has become democratised and universally accepted as a stage of life – so much so, that old age has increasingly become a welfarist concept, associated with permanent withdrawal from paid work and receipt of a state pension. Yet it was not always so. As noted in Chapter 1, in the predominantly rural economy that existed before the nineteenth century, male and female agricultural workers continued working for as long as they could, generally moving to less physically demanding jobs as they aged with Poor Law outdoor relief supplementing their diminishing earnings, terminating in 'infirmity' retirement. To some extent, this practice was observed in small industrial enterprises in the nineteenth century: 'old servants' whose individual productivity was declining but who had been with the firm for a long time would be kept on and allotted light tasks (such as storekeeper).

With industrialisation and the greater separation of home and formal work, the labour force participation of married women fell, so that by the end of the nineteenth century the concept of retirement had little meaning for them. From the 1880s onwards, a new kind of retirement gradually spread down the age structure, affecting first men – and then women, as their participation in the labour force increased in the second half of the twentieth century. This was 'jobless' retirement, caused primarily by a gradual shrinking of those labour market sectors that employed older workers and secondarily by an increasing emphasis in personnel practices on individual productivity: older workers deemed to be 'past their best' when aged in their mid- or late sixties would be eased out of employment by various means. Of course, 'jobless' and 'infirmity' retirement have always overlapped – ill-health is today the most frequently cited reason for labour force exit, and there is a merging of disability, unemployment and male 'early' retirement[1] – but the distinction between the two is heuristically useful.

[1] The inverted commas will be used only once at this stage, and subsequently, to denote the artificiality of state pension ages as a marker of 'normal' retirement – which, of course, they have never been.

Mass retirement is therefore a phenomenon of the last 130 years. Its principal cause has been long-run economic restructuring, or diminishing labour market demand in those sectors in which older workers have predominated. Yet the neoliberalisation of old age that has taken place since the 1970s has given rise to exactly the opposite kind of explanation – that, instead, the historic spread of retirement can be attributed to supply-side factors and human volition, and can therefore be reversed. These causal factors would include: the incentive effect of state, occupational and private pension schemes; accumulated saving making retirement more affordable; a 'retirement expectation' or 'retirement tradition' becoming culturally embedded; and so on. For example, it is often stated that an 'early retirement culture' has developed since the 1970s, and needs to be eradicated. Hence Smeaton and Vegeris assert that 'One of the key labour market trends that characterised the late 20th century was the emergence of an early retirement culture leading to a steady decline in employment participation rates of people (men in particular) in their 50s and 60s.'[2] What is striking about such 'explanations' is how much is actually left *un*explained – not least, how and why culture is formed, why it becomes all-powerful, why this 'early retirement culture' diminished in influence from the early mid-1990s (as older people's employment rates rose), why it affected some regions more than others and why it apparently influenced men more than women.

Supply-side, behavioural explanations have now become the new orthodoxy. One apolitical reason for this has been that, as male early retirement spread with particular rapidity from the 1970s onwards, economists and social scientists became increasingly interested in what determined the precise timing of labour force exit. The fact that this spread of retirement coincided with a rise in the value of the Social Security pension in the USA also made a 'pension as incentive' argument appear more convincing than it had been in the 1950s. In 1972 the value of Social Security benefits to retirees was increased by 20 per cent and the cost of living adjustment (COLA) was introduced to ensure that from 1975 benefits would rise in line with inflation. Interestingly, this was introduced by a Republican President, Richard Nixon, who expressed pride that retirees were being protected against inflation. (Nixon was a corporatist conservative, who believed in using the power of the state; his was a very different Republicanism to that of Ronald Reagan.) Again, there were striking reductions in absolute poverty among American retirees that made retirement appear less of an unwelcome

---

[2] Deborah Smeaton and Sandra Vegeris, *Older People Inside and Outside the Labour Market: A Review* (2009), p. 14.

prospect and therefore more likely to be chosen: as will be shown in the next chapter, between 1959 and 2005, the poverty rate for Americans aged 65+ fell from one in three to one in ten.[3] But the most important causal factor in the ascendancy of supply-side explanations of retirement has been the growth of low-paid and part-time jobs and the associated strategy (outlined in an earlier chapter) of maximising labour supply – illustrating perfectly Howard Becker's truism that 'the definition of a problem usually contains, implicitly or explicitly, suggestions for how it may be solved'.[4] In other words, definitions of social problems are often constructed with regard to envisaged solutions: in this case, the anticipated solution of freeing up labour supply by withdrawing benefits has determined the identification of benefits as the main cause of retirement. To this has been added the stranglehold that neoliberal, behavioural economics now exerts over the economics profession. The paradigm shift that occurred in the 1970s was therefore less to do with actual changes in the circumstances of older people than with the rise of neoliberalism, which has caused all social problems to be viewed through its distorting lens. The result has been that the effect of all social security benefits on work incentives, wage rigidities and labour mobility has come under increasingly critical scrutiny, and a growing emphasis has been placed upon human agency in the aetiology of social problems. If the historic spread of retirement has been mainly a matter of financial incentives, so the argument goes, then it is a trend that can be reversed merely by changing those incentives by withdrawing benefits. As a recent NBER press release asserts, with disarming simplicity, and confidence: 'Give male workers in industrial nations enough pension money to retire early, and they do. Delay the age at which they are eligible for retirement under national social security programs, and many older employees will keep working.'[5]

To an extent, this view might seem intuitive because the spread of modern mass retirement presents us with a paradox. As health status and working capacity have improved over the last 130 years, so has there occurred the increasing withdrawal of older men from paid employment. It is a paradox that has a significance well beyond the pages of obscure academic journals, being central to one of the most difficult dilemmas now troubling western governments as they face a future of ageing

---

[3] Barbara A. Butricia, Daniel P. Murphy and Sheila R. Zedlewski, 'How Many Struggle to Get By in Retirement?', *The Gerontologist*, 50, 4, 2010, p. 483.

[4] Howard S. Becker, 'Introduction', in Becker (ed.), *Social Problems: A Modern Approach* (1966), p. 10.

[5] David R. Francis, 'Social Security Causes Earlier Retirement', National Bureau of Economic Research Press Release, 24 Feb. 2014, www.nber.org

populations and rising pension costs in the medium term. Can the very long-run trend to male retirement be reversed? Does the modest rise in older people's employment rates over the past twenty years form the basis for a significant extension of working lives in the future? Has a 'retirement expectation' or a 'right to retirement' become so deeply embedded in popular consciousness that radical action is now needed to force people to work later in life?

There has always been a third kind of retirement, along with infirmity and joblessness. It is appropriate to term this 'elite' retirement, since it applied only to a small, privileged group at the top of society who would withdraw voluntarily from active professional life and had the means (savings or an occupational pension) to do so. Politicians, government officials, military officers and servants of the wealthy would often be 'pensioned off' at a certain age and would enjoy a quality of life in retirement equivalent to the amount of their means. They would 'retire from public life', and withdraw into private activities. There are innumerable historical examples of such elite retirement. One engaging one is that of Warren Hastings, as recorded by his early biographer, Lord Macaulay:

The last twenty-four years of his life were chiefly passed at Daylesford. He amused himself with embellishing his grounds, riding fine Arab horses, fattening prize-cattle, and trying to rear Indian animals and vegetables in England. He sent for seeds of a very fine custard-apple, from the garden of what had once been his own villa, among the green hedgerows of Allipore. He tried also to naturalise in Worcestershire the delicious leechee, almost the only fruit of Bengal which deserves to be regretted even amidst the plenty of Covent Garden.[6]

The financial expectations of those who enjoyed this elite retirement were, of course, high. For example, when the Archbishop of Canterbury, Cosmo Lang, retired in 1942, he received a pension of £1,500 a year[7] – fifty-eight times what the basic state pension then was. Relative to today's basic state pension, this would now amount to nearly £330,000 per annum. Elite retirement flourishes today, in the form of exceptionally generous severance packages to senior company executives. In the year 2013, 294 directors of the UK's top 100 publicly listed companies were in line to receive pensions averaging £259,947 per annum, with most still able to retire at age 60; by contrast, the average employee occupational pension for that year was £10,452 per annum.[8] As has already been argued, only a small elite of privileged retirees – at most, no more than

---

[6] Thomas Babington Macaulay, *Warren Hastings*, edited by Arthur D. Innes (1916), p. 137.
[7] J. G. Lockhart, *Cosmo Gordon Lang* (1949), p. 440.
[8] Trades Union Congress, *Pensions Watch 2013: A TUC Report on Directors' Pensions in the UK's Top Companies* (2013). This refers to occupational pensions only.

the top 10 per cent – are able to enjoy the consumption-rich, 'Third Age' retirement so often presented as the norm.

Definitions

Defining retirement has always been challenging. In its most conceptually robust form, the term implies complete and permanent withdrawal from the workforce and reliance upon a pension and/or savings. Yet this definition is too austere, and it has long been recognised that the transition can be gradual, via part-time working in some kind of post-career 'bridge' job.[9] Some retirees even return to fulltime employment. As has often been observed, retirement is a dynamic *process*, rather than a static event, best studied longitudinally.

Early retirement is really indistinguishable from 'hidden' or 'disguised' unemployment, and some have argued that it should be called just that.[10] Nearly one-third (29 per cent) of people in the UK aged 50–64 are economically inactive; of these, 41 per cent consider themselves retired. Therefore, only 12 per cent of the total age group consider themselves retired.[11] It is a situation extraordinarily similar to the 1930s, when social researchers noticed that older, unemployed men were reluctant to classify themselves as 'retired' because to do so would be to admit that they would never again return to fulltime employment: only in retrospect could their true situation be understood.[12] By contrast, those recorded by the census as 'retired' have always undertaken some part-time work in the informal economy, including unpaid domestic caring duties. The 'true' level of retirement is therefore difficult to measure, as is the precise age of final labour force disengagement. These and other difficulties are said to have intensified with the emergence of more complex work-histories and a diversification of pathways into retirement.

Retirement has always been an ambiguous and contradictory social experience,[13] highly differentiated in its impact and engendering a continuum of reactions, between crisis and opportunity. Something of this ambiguity was captured by the Acton Society Trust in 1960 when it observed that, for an employer, a retiring worker 'is, at once, or

---

[9] Robert C. Atchley, *The Sociology of Retirement* (1976), pp. 1–2.
[10] Chris Phillipson and Allison Smith, *Extending Working Life: A Review of the Research Literature* (2005), p. 13.
[11] DWP, *Older Workers 2013*, p. 15.
[12] Political and Economic Planning, Employment Group Memorandum, 'A Retirement Policy for Industry', 21 Jan. 1935, Political and Economic Planning Archives WG 3/5.
[13] Macnicol, *Politics of Retirement*, p. 20.

alternatively, an asset whose loss will be felt, a liability blocking the flex-ible flow of promotions, and, where occupational pension schemes are in force and sometimes even where they are not, a responsibility'.[14] As a major life transition, retirement can be a profoundly emotional expe-rience, representing a harbinger of future mortality, and therefore not easily captured by rational analysis.

Researching retirement

Exploring the complexity of motivation behind retirement is highly prob-lematic, raising enormously complex questions about the ways in which human beings absorb and subtly internalise background socio-economic factors. The cognitive processes deployed by individuals to assimilate information and make decisions are also highly complex – far more so than has ever been encapsulated by rational choice theory or behavioural economics. There are many other intriguing aspects, such as Henry Aaron's point that retirement generally occurs only once in a lifetime, and cannot be rehearsed: there can be no trial-and-error experimen-tation to get it right.[15] It is therefore a decision made on the basis of imperfect knowledge, which casts doubt on whether it can ever be a truly well-informed rational choice.

A thorough investigation would have to consist of three stages. The first stage would draw conclusions from observations of labour market, economic, social and cultural change. Most historical studies of retire-ment have remained at this rather general, broad-brush level, given the limitations of evidence. There have been some attempts – but, alas, not many – to examine changes in economic activity rates by labour mar-ket sectors (for example, Clark and Dunne's interesting analysis of age-compositional changes in different industries between 1931 and 1951).[16] Nevertheless, an understanding of economic and social history is essen-tial. A major problem in much of the recent literature on retirement is that it is infused by a kind of apocalyptic sociology that seeks to present current features of retirement as entirely novel. In fact, there is much continuity with the past. Again, much of the econometric literature and mathematical modelling from behavioural economists is so divorced from the socio-economic context and everyday realities of ordinary people that it is of little use.

[14] Acton Society Trust, *Retirement: A Study of Current Attitudes and Practices* (1960), p. 1.
[15] Henry J. Aaron, 'Retirement, Retirement Research, and Retirement Policy', in Aaron (ed.), *Behavioral Dimensions of Retirement Economics* (1999), p. 67.
[16] F. Le Gros Clark and Agnes C. Dunne, *Ageing in Industry* (1955).

A second stage would be to conduct opinion surveys of retirees, in order to ascertain their motives for leaving work and their subsequent experiences. One example of such a longitudinal survey was the USA Social Security Administration's Retirement History Study, which commenced in 1969 with c. 11,000 subjects then aged 58–63; these were interviewed at two-yearly intervals thereafter. The USA's Health and Retirement Study and National Longitudinal Survey have also been the basis of several studies. In the UK *The Dynamics of Retirement* (1997) was based upon interviews with c. 3,500 people aged 55–69 in 1988/9 and 1994 in the Office for National Statistics Retirement Survey.[17] There have also been many projects tracking changes in income, health, occupation and so on longitudinally, such as the Irish Longitudinal Study on Ageing, the English Longitudinal Study on Ageing (ELSA), the Survey of Health, Ageing and Retirement in Europe (SHARE) and so on. In addition, the last ten years have seen the publication of many small-scale, survey-based studies exploring attitudes to work and retirement.

However, such investigations present considerable interpretative problems. First, they tend to focus on the personal and circumstantial characteristics of the respondents, and not the background economic and social factors that shape consciousness and determine the range of available 'choices'. As will be argued later, these circumstantial factors have some contributory effect, but are only of major significance when they interact with wider socio-economic, labour market and health-related factors.

Second, the results of such opinion surveys cannot necessarily be taken at face value, given that human beings have a natural tendency to adapt to new circumstances, justify the inevitable and impose retrospective rationalisations that may be misleading with regard to the initial motivation. This has long been understood by researchers into retirement. Surveys of retirees in the 1950s and 1960s revealed that interview-based responses could be internally contradictory, could conceal other motives and could change over time as individuals adjusted to their new lives.[18] In her excellent survey of the ageing and social policy debate in the 1950s, Barbara Shenfield pointed out that the 'reasons given' for retirement in surveys needed to be scrutinised carefully, to ascertain what hidden factors lay beneath: apart from clear cases of ill-health, most firms consulted in such surveys felt that there was 'no reliance to be placed on the explanations

---

[17] Richard Disney, Emily Grundy and Paul Johnson (eds.), *The Dynamics of Retirement: Analyses of the Retirement Surveys* (1997).

[18] Margaret Pearson, 'The Transition from Work to Retirement (1)', *Occupational Psychology*, 31, 2, April 1957, pp. 85–86; Pearson, 'The Transition from Work to Retirement (2)', *Occupational Psychology*, 31, 3, July 1957, p. 148.

given by the employee for retirement, and in any case these are usually very vague'.[19] In 1964, I. M. Richardson perceptively commented that 'Since experience after an event may modify memory of the event itself, too much should not be made of these retrospective reasons for retiring.'[20]

Another study of the early 1990s described this problem at greater length:

The reasons people gave for their choice may not always reveal their motivation for taking early or late retirement, some reasons may be regarded as more acceptable than others; for example, retiring early to spend more time with one's partner may be felt to be more acceptable than taking early retirement because of being offered a financial inducement or being dismissed. Moreover, the reasons people gave for their choice may conceal other, more influential factors of which they may have been unaware, or did not mention because they took them for granted. These might include labour market conditions at the time, the policy of employers, the plans of spouses, and the ages and educational careers of children.[21]

A third problem can be that longitudinal surveys of older people and their attitudes are particularly vulnerable to attrition through mortality, which will tend to winnow out those with the poorest health and lowest incomes: a sample who retire when aged in their early fifties will be considerably depleted by the time they are in their mid-seventies, making longitudinal comparison difficult.[22] Again, older people's subjective definitions of concepts like adequate income and good health tend to become more austere in relation to objective measures as they age.

Finally, survey-based testimonial evidence is too blunt an instrument to draw the vexatious distinction between 'voluntary' and 'involuntary' retirement. Employees are often unaware of all the internal machinations that occur within a firm. Early retirees may be obliged (as part of the contract of severance) to define their retirement as voluntary where in fact it was impelled by an employer's desire to achieve workforce reductions. (This occurred frequently in the downsizings by large American corporations in the 1980s, which sought to thin out their workforces in response to global economic forces.) Subtle pressures may be put on employees by a 'too good to refuse' early exit offer that must be taken up quickly, or lost forever. The processes whereby an 'early exit culture' is

[19] Shenfield, *Social Policies*, pp. 62–63.
[20] I. M. Richardson, *Age and Need: A Study of Older People in North-East Scotland* (1964), pp. 74–75, 77.
[21] Margaret Bone, Janet Gregory, Baljit Gill and Deborah Lader, *Retirement and Retirement Plans: A Survey Carried Out by the Social Survey Division of OPCS on Behalf of the Department of Social Security* (1992), p. 55.
[22] Pamela Meadows, *Early Retirement and Income in Later Life* (2002), p. 15.

created in an individual firm, thus affecting the consciousness of its older employees, are exceedingly complex: there are numerous endogenous and exogenous factors to be considered. A striking example was cited in 1991 by Michael Young and Tom Schuller, in their investigation of retirees from the Ford car factory at Dagenham. The plant was served by a smaller factory at Woolwich making a few engine components, which found itself increasingly under threat from global competition:

In a new era of Japanese competition and labour surplus what had made sense then no longer did. The Woolwich factory was thought too small. Higher management might at any moment decide to reverse their earlier policy of dispersal and close the plant completely. At the time of our study they had not yet reached that but they were offering older men inducements to retire. The men would not necessarily get such generous terms again. An opportunity had come it would be foolhardy not to seize. As soon as it was announced, most of the workers at Woolwich with a chance rushed to put their names down for this 'Special Early Retirement', as the scheme was called. The name also gave them a label, 'early retired', which they would mostly be glad to adopt, even though they would all also register officially as unemployed in order to draw unemployment benefit.[23]

The third stage of investigation would be to mount a complex examination of macro- and micro-level factors at work – factors such as changes in the personnel structure of a particular firm, the policies and motives of employers and personnel managers, the long-term work-histories of individual employees, the effect of new technology and working practices, or shifts in global demand for the firm's products. These would have to be carefully cross-checked and triangulated with survey-based evidence, and the chain of cause and effect painstakingly traced back. Only then could one uncover what Edward Lazear has rightly noted is the key question: exactly who initiated the retirement?[24] As will be shown later in this chapter, what appears to be a freely chosen 'retirement decision' by an employee can often be their response to employer pressure caused by economic restructuring or to a lack of suitable alternative jobs. The extent to which individuals are able to exert control over their retirement has always intrigued researchers.

The above suggestion of a three-stage enquiry is of course a counsel of perfection. In practice, such an exercise would be immensely difficult and costly. All we have at the moment are studies that fall into one of the three categories above (and generally the first two). Given these methodological problems, it is not surprising that two American scholars have

[23] Michael Young and Tom Schuller, *Life After Work: The Arrival of the Ageless Society* (1991), pp. 28–29.
[24] Edward Lazear, 'Comment', in Gary Burtless (ed.), *Work, Health and Income Among the Elderly* (1987), p. 180.

remarked that analysing and explaining the diversity of today's retirement patterns 'strains the capacities of economic theory and statistical technique'.[25]

Historical developments

At this point, it is useful to summarise historical trends in retirement with regard to both the UK and the USA. Beginning in the 1880s, UK men aged 65+ began to experience a decline in their employment rates. Having been 73.6 per cent in 1881,[26] the rate fell to 56.8 per cent in 1911. The First World War produced a temporary rise, caused by the intensified labour market demand of a wartime economy. This economic boom continued after the war, resulting in a figure for 1921 of 58.9 per cent, two percentage points *above* the 1911 level.

By 1931, the rate had fallen to 47.9 per cent. For the next twenty years, reliance has to be placed on sources other than the decennial census since it had to be suspended in 1941 owing to wartime disruption. Testimonial and social survey evidence indicates that older workers suffered disproportionately in the 1930s recession, being concentrated in the depressed areas and in long-established industrial sectors that were relatively labour-intensive and therefore slowly declining; they were therefore much more likely to be rendered jobless by economic restructuring in the name of higher productivity and improved efficiency. The unemployment rates of older workers were not necessarily higher than those of younger workers but their spells of unemployment were longer. Hence of applicants to the Unemployment Assistance Board aged 25–34 in 1937, 15.8 per cent had been unemployed for three years or more, but of those aged 55–64 this proportion was more than double – 34.1 per cent.[27] Indeed, by the late 1930s there was great concern that many of these older men would never work again – a looming crisis that was unexpectedly resolved by the Second World War. In the USA, mass unemployment and economic restructuring in the 1930s had a similar effect on older workers.

---

[25] Henry J. Aaron and Gary Burtless, 'Introduction and Summary', in Henry J. Aaron and Gary Burtless (eds.), *Retirement and Economic Behaviour* (1984), p. 22.

[26] The 1881 census was the first to include the category 'retired', but we can be confident that this coincided with the commencement of a decline. See Paul Johnson, 'The Employment and Retirement of Older Men in England and Wales, 1881–1981', *Economic History Review*, XLVII, 1, 1994, p. 109.

[27] *Report of the Unemployment Assistance Board for the Year Ended 31st December 1937*, Cmd. 5752 (1938), pp. 71–74.

There is fragmentary but powerful evidence that the 1930s recession caused a sharp drop in older people's employment rates. In 1935–1936, Seebohm Rowntree discovered that the employment rate of working-class men aged 65+ in York had fallen to c. 30 per cent. That of women aged 60+ was c. 16 per cent.[28] Ignoring the focus only on the working class, this employment rate for men was almost exactly the same as that for all UK men recorded sixteen years later by the census in 1951, indicating that diminished labour market demand in the 1930s, caused by the recession, had temporarily 'speeded up' the spread of retirement. Poorer working-class areas were particularly hard hit by the recession, with adverse consequences for older men's employment, for the *New Survey* of East London found that the proportion of men aged 65+ receiving an income from employment in the early 1930s was only 32 per cent and that of women 11 per cent (when the 1931 census figures for the UK were 47.9 per cent and 8.2 per cent respectively).[29] Conversely, buoyant labour demand during the Second World War greatly increased the employment rates of older people (and others previously marginal to the labour force). Stimulated by a wartime economy, heavy industry in both the UK and the USA expanded rapidly, drawing older workers back into jobs that had disappeared during the previous decades. Thus in the UK the employment rates of older men more or less doubled (as far as can be estimated) during the War – indicating that, when industrial production increased, and demand for labour rose, older workers willingly took the available jobs.[30] In the USA, there was a 40 per cent increase in the number of men and women aged 65+ in the labour force between 1940 and 1945.[31]

By 1951, just under one-third (31.1 per cent) of UK men aged 65+ were in gainful employment. On the face of it, there was then a steady fall to 24.4 per cent in 1961. This has led some commentators to argue that, in the 1950s, retirement became elevated into an expectation or a social right – the 'consolidation of old age'. The power of this expectation is said to have neutralised both governmental inducements to later-life working and the job offerings of a full-employment economy (indicating, it is argued, that declining sectoral labour market demand was not a major

---

[28] Rowntree was obsessed with the second decimal place, so these figures are here rounded up. They do not actually appear in Rowntree's second survey of York – reflecting the low priority he gave to old age poverty – but they are cited in Nuffield Foundation, *Old People: Report of a Survey Committee on the Problems of Ageing and the Care of Old People Under the Chairmanship of B. Seebohm Rowntree* (1947), p. 85.

[29] Chris Gordon, *The Myth of Family Care? The Elderly in the Early 1930s* (1988), p. 34.

[30] Macnicol, *Politics of Retirement*, pp. 23–24.

[31] Macnicol, *Age Discrimination*, pp. 216–217.

Thousands

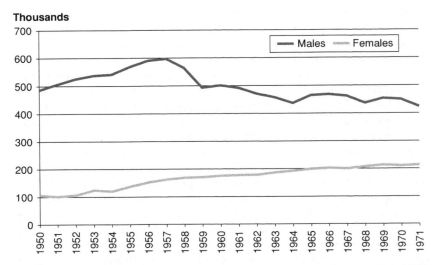

Figure 5.1 The number of UK male employees aged 65+, 1950–1971.
Sources: 'Age-Analysis of Employed Persons', *Ministry of Labour Gazette*,
LIX, 6, June 1951, p. 224; Central Statistical Office, *Annual Abstract of
Statistics No. 99 1962* (1962), p. 105; Central Statistical Office, *Annual
Abstract of Statistics No. 109 1972* (1972), p. 131.

causal factor and that, by the 1950s, retirement had become largely
voluntary).[32] However, this view is mistaken. Economic growth and a
tight labour market resulted in a steady *increase* in the number of UK
employees aged 65+ for much of the 1950s (see Figure 5.1). ('Employees'
excludes the self-employed but can be taken as an accurate proxy for
economic activity: in the case of men, it was about four-fifths of all
economically active men aged 65+.) The number of male employees
aged 65+ rose from 486,000 in 1950 to 597,000 in 1957. However, the
late 1950s mild recession then caused a decline, to 492,000 in 1961.
There were then slight fluctuations in the 1960s, but an overall decline
to 424,000 in 1971. For women aged 65+, the equivalent numbers were
106,000 (1950), 162,000 (1957), 177,000 (1961) and 213,000 (1971) –
a steady rise that reflected the overall increase in women's employment.
These were increases or decreases in both numbers and rates.

---

[32] Pat Thane, *Old Age in English History: Past Experiences, Present Issues* (2000), pp. 404–
405; Pat Thane, 'Social Histories of Old Age and Ageing', *Journal of Social History*, 37,
1, Fall 2003, p. 100.

In addition, there were pronounced regional variations in older men's employment rates.[33] Their employment levels were directly related to the state of the economy, and therefore labour market demand, both nationally and regionally.

The employment rates of British men aged 50–64 more or less stabilised between 1951 and 1971, during the long postwar economic boom. This led social commentators in the 1950s to express relief that the inter-war trend to male early retirement had been 'arrested and perhaps even reversed', as the 1954 Phillips Committee report put it.[34] Likewise, in their social survey of England and Wales Carr-Saunders et al. observed in 1958 that 'recent years have shown indications of a slight reversal of the trend towards early retirement'. However, they predicted that retirement at later ages would continue to spread because of the growth of occupational pensions and the effect of the retirement condition attached to the state pension.[35] As in the UK, the USA in the 1950s experienced a lively debate on older workers and their labour market problems, yet by the end of the decade there was an acknowledgement that the long-run trend to retirement could not be reversed.[36] Indeed, more prescient social commentators in both countries realised that 'an extra span of life' was emerging with its own needs and challenges.[37] In a telling phrase, Richard Titmuss warned of a 'functionless interregnum' opening up between the end of work and the beginning of formal retirement.[38]

The 1960s present an intriguing picture, since the employment rates of UK men aged 65+ dropped only one percentage point between 1961 (24.4 per cent) and 1971 (23.5 per cent). In addition, the rates for men 50–64 remained unchanged. Clearly, the continuing prosperity of manufacturing boosted labour market demand in those sectors employing older workers. By contrast, since 1930 the USA has had employment rates for men aged 65+ higher than those in the UK, despite a sharp drop between 1960 and 1970 – from 30.5 per cent to 24.8 per cent. Thereafter, the USA maintained consistently higher rates than the UK, but probably not because of its 1967 Age Discrimination in Employment

[33] Macnicol, *Age Discrimination*, pp. 171–172.
[34] *Report of the Committee on the Economic and Financial Problems*, p. 24.
[35] A. M. Carr-Saunders, D. Caradog Jones and C. A. Moser, *A Survey of Social Conditions in England and Wales as Illustrated by Statistics* (1958 edn.), p. 200.
[36] John Macnicol, 'The American Experience of Age Discrimination Legislation', in Wendy Loretto, Sarah Vickerstaff and Phil White (eds.), *The Future for Older Workers: New Perspectives* (2007), p. 30.
[37] Richard M. Titmuss, 'Social Administration in a Changing Society', in Titmuss, *Essays on 'The Welfare State'* (1958), p. 29.
[38] Quoted in Pearson, 'The Transition (2)', p. 149.

Table 5.1 *UK Males aged 45–64, economic activity rates (percentages)*

Year	1891	1901	1911	1921	1931	1951	1961	1971	1981[a]	1991[a]	2001[a]	2011[a]
Rate	93.7	93.5	94.1	94.9	94.3	95.2	97.6	95.8	88.0	80.9	77.2	80.2

Sources: Department of Employment, *British Labour Statistics Historical Abstract 1886–1968* (1971), p. 206; Central Statistical Office, *Social Trends No. 3 1972* (1972), p. 74; personal communication.
[a] I am most grateful to Professor Jonathan Wadsworth for supplying me with the calculations for 1981, 1991, 2001 and 2011, based upon the Labour Force Survey.

Act.[39] Hence the respective labour force participation rates of men aged 65+ in 2000/1 were 17.7 per cent (USA) and 7.5 per cent (UK).

The 1970s and after constitute a period that has been subject to much scrutiny, since it witnessed a sharp fall in the employment rates of older men. This was not entirely unprecedented, since job insecurity at later ages had been something of a problem for working-class men before the Second World War. However, it was a significant change, with a fall of over eighteen percentage points between 1971 and 2001. This can be seen clearly if we compare the employment rates of UK men aged 45 to 64 for every census year between 1891 and 1971 (see Table 5.1).

The twenty-five-year boom after 1945 boosted the economic activity rates of middle-aged men – but only temporarily. The extent to which the 1930s recession caused job opportunities to melt away as workers aged can be seen even more clearly if one makes a comparison between 1931 and 1951 by smaller age group (see Table 5.2).

From Table 5.2 it can be seen that male economic activity rates in 1931 started to fall from a remarkably early age (35–44) and were lower than in 1951 at every age thereafter, apart from men aged 65+. What we call male early retirement (between the ages of 35 and 65) was therefore *higher* in 1931 than in 1951.[40] It is also significant that there was a lower overall employment rate for men in 1951 (a year of prosperity) than in 1931 (a year of recession), indicating that numbers in a workforce matter less than total productivity.

What occurred in the 1970s and 1980s was that the long-run pattern of middle-aged men experiencing employment insecurity re-established itself – but in a more extreme form, owing to permanent deindustrialisation. By the early 1990s it seemed that the average age of permanent labour market exit was going to continue to fall indefinitely, raising the disturbing prospect of a growing group of economically inactive people

[39] Macnicol, 'American Experience', pp. 35–39.
[40] The slightly lower rates for men aged 15–34 are a consequence of compulsory military service resulting in men being abroad and therefore absent from the population census.

Table 5.2 *Percentage of males and females at each age gainfully occupied (including out of work), England and Wales, 1931 and 1951*

	Males		Females	
Age	1931	1951	1931	1951
15–19	89.9	83.7	75.1	78.7
20–24	97.3	94.9	65.1	65.5
25–29	98.4	97.6	42.7	40.6
30–34	98.5	98.3	29.6	33.9
35–44	98.2	98.6	24.5	35.8
45–54	96.7	98.6	21.1	35.0
55–59	93.9	97.8	18.9	27.0
60–64	87.2	95.0	16.4	15.0
65–69	64.9	47.2	12.3	8.9
70–74	41.7	27.4	7.2	4.7
75+	22.7	12.6	3.8	2.0
All	90.5	87.5	34.2	34.9

Source: A. M. Carr-Saunders, D. Caradog Jones and C. A. Moser, A Survey of Social Conditions in England and Wales as Illustrated by Statistics (1958 edn.), p. 90.

aged 50+ whose numbers would be swelled by the large baby boom cohorts.[41]

However, the economic recovery that began in the early 1990s (in the UK, as in most industrialised societies) produced rising employment rates among lone parents, the conventional unemployed and people aged between 50 and state pension age. From 2001 onwards, those aged 65+ experienced a rise: employment rates for men aged 65+ fell from 8.7 per cent to 7.5 per cent between 1991 and 2001 and then rose, to 13.0 per cent in 2013.

Opposed explanatory models of retirement

Standing in opposition to each other are broadly supply-side and demand-side explanations of retirement.[42] Has the spread of modern

---

[41] For a good contemporary discussion of this concern, see Frank Laczko and Chris Phillipson, *Changing Work and Retirement: Social Policy and the Older Worker* (1991).

[42] John Macnicol, 'Retirement', in Joel Mokyr (ed.), *Oxford Encyclopedia of Economic History*, *Vol. IV* (2003), pp. 371–375. The rather different division in current retirement research is between 'push' factors (negative, such as ill-health) and 'pull' factors (more positive, such as financial incentives).

jobless retirement over the past 130 years occurred because retirement has been collectively chosen? Or has it been a consequence of economic restructuring, largely independent of human agency?

Few serious analysts would offer only one of these alternatives. Supply and demand are not autonomous: they have an interactive, symbiotic relationship, and there are complex feedback processes at work. However, in today's political culture labour market demand is little mentioned. This is strikingly illustrated in UK government publications. In 1980, the *Department of Employment Gazette* analysed the recent trend to male early retirement and emphatically rejected supply-side factors like ill-health, improved occupational pension provision or the Job Release Scheme. It identified demand-side factors as the main cause – diminished job opportunities, unemployment among older workers and so on.[43] Yet now UK government departments – most notoriously, the DWP – and supranational bodies like the World Bank and the OECD offer overwhelmingly supply-side explanations. The most powerful causal factor – labour market demand – is rarely, if ever, mentioned. All the evidence shows that most early retirements are involuntary, yet the prevailing assumption is that people in late middle age have complete control over their lives, and that there is an abundance of available jobs.

Supply-side explanations

Since the 1970s, therefore, neoclassical economists have increasingly used the value-loaded terms 'retirement decision' and 'retirement behaviour' to imply human volition and have fashioned behavioural explanations by reference to the effect of economic incentives, such as accumulated wealth and savings, or state, occupational and private pensions. Typical of this view is Steven Sandell's assertion, regarding the USA, that the spread of retirement has been 'primarily due to voluntary decisions by older persons. The increased affluence of older Americans, often channelled through public and private pension benefits, is perhaps the most important factor behind this trend.'[44] In an oft-cited verdict on the UK, Leslie Hannah identified 'the increased capacity to finance retirement and the reduced dependence of the old on income from employment' as a major causal factor, concluding that 'Voluntary retirement is, in a sense, a luxury good whose incidence would be expected to

---

[43] 'An Increase in Earlier Retirement for Men', *Department of Employment Gazette*, April 1980, pp. 366–369.

[44] Steven H. Sandell, 'Introduction', in Sandell (ed.), *The Problem Isn't Age: Work and Older Americans* (1987), p. 8.

grow in a hundred year period in which general living standards have perhaps tripled.'[45] More recently, Joseph Quinn has declared that retirement in the USA has been caused by 'wealth and (later) the financial incentives buried in public and employer pension plans. As citizens become wealthier over time, they spend these additional resources in many ways, including staying in school longer, entering the labour force later, working fewer hours per year, and "purchasing" more leisure later in life, i.e. retiring earlier.'[46]

There have also been attempts to offer broadly cultural explanations – that there has been 'a growing acceptance of retirement as a legitimate stage of life', and the stigma of non-working in later life no longer exists.[47] As two American commentators have put it, 'in the relatively short period of approximately forty years, Americans have adopted policies, a supporting value system and social norms which have institutionalised relatively early retirement as a fundamental and expected part of the life course'.[48] Likewise, two British authors argued in 2000 that the last twenty years of the twentieth century witnessed the growth of 'an expectation to leave work early and live a long and active retirement on a reasonable income'.[49] One of the most convincing presentations of this argument was by Jonathan Scales and Richard Scase, who suggested that, for those in managerial and professional occupations, 'an expectation of early retirement has become entrenched which will be difficult to change'. They viewed this as part of a wider quest for personal autonomy ('a cultural feature of the information age').[50]

Supply-side explanations tend to present 'the retirement decision' as the ultimate rational choice. Far-sighted individuals, in possession of a stock of perfect knowledge and living in a world of certainty, are said to be able to plan lifetime spending, consumption and saving so that they do not use up all their resources before death. They are able to avoid systematic forecast errors, and can thus achieve the smoothing of consumption over the lifecourse, balancing the benefits of saving during the working life against the hazards of dissaving during retirement by trading off the pros and cons of a wide range of variables

---

[45] Leslie Hannah, *Inventing Retirement: The Development of Occupational Pensions in Britain* (1986), p. 124.

[46] Joseph F. Quinn, 'Work and Retirement: How and Why Older Americans Leave the Labor Force', Boston College Working Paper 743 (2010), p. 2.

[47] 'America's Aging Workforce', *AARP Brief No. 3*, March 1991, p. 9.

[48] Malcolm H. Morrison and Victor S. Barocas, 'The Aging Work Force – Human Resource Implications', in The Ageing Society Project, *Human Resource Implications of an Ageing Work Force* (1984), p. 119.

[49] Jessica Bone and Samantha Mercer, *Flexible Retirement* (2000), p. 5.

[50] Jonathan Scales and Richard Scase, *Fit and Fifty?* (2000), p. 7.

against each other – income, savings, working, job satisfaction, leisure, hobbies, family obligations, health status, anticipated life expectancy, social security benefits, occupational pensions, income taxes and so on. The claim is that citizens, deploying some kind of Benthamite felicific calculus, invariably prefer leisure to working, and the attractions of leisure will increasingly outweigh the disbenefits of working as a person ages and (presumably) accumulates more and more savings. Typical of this approach is the a priori statement by Barrell *et al.*: noting vaguely that for 'some' people, earning capacity 'may' decline with age, they conclude: 'This means that, as people age, the cost of work, in terms of leisure forgone, becomes increasingly expensive relative to the benefit they gain from working. Working becomes less attractive and, when people feel they can afford an acceptable living standard without working, they retire.'[51] Even more boldly, Pamela Meadows states that 'in practice most retirement in most countries is voluntary. Most people regard leisure as more desirable than work, and they prefer to be retired than continuing in paid employment.'[52]

It is perhaps instructive to pause and take note of the intriguing implications of such statements. The first is common to all econometric modelling. Rational economic men and women are said to take personal decisions according to highly complex econometric formulae, but are unable to explain or formularise their own decision-making processes: only trained economists can do that. The second is that rational choice, behavioural explanations tend to be supported by neoclassical economists who are enthusiasts for free market capitalism; yet the explanation offered by them is that those who work in the capitalist economy so dislike it that they cannot wait to retire from it. While many citizens undoubtedly have to endure boring, repetitive, low-paid jobs, and therefore look forward to retirement at the end of a long working life, most serious research into public attitudes finds that people want to work and desperately need the higher incomes that come from working.[53] As will be shown later in this chapter, surveys also demonstrate that people try to work as late in life as possible, but are prevented from doing so by structural barriers not of their own making (most notably, ill-health or redundancy); once retired, they may not wish to return to work – but that is largely a rationalisation of the inevitable or a reflection of the inherent unattractiveness of the few jobs that are available. In short, choice and control over 'the retirement

[51]   Barrell *et al.*, *Macroeconomic Impact*, p. 4.
[52]   Pamela Meadows, *Retirement Ages in the UK: A Review of the Literature* (2003), p. 34.
[53]   See, for example, Tracy Shildrick, Robert MacDonald, Andy Furlong, Johann Roden and Robert Crow, *Are 'Cultures of Worklessness' Passed Down the Generations?* (2012).

decision' are enjoyed by only a small elite. Third is the curious volte-face in behavioural economics: in the 1980s, it was maintaining that people made rational choices, in response to economic incentives; by the 2000s, people were seen as making *irrational* choices, and needed to be 'nudged' in the right direction by paternalistic state policies. A fourth point is that supply-side explanations assume a world of complete certainty, in which individuals are able to predict the future and plan ahead. In fact, later life is full of unwelcome surprises – a sudden health crisis, for example – that render such forward planning impossible. Finally, behavioural economics spares no effort to analyse the behaviour of human beings, but completely ignores the behaviour of private capital.

On the face of it, there appears to be considerable survey-based evidence since the 1970s that retirement in the USA has been increasingly 'chosen'. Analysis by Joseph Quinn showed that, in the 1940s, fewer than 5 per cent of American new retirees cited voluntary factors as their reason for leaving work; by the 1980s, however, voluntary factors accounted for nearly half of all retirements, with involuntary layoff only about 15 per cent.[54] Similarly, among newly retired Social Security beneficiaries in the USA in 1982, the desire to retire accounted for 40 per cent of cases and health problems 27 per cent, with loss of a job only 10 per cent and compulsory retirement a mere 7 per cent.[55] One must of course be very wary of taking such opinion-based evidence at face value: a stated wish to retire may well conceal other factors. Fantasising about early retirement may merely be a device to offset higher levels of stress and burn-out in a more competitive workplace environment and, as has been shown, retrospective rationalisations can be inaccurate. Nevertheless, most American researchers into retirement take the view that up to the 1970s retirement was driven largely by involuntary factors (notably, ill-health, mandatory retirement and redundancy), but after the 1970s voluntary factors predominated.[56] This may appear to be so, but one must bear in mind that this seeming change coincided with the beginnings of the neoliberal revolution (especially in the economics profession), which viewed social problems as driven by human agency.

It is a central tenet of neoliberalism that state pensions and social security benefits have encouraged retirement. Hence the OECD declares

[54] Cited in Gary Burtless, 'An Economic View of Retirement', in H. J. Aaron (ed.), *Behavioural Dimensions of Retirement Economics* (1999), pp. 11–13.
[55] Herbert S. Parnes, 'The Retirement Decision', in Michael E. Borus, Herbert S. Parnes, Steven H. Sandell and Bert Seidman (eds.), *The Older Worker* (1988), p. 133.
[56] Well discussed in Joseph F. Quinn and Richard V. Burkhauser, 'Work and Retirement', in Robert H. Binstock and Linda K. George (eds.), *Handbook of Aging and the Social Sciences* (3rd edn., 1990), pp. 310–311.

boldly that 'Individuals' decisions about work and retirement depend on the financial incentives embedded in retirement-income systems.'[57] This article of faith is reasserted in every OECD report on old age: old age pension systems are said to 'discourage work at older ages in virtually all OECD countries'; state pension replacement rates 'will tend to influence the decision to retire. For workers who have reached pensionable age, retirement is more likely if the pension replacement rate is high.'[58] Similarly, a recent Institute of Economic Affairs publication argues that state pension systems play a major part in disincentivising later-life working while disability benefits encourage early retirement.[59] In a 1977 article pioneering this view Michael Boskin argued that 'Recent increases in Social Security benefits and coverage, combined with the earnings test, are a significant contributor to the rapid decline of the labour force participation of the elderly in the United States',[60] and David Wise's similar verdict twenty years later was that 'economic analysis reveals that public and private pension provisions themselves have contributed to the decline in labour force participation'.[61]

Both authors above argue that Social Security has a contributory effect – but by exactly how much they cannot say. Two important US histories of retirement have likewise argued that the Social Security pension and increasing real wealth have given older citizens greater disposable income, and thus the freedom to leave work: Carole Haber and Brian Gratton identified federal Social Security as 'the decisive catalyst of change'[62] and Dora Costa singled out increasing levels of accumulated personal savings.[63] In the USA, the lowering of pension eligibility age for men to 62 in 1961 (with actuarially reduced benefits) is often credited with hastening earlier retirement,[64] and the apparent

---

[57] Organisation for Economic Co-operation and Development, *Pensions at a Glance 2011: Retirement-income Systems in OECD and G20 Countries* (2010), p. 49. Throughout this report, the assumption is that the answer is to withdraw these alleged financial incentives.

[58] Sveinbjorn Blondal and Stefano Scarpetta, *The Retirement Decision in OECD Countries: Economics Department Working Papers No. 202* (1999), pp. 7, 16. See also, Gruber and Wise (eds.), *Social Security*.

[59] Gabriel Heller Sahlgren, *Income from Work – the Fourth Pillar of Income Provision in Old Age* (2014), pp. 21–33.

[60] Michael J. Boskin, 'Social Security and Retirement Decisions', *Economic Inquiry*, XV, 1, Jan. 1977, p. 19.

[61] David A. Wise, 'Retirement Against the Demographic Trend: More Older People Living Longer, Working Less, and Saving Less', *Demography*, 34, 1, Feb. 1997, p. 87.

[62] Carole Haber and Brian Gratton, *Old Age and the Search for Security: An American Social History* (1994), p. 88.

[63] Dora L. Costa, *The Evolution of Retirement: An American Economic History, 1880–1990* (1998), esp. pp. 14–21.

[64] See, for example, Harold Sheppard and Sara E. Rix, *The Graying of America: The Coming Crisis in Retirement-Age Policy* (1977), p. 4.

'bunching' of labour force exits at ages 62 and 65 (the age for full bene-fits) has been cited as evidence of this incentive effect.[65]

Attributing the spread of retirement to the state pension is less com-mon in the UK – hardly surprising, given its low value. Between the late 1940s and the mid-1970s the relative value of the UK's basic state pension did not change (remaining at about 19 per cent of average male manual earnings); this relative value then declined, from 1980 onwards. Yet age-65 retirement continued to spread during both of these periods. There have been slight fluctuations in the average age of labour market withdrawal in the UK, and these bear no relation to any changes in the value of social security benefits. The UK now has one of the worst state pension schemes in the developed world. As a percentage of average pre-retirement gross earnings for a single male, the UK's state pension in 2013 was 37.9 per cent, compared with an OECD average of 57.9 per cent. The levels for comparable countries were: France, 59.1 per cent; Germany, 42.0 per cent; Italy, 71.2 per cent; Spain, 73.9 per cent.[66] Contrary to OECD assertions, the average effective ages of retirement in each of these countries do not correlate with the generosity or parsimony of their state pension replacement rates – for example, Spain has a much higher replacement rate than the UK yet an average age of retirement for men in 2012 of 62.3 (only slightly lower that the UK's 63.7).

Looking across the industrialised world, one can see that the historic spread of retirement has followed a similar pattern despite these varying replacement rates. Hence between 1970 and the 1990s, average ages of retirement for men fell in both the UK and the USA: for the UK, the fall between 1970 and 1998 was from 67.7 to 61.7; for the USA between 1970 and 1994 it was from 68.5 to 64.1. Average ages of retirement then rose slightly, to 63.7 (UK) and 65.0 (USA) in 2012. In other words, between 1970 and 2012, this net fall was 4.0 years for the UK and 3.5 years for the USA – a remarkably similar amount, despite very different social security systems.[67] Cross-national data show similar retirement trends shared by different countries, albeit with slight differences in tim-ing. Among OECD member states, there was an increasing withdrawal of people from paid employment from 1970 to the mid-1990s, then a

[65] Henry J. Aaron and Jean Marie Callan, *Who Retires Early?* (2011), n.p.; Sandell, 'Intro-duction', p. 8; Michael V. Leonesio, 'The Economics of Retirement: A Nontechnical Guide', *Social Security Bulletin*, 59, 4, Winter 1996, p. 30; Jonathan Gruber and David Wise, 'Introduction and Summary', in Gruber and Wise (eds.), *Social Security*, pp. 16–20.
[66] OECD, 'Gross and Net Pension Replacement Rates', in OECD, *Pensions at a Glance 2013: OECD and G20 Indicators* (2013), www.oecd-library.org
[67] 'Trends in Retirement and in Working at Older Ages', in OECD, *Pensions at a Glance 2011.*

rise in their employment rates. The average age of labour market exit in all OECD countries is now 64.2 for men and 63.1 for women.[68] This average age of exit is lower than the pensionable age in most OECD countries, also undermining the 'pension as incentive' argument. All in all, the remarkably common experience shared by the industrialised nations largely absolves any one country's state pension provision from blame: after all, why would a social security benefit in one country affect 'retirement behaviour' in many other countries?

The UK's state pension scheme is also one that is riddled with complexity – 'arguably the most complex of any industrialised country', as a House of Lords Select Committee put it in 2003.[69] Some sixty years previously, similar complaints were being made[70] and all that has happened since then has been that more layers of provision have been added. This complexity makes it extremely difficult for UK citizens to make well-informed choices – a situation that has encouraged governments to blame consumers. Hence the 2002 Green Paper lamented: 'Evidence suggests that most people have only a limited understanding and awareness of pensions and the pensions system . . . both public and private pensions are poorly understood and seen as complex.'[71] Recent studies have re-emphasised that UK citizens are strikingly ignorant of their likely pension income and, indeed, display a deep lack of trust in financial institutions.[72] Consumers feel so baffled by the complexity of private pensions that they have little or no idea what they will receive in retirement.[73] Whether this has been caused by path dependency or political factors, it still amounts to a Byzantine structure that individuals find difficult to understand, let alone exploit (although they tend to be blamed for making poor choices if the financial products they purchase turn out to be a disappointment). Some attempts to implicate welfare benefits have been made, such as Blundell and Johnson's claim that state benefits encourage early retirement, whereas occupational pensions encourage longer working.[74] As will

[68] OECD, *Pensions at a Glance 2013*, pp. 128–129.

[69] House of Lords. Select Committee on Economic Affairs, *Aspects of the Economics of an Ageing Population: Vol. I – Report* (2003), p. 45.

[70] W. A. Robson, 'Introduction: Present Principles', in W. A. Robson (ed.), *Social Security* (1943), p. 15.

[71] Department for Work and Pensions, *Simplicity, Security and Choice: Working and Saving for Retirement*, Cm 5677 (December 2002), p. 36.

[72] Phillipson and Smith, *Extending Working Life*, pp. 41–42; Sarah Vickerstaff, Wendy Loretto, Jenny Billings, Patrick Brown, Lavinia Mitton, Tina Parkin and Phil White, *Encouraging Labour Market Activity Among 60–64 Year Olds* (2008), pp. 28, 57–59.

[73] Effectively summarised in Price and Livsey, 'Financing Later Life', p. 74.

[74] Richard Blundell and Paul Johnson, 'Pensions and Retirement in the United Kingdom', in Gruber and Wise (eds.), *Social Security*. See also, Richard Blundell, Costas Meghir

be shown later in this chapter, in the UK there is some bunching of retirements around the respective male and female state pension ages. This has been used as evidence of the incentive effect of the state pension,[75] but the opposite interpretation is also possible since the bunching is over quite a wide age range.

A final supply-side factor is that older workers may retire semi-willingly because they perceive themselves to lack the skills and adaptability to compete with younger workers for available jobs – often termed the 'discouraged worker' syndrome. This is often rationalised as ill-health and work-disability.

Demand-side explanations

A very different group of explanations form what can loosely be called a 'demand-side' view – that the evolution of western economies has slowly marginalised older workers. Modern mass retirement is associated with the enormous structural changes that affected all industrialised economies from the late nineteenth century onwards, which in turn gave rise to more 'scientific' personnel management and scrutiny of each worker's productivity. Retirement became a useful managerial device, terminating a contract of employment just when an individual worker's productivity began to diminish. Technology-driven innovations over the course of the twentieth century continued the displacement of older workers, and at progressively younger ages (the decline in agriculture being a contributory factor). In other words, more was possible with fewer workers. Older workers have tended to be concentrated in old industrial sectors that are in decline and are likely to close or contract and shed labour. New economic growth has tended to take place in sectors with youthful workforces. Only recently – since the 1990s, with the expansion of low-grade service jobs, many of them part-time – has the demand for older workers improved, and the improvement is slight.

The balance between the two models

Any polarisation between 'supply' and 'demand' is, of course, too simplistic. A correct explanation would have to offer some combination between the two, such as Stephen McConnell's conclusion in 1983 that, in the USA, the declining labour force participation rates of older men

and Sarah Smith, 'Pension Incentives and the Pattern of Early Retirement', *Economic Journal*, 112, March 2002, pp. C153–C170.
[75] Barrell *et al.*, *Macroeconomic Impact*, pp. 5, 7.

have been 'in large part a direct result of public policies that have long encouraged early retirement and allowed (even created) obstacles to continued employment. In addition, eight major recessions or depressions since 1948 have wracked the economy, resulting in a dramatic decline in labour force participation rates among older workers.'[76] There are also some explanations that fit neither 'supply' nor 'demand', such as the theory often credited to the economist Edward Lazear (although, interestingly, not actually invented by him[77]) that mandatory retirement rids a firm of older workers when they become too expensive to employ in relation to their productivity.[78] (This, of course, assumes that employers can accurately measure both an individual's productivity and their labour costs.)

Clearly, what is at issue is the nature of a 'cause'. Economic restructuring may create an immensely powerful set of forces operating at the macro-level, displacing older workers from the labour force; however, the precise *timing* of their exit – this year or next year – may be determined more by micro-level incentives or personal circumstances. Perhaps the most ingenious interpretation in this regard is the contention that health problems and socio-economic status (structural factors) are drivers of 'the retirement decision': in other words, if poor health or a factory closure prevents an individual from working in later life, and they are forced to retire, that apparently constitutes their voluntary 'choice'.[79]

Supply versus demand models: the pros and cons

'Demand-side' explanations tend to be very general and contextual, lacking in explanatory precision. They do not reveal what happens at the micro-level of the firm, they can lapse into crude economic determinism and their emphasis on work-based identities can throw little light on the past retirement experiences of women. However, there are a number of reasons for according them greater importance: the long-term historical evidence certainly warrants this. The case made here will be that demand-side factors have accounted for most of the fall in older men's

[76] Stephen R. McConnell, 'Age Discrimination in Employment', in Herbert S. Parnes (ed.), *Policy Issues in Work and Retirement* (1983), p. 159.

[77] For an earlier version, see Edwin Shields Hewitt, 'Industrial Retirement Plans As Viewed by Management', in George B. Hurff (ed.), *Economic Problems of Retirement: A Report on the Fourth Annual Southern Conference on Gerontology held at the University of Florida January 1954* (1954), pp. 100–101.

[78] Edward P. Lazear, 'Why Is There Mandatory Retirement?', *Journal of Political Economy*, 87, 6, Dec. 1979, pp. 1261–1284.

[79] Melissa Knoll, 'Behavioural and Psychological Aspects of the Retirement Decision', *Social Security Bulletin*, 71, 4, 2011, www.ssa.gov

economic activity in the past 130 years, and supply-side factors for only some – as a contributory cause. What arguments can be marshalled to demonstrate this?

First, perusal of the contemporary literature shows that social observers in the 1880s and 1890s noticed that jobs for older workers were disappearing. In subsequent decades, trades unionists and pensioners' organisations campaigned for improved state pensions as a recognition of the fact that the working lifecourse had changed, and was going to be terminated by a lengthening period of enforced retirement.[80]

Second, how does the 'pension as incentive' argument stand up against the evidence? As Gary Burtless has observed, most of the theorising on the behavioural effects of Social Security benefits 'is based on the casual empirical observation that retirements have occurred earlier as Social Security benefits have become more generous'.[81] By 'casual' is meant an observed correlation, without a clear, demonstrable flow of causation: we might just as well assert that retirement has spread as car ownership has increased. Vague and allusive language is frequently used by those who argue this case: David Wise, for example, suggests that 'the accelerated decline in labour force participation rates after about 1940' in the USA 'roughly corresponds' to the implementation of Social Security and federal tax incentives for private pensions; the noticeable rises in labour force departure rates (at ages 55, 60, 62 and 65) 'coincide', he argues, with economic incentives in company pension plans and in federal Social Security.[82] Along with Jonathan Gruber, Wise claims that 'one explanation' for early retirement is that Social Security benefits 'provide enormous incentives to leave the labor force early'; however, the authors never consider any other possible explanations.[83] Leonesio similarly views Social Security as 'probably' causing 'a reduction' in the labour force activity of older Americans (by exactly how much he does not say).[84] However, this observed correlation confuses cause and effect and may therefore be a classic case of reverse causality – rather like saying that wet pavements cause rain. It is much more likely that the spread of retirement has been the *cause* of more generous pension provision in the USA (particularly the lowering of the eligibility age), rather than the other way round.

[80] Macnicol, *Politics of Retirement*, pp. 48–59.
[81] Gary Burtless, 'Introduction and Summary', in Burtless (ed.), *Work, Health and Income*, p. 15.
[82] Wise, 'Retirement Against the Demographic Trend', pp. 86, 87, 93.
[83] Gruber and Wise, 'Introduction and Summary', p. 1.
[84] Michael V. Leonesio, 'Social Security and Older Americans', in Olivia S. Mitchell (ed.), *As the Workforce Ages: Costs, Benefits and Policy Challenges* (1993), p. 201.

Much has been made in the USA of the reduction in the minimum Social Security entitlement age for men to 62 in 1961 'causing' earlier retirement. Yet it was not followed by an immediate fall in the average age of retirement. The fall was gradual, implying that earlier retirement was cause and not effect.[85] Between 1963 and 1983, the labour force participation rates for American men aged 62 fell by 31.8 per cent – faster than that for men aged 55 (7.6 per cent) or 60 (18.7 per cent). However, the rate of fall increased for every one-year age group between 55 and 65: for men aged 63, it was 38.2 per cent and for men aged 65 it was 43.0 per cent.[86] There was indeed a small spike of retirements at age 62, but this is most likely because taking Social Security early was a last resort for those whose hold on the labour market was precarious anyway. The inconvenient fact is that labour force participation rates for American men aged 62 to 72 *rose* between 1985 and 2009, despite this alleged incentive to retire at age 62. Joseph Quinn's supply-side explanation for this is that the delayed retirement credit in Social Security changed and incentivised later-life working, that defined benefit pension schemes have declined and that older Americans are living longer and healthier lives.[87] The tendency in such calculations is to ignore labour market demand, and focus instead on observed correlations between changes in Social Security eligibility and 'people's labour supply behaviour'.

Historical evidence shows that older workers' past rates of economic activity or inactivity across different societies did not correlate with changes in the availability or value of state pensions. In the UK, modern retirement began in the 1880s, yet the first state pension payments (under the 1908 Old Age Pensions Act) were not made until 1 January 1909 – some three decades later. In any case, nearly two-thirds of recipients were women with little or no formal labour market attachment and minimal earnings. The doubling in the value of the state pension in 1919 did not accelerate the trend to retirement. As we have seen, buoyant labour market demand meant that the 1921 census recorded an *increase* in the employment rates of men aged 65+ compared with 1911. In the UK in the 1930s, all the evidence from social surveys showed that older workers clung tenaciously on to jobs for as long as they could, rather than 'retiring' on a basic state pension of only 10s0d (50p) per week (about one-fifth of a low industrial wage in the 1930s). While the state pension might have

[85] Henry J. Aaron, 'Introduction', in Aaron, *Behavioral Dimensions*, p. 2.
[86] Philip L. Rones, 'Using the CPS to Track Retirement Among Older Men', *Monthly Labor Review*, 108, Feb. 1985, p. 47.
[87] Quinn, 'Work and Retirement', pp. 4–5 and table 3.

made it possible for some very low-paid, marginal workers aged 65+ to relinquish fulltime employment, or to have small earnings from casual work topped up, complete retirement would have brought a serious drop in income. Unless a pensioner had substantial savings, or assistance from relatives, his or her poverty would be extreme. It would have been myopic behaviour of the most self-destructive kind – at odds with any rational choice econometric modelling – to 'choose' to leave waged employment and retire into such extreme poverty. Yet the economic activity rates of older men fell sharply. Surveying the working-class population of York in 1935–1936, Seebohm Rowntree surmised that the existence of the state pension might have made employers more inclined to dismiss older workers than in 1899 (the date of his previous survey, and a time of strong demand for labour), but he firmly declared that, of those men aged 60+ and unlikely to work again, 'the great majority would be employed if there was a labour shortage'.[88]

The marked rise in the value of the UK state pension in 1946 appears not to have increased the rate of labour force disengagement (though it was initially believed to have done so, along with the new retirement condition). Again, in 1940 the pensionable age for women was lowered from 65 to 60 – yet the employment rates of women aged 60–64 rose thereafter, from 14.1 per cent in 1951 to 28.8 per cent in 1971. On the face of it, therefore, the state pension encouraged older women to work *more*. It might just be plausible to argue that a 'cohort effect' operated, and that the progressively higher levels of women's education caused successive cohorts to gain more jobs; but such a cohort effect should also have applied to older men, and during every decade. The state pension also cannot be held responsible for the gradual fall in the average age of male retirement up to the mid-1990s: in the early 1950s, roughly six out of ten British men continued to work on past the state pensionable age of 65 (albeit not for very long), mainly for reasons of financial hardship; by the late 1990s, six out of ten British men had retired by the age of 64.[89] Looking at very recent data (taking into account the rise in employment rates since the early 1990s), in 2012 51.9 per cent of men and 26.3 per cent of women left the labour market before state pension age; 37.6 per cent of men and 22.4 per cent of women after it. Only 10.5 per cent of men but fully 51.3 per cent of women left exactly at

[88] B. Seebohm Rowntree, *Poverty and Progress: A Second Social Survey of York* (1941), pp. 44, 114.

[89] *National Advisory Committee on the Employment of Older Men and Women. Second Report*, Cmd. 9628 (1955), p. 10; Office for National Statistics, *Social Focus on Older People* (1999), pp. 25–26.

state pension age.[90] The state pension appears to have had little direct incentive effect,[91] although it may act indirectly, both in prospect and in retrospect, since there is some bunching around those ages. On the face of it, the effect is stronger on women. However, most of the recent UK research into retirement transitions has not seen financial factors as of major importance in people's decisions to leave work.[92] As will be shown, other factors are more important. Donald Hirsch comments that most exits from work 'are not led by considerations of what non-work income is available but by the interplay of labour market difficulties and other constraining factors'.[93] In other words, it is the way that financial incentives interact with a myriad of other circumstantial factors that is crucial.[94]

The US historical evidence on the 'pension incentive' argument is also unconvincing. By the time that the first federal Social Security pension payments were made in 1940, 58 per cent of the total decline in labour force participation rates of men aged 65+ between 1880 and 1990 had already taken place.[95] In the first ten years of its existence, Social Security had no measurable effect on the labour force participation rates of American men aged 65+: these remained virtually unchanged between 1940 (41.8 per cent) and 1950 (41.4 per cent), owing to the postwar economic boom, assisted by the Korean War. An interesting and seemingly convincing argument is offered by Haber and Gratton, who maintain that, after 1950, 'OAA [Old Age Assistance] had a sharply negative impact on the labour force participation of elderly men . . . In states where Social Security benefits were high, fewer old men worked. The strongest variable in explaining decline in the elderly's labour force activity between 1930 and 1950 was the ratio of OAA payments to median income.'[96]

However, Haber and Gratton's thesis appears to be contradicted by the contemporary evidence, which shows no correlation between levels of old age assistance payments and the proportions aided by OAA, analysed by region. The latter may not be a precise proxy for lack of labour force participation, but it is strongly suggestive. The few examples in Table 5.3 of 'generous' and 'ungenerous' states in June 1951 will suffice.

---

[90] Office for National Statistics, *Pension Trends. Chapter 4: The Labour Market and Retirement, 2013 Edition* (2013), pp. 21–22.

[91] Craig Berry, *The Future of Retirement* (2010), p. 7.

[92] For example, Sue Arthur, *Money, Choice and Control: The Financial Circumstances of Early Retirement* (2003), p. 41.

[93] Donald Hirsch, *Crossroads After 50: Improving Choices in Work and Retirement* (2003), p. 24.

[94] Berry, *Future of Retirement*, p. 9.   [95] Costa, *Evolution*, p. 20.

[96] Haber and Gratton, *Old Age*, p. 111.

Table 5.3 *Old age assistance recipient rates in the USA and average monthly payments in June 1951, by region*

State	Average monthly OAA payment	Persons aided per 1,000 population aged 65+
(Generous):		
Colorado	$76.41	416
California	$67.02	317
Washington	$62.13	331
Massachusetts	$61.78	225
Connecticut	$60.58	112
Wyoming	$55.89	238
(Ungenerous):		
Virginia	$22.09	91
Alabama	$21.21	448
Arkansas	$20.90	425
Kentucky	$20.67	285
Mississippi	$18.41	416
Puerto Rico	$7.66	210
US average:	$43.23	220

Source: Wilbur J. Cohen, 'Economics, Employment and Welfare', in Nathan W. Shock (ed.), *Problems of Aging* (1951), pp. 83–84.

Moving to the more recent past, there are several empirical studies that challenge the link between Social Security provision and retirement: for example, Robert Moffitt examined changes in the value of Social Security retirement benefits and concluded that, at most, only about 20 per cent of the decline in labour supply between 1965 and 1975 could be attributed to the incentive effect of Social Security. Besides, Social Security rose more in value in the 1950s than in later periods, yet did not induce a more rapid rate of retirement.[97]

The 'pension as incentive' argument is also rendered unconvincing by the substantial regional variations in the employment rates of people aged 65+ in the UK. Higher combined pensioner incomes are received by those in more prosperous regions – and in such regions employment rates are highest. Analysis of the 'geography of early retirement' shows that, in the UK, those regions with the lowest levels of economic activity among

[97] Robert A. Moffitt, 'Life-cycle Labour Supply and Social Security: A Time-series Analysis', in Burtless (ed.), *Work, Health and Income*, pp. 183–220.

men aged 50–64 are regions that were once based upon manufacturing (now in recession).[98]

Is it likely that middle-aged workers would be willing to trade the benefits of increased leisure against the disbenefits of reductions in consumption? If so, the price they pay is very high. Numerous studies in the UK have documented the poverty of most recent early retirees, and the marked reductions in income and consumption that they experience. In the majority of cases, early retirement is involuntary, most affecting those with lower socio-economic status and poorest health. It brings material hardship, psychological adjustment, a fall in self-esteem and a loss of social roles.[99] In the UK, *Winning the Generation Game* (2000) found that almost half of those aged 50–64 who were not working depended upon social security benefits for most of their income.[100] Longitudinal studies have also tracked the falls in income that accompany retirement.[101] Indeed, a powerful argument used by recent British governments to justify action against age discrimination is that early retirement is damaging to individuals: it is said to impoverish and socially exclude those who experience it, and worsen their health.

There have also been many studies in the USA. For example, in the early 1980s Hausman and Pacquette surveyed a sample of American early retirees from the Retirement History Survey and found substantial decreases in income and food consumption inconsistent with a well-informed rationality: the younger the early retirement, the more likely it was to be involuntary.[102] Again, in a 1998 article in *The Gerontologist*, Kenneth Crouch examined the impact of job displacement on a sample of US workers aged 51–60 (thereby ineligible for Social Security, and generally not receiving private pensions). The greatest risk of job displacement was among ethnic minorities and/or those with the lowest educational qualifications plus those least likely to qualify for a private pension; and displacement brought with it a significant (average of 39 per cent) drop in income (as well as loss of health insurance

---

[98] John Macnicol, 'Older Men and Work in the Twenty-First Century: What Can the History of Retirement Tell Us?', *Journal of Social Policy*, 37, 4, Oct. 2008, pp. 587–588.

[99] Hirsch, *Crossroads*, pp. 41–46.

[100] Cabinet Office. Performance and Innovation Unit, *Winning the Generation Game: Improving Opportunities for People Aged 50–65 in Work and Community Activity* (2000), p. 19.

[101] Elena Bardasi, Stephen P. Jenkins and John A. Rigg, 'Retirement and the Income of Older People: A British Perspective', *Ageing and Society*, 22, 2, March 2002, pp. 131–159.

[102] Jerry A. Hausman and Lynn Pacquette, 'Involuntary Early Retirement and Consumption', in Burtless (ed.), *Work, Health and Income*, pp. 151–175.

benefits).[103] Very recently, Aaron and Callan found that the character-istics of those with the greatest propensity to retirement were: ethnic minority status, lower educational qualifications, poorer or deteriorating health, functional limitations and low income. It was the familiar picture of early retirement affecting mainly those at the bottom (involuntary) and to a lesser extent those at the top (voluntary), for other predisposing characteristics were belonging to a defined pension scheme and having greater assets.[104]

Let us now consider the effect of personal wealth. There has of course been increased wealth-holding in the UK and the USA over the course of the twentieth century. This has coincided with the spread of retirement and must have had some effect on that minority of late-middle-aged workers who had the power to make their own 'retirement decision'. But this argument needs to be examined critically. While households headed by a person aged 65+ have accumulated greater measurable wealth, much of this wealth has been in non-realisable form (notably housing) – the classic old age conundrum of being 'asset-rich but income-poor'. In addition, such wealth has always been held very unequally. In their history of retirement in the USA, Haber and Gratton cite evidence purporting to show that older-person households had mean assets worth on average $227,464 in 1983, while those headed by a person aged under 65 had on average $133,820. Yet the authors acknowledge that, in 1983, the top 5 per cent of such older-person households owned more than half of the wealth in that age group.[105] We can assume that a high proportion of households at the bottom end of this distribution held little in the way of assets – yet they still participated in the retirement trend. Haber and Gratton are also unable to explain why retirement progressed in the 1950s, when the overwhelming evidence from such respected bodies as the Social Security Administration revealed that retirees possessed few assets, and endured very low incomes.[106]

The assertion that increased wealth-holding is the key also sits rather uneasily alongside current concerns over the low levels of aggregate sav-ings in the UK and the USA. This has given rise to regular governmental exhortations that citizens should save more for their old age – gener-ally delivered as stern admonishments in which the general public is blamed for their ignorance. Hence in 2009 the UK pensions regulator, David Norgrove, warned that the state pension age would have to rise

---

[103] Kenneth A. Crouch, 'Late Life Job Displacement', *The Gerontologist*, 38, 1, 1998, pp. 7–17.
[104] Aaron and Callan, *Who Retires Early?*
[105] Haber and Gratton, *Old Age*, p. 82. This must include the value of property.
[106] Macnicol, *Age Discrimination*, pp. 219, 222–223.

higher than the then-planned 68 and that 'people are going to have to work longer' and save more: there was a 'lack of knowledge among the public about how to save' and the evidence was that 'people generally are frightened of saving for pensions'.[107] The lack of saving for retirement was one of the stated impulses behind the establishment of the Turner Commission on state pension reform. Its first report estimated that some 9,600,000 people in the UK were either not saving or under-saving for retirement and also tended to blame them for procrastination, inertia and caution.[108] Before that, the 2002 UK Green Paper *Simplicity, Security and Choice* showed that one-quarter of the population had negative net financial wealth in the year 2000; only the top decile had any meaningful amount, and this averaged £35,000. The level of liquid savings was even lower, with the top decile having only £18,000 on average. Savings were very unequally distributed by class and gender: 70 per cent of non-savers were women.[109] The UK financial services industry has understandably voiced concern over the inadequate savings for retirement, and the fact that savings levels have fallen recently (because of a short-term drop in real incomes caused by the recession): Scottish Widows found in 2013 that only 46 per cent of people interviewed were saving enough for retirement, compared with 54 per cent in 2008; 22 per cent were saving nothing. The gap between expected income in retirement and likely income had widened: an adequate individual income at age 70 was put at £24,500 per annum, though only a small minority were likely to receive this. The harsh reality was that an income of £25,000 per annum from combined private and state pension schemes to fund retirement at age 66 would require savings of £1,000 per month from the age of 30. Unsurprisingly, other expenditure took priority over saving for retirement.[110] Similarly, the Prudential Insurance Company found that fewer than two in five people surveyed expected a financially comfortable retirement.[111] Interestingly, Wise – though broadly supporting a 'rational choice' explanation – adamantly insists that 'increased saving is not the explanation for earlier retirement' in the USA and cites wealth-holding statistics for older-person households much lower than those of Haber and Gratton.[112] A theme running through several US studies is

107 Alastair Jamieson, 'State Pension Age Could Climb to 70', *Telegraph*, 8 Aug. 2009, www.telegraph.co.uk
108 Pensions Commission, *First Report*, pp. 159, 208–209.
109 DWP, *Simplicity, Security and Choice*, p. 154; for slightly different estimates, see Office for National Statistics, *Social Focus on Older People*, p. 60.
110 Scottish Widows, *Retirement Savings*.
111 Prudential press release, 'Expected Retirement Incomes Hit Five-Year Low', 11 Jan. 2012, www.prudential.co.uk
112 Wise, 'Retirement Against the Demographic Trend', pp. 83, 85.

that older Americans display a remarkable degree of *un*preparedness for retirement, in terms of their likely income and adequacy of savings.[113] For example, in a McKinsey & Co. study of 2006, 43 per cent of retirees surveyed reported that they had underestimated their retirement spending needs.[114]

From the perspective of behavioural economics, the only possible explanations are that people are financially myopic, underestimating the level of resources they will actually need in retirement, that they procrastinate endlessly or that they operate by short-term rather than long-term rationality – in other words, that the decision to retire is made on the basis of exceedingly imperfect knowledge. A more plausible explanation is that in youth and middle age individuals have much more urgent expenditure claims, notably mortgages, children, food and essential consumer items. All in all, the evidence of under-saving does not fit easily with a model of rational, well-informed economic men and women pursuing their own enlightened self-interest and choosing to retire when they can afford to.

Over the past sixty years, research has consistently shown that those most able to postpone retirement are those with the greatest control over their workplace situation (notably the self-employed). Three contrasting examples will suffice. In the USA in April 1948 those most likely still to be in employment after age 65 were (with employment rates): farmers and farm managers (26 per cent); proprietors, managers and officials (15 per cent); craftsmen, foremen and kindred workers (13 per cent); and service workers (11 per cent).[115] In the UK in the mid-1960s, F. Le Gros Clark found that the self-employed were the only occupational group able to find work after the age of 65.[116] And in 2013, fully 43 per cent of British men aged 65+ who were still in employment were self-employed.[117]

To conclude, what of the growth of a 'retirement expectation'? As argued earlier in this chapter, it is undeniable that such an expectation has become firmly embedded in public consciousness over the past hundred years, and that an adequately funded retirement is now seen as a social right – particularly if older people perceive there to be a lack of suitable jobs. Recent years have seen waves of industrial action and street protests

---

[113] For example: David J. Ekerdt and Jennifer Kay Hackney, 'Workers' Ignorance of Retirement Benefits', *The Gerontologist*, 42, 4, 2002, pp. 543–551; Annamari Lusardi, 'Information, Expectations and Savings for Retirement', in Aaron, *Behavioral Dimensions*, pp. 81–115.

[114] McKinsey & Company, *Cracking the Consumer Retirement Code* (2006), p. 10.

[115] Nathan W. Shock, *Trends in Gerontology* (1951), p. 18.

[116] F. Le Gros Clark, *Pensioners in Search of a Job* (1969).

[117] DWP, *Older Workers 2013*, p. 17.

in many European countries against proposals to raise state pension ages and in defence of the right to an adequately funded retirement. However, one must probe deeper. Human beings certainly make choices; but they do so as best they can, on the basis of limited knowledge, within a particular economic context, usually from a very restricted range of options and constrained by factors not of their making. People may have an expectation – but it may not materialise in the way they hoped.[118] A striking example of this was the 2006 finding by the McKinsey & Co. survey of 3,000 pre-retirees aged 40 to 68. Nearly half of the sample had planned to work past the age of 65, but only 13 per cent had actually been able to do so: 40 per cent had been forced out of work – on average, between the ages of 54 and 59. Of this 40 per cent, 47 per cent had left for health reasons, 44 per cent through job termination and 9 per cent because of caring responsibilities. The financial ability to retire played virtually no part in their early exit.[119]

All in all, therefore, it is most likely that this 'retirement expectation' is essentially an attitudinal adjustment by citizens to the inevitability of joblessness at older ages, caused by the slow contraction of the labour market niche employing older men. There is therefore no contradiction between economic *causes* and cultural *effects*. It should not be surprising that financial protection against an economic inevitability like retirement has increasingly been viewed as a social right.

Analysis of patterns of retirement must, therefore, examine the economic context at both macro- and micro-levels. For example, at the micro-level of the firm, the introduction of early exit incentives by an employer always takes place within a particular economic context – generally, the need to reduce the size of a workforce because of external economic pressures (such as the outsourcing of labour to another part of the world).[120] The role of employers is strikingly neglected in retirement research, the focus of which is usually on the decontextualised 'retirement behaviour' of employees. Yet employers play a vital role. As Harold Sheppard rightly commented:

Conventional wisdom has it that workers retire earlier than otherwise because of attractive pension benefits. Little thought has been given to the possibility that there is a policy underlying this, that the very purpose of certain types of pension

---

[118] Wendy Loretto, Sarah Vickerstaff and Phil White, *Older Workers and Options for Flexible Work* (2005), p. 38.

[119] McKinsey, *Cracking*, esp. pp. 8–9.

[120] Sarah Vickerstaff, John Baldock, Jennifer Cox and Linda Keen, *Happy Retirement? The Impact of Employers' Policies and Practice on the Process of Retirement* (2004).

provisions is exactly to achieve this result – to rid the enterprise or the economy in general of an unwanted class of employees.[121]

Similarly, Michael Fogarty observed in 1980 that the encouragement of early retirement might originate with an employer, but, once established, would then set up 'a new pattern of custom and practice' that would affect the attitudes, expectations and choices of the whole workforce.[122] More recently, Donald Hirsch has stressed that employers in the 1980s used early retirement as an easy method of restructuring their work-forces. This may have caused them 'to lose control of the retirement process' such that, by the 1990s, they sought to regain control and reverse this process: but the original impulses were economic, and in their interests.[123]

As already noted, older employees targeted in downsizings may well be persuaded to agree to leave 'voluntarily'; but the prime causal factors will be outside the control of either employer or employees. Supply-side explanations are certainly relevant to the minority who have some influence over their retirement – middle-class beneficiaries of final-salary pension schemes with, perhaps, some years of pension enhancement and an attractive 'golden handshake' – but they do not fit very easily with the majority, working-class retirement experience. Plant closures are not generally brought about by the rational choices of their own workers.

Social divisions in retirement

It is clear, therefore, that the overarching economic context within which retirement has historically spread has been declining sectoral labour market demand. However, this has had a differentiated impact on individuals according to many personal and circumstantial factors. The retired population has always been extremely heterogeneous, divided by factors such as income, gender, social class, ethnicity and family circumstance. This is certainly the case today. Whether or not this heterogeneity has increased historically is difficult to demonstrate conclusively, as is the question of whether transitions into retirement have become more complex. What we do know is that the resurgence of interest in older workers in the last

---

[121] Harold L. Sheppard, 'Work Continuity Versus Retirement: Reasons for Continuing Work', in Robert Morris and Scott A. Bass (eds.), *Retirement Reconsidered: Economic and Social Roles for Older People* (1988), p. 130.
[122] Michael P. Fogarty, *Retirement Age and Retirement Costs* (1980), p. 11.
[123] Hirsch, *Crossroads*, p. 15.

fifteen years has produced an abundance of research attempting to capture this complexity. Initiatives in the UK have included the Economic and Social Research Council's 'Growing Older' and 'Rethinking Retirement' programmes, the Joseph Rowntree Foundation's 'Transitions After 50' and reports commissioned by government departments such as the DWP.[124] This research has demonstrated that no two retirement experiences are alike.

The social divisions in retirement are complex, cross-cutting and interactive; they also merge into structural economic factors, and are difficult to rank in order of importance. What follows below can only be a brief summary. In no particular order, therefore, the main personal/circumstantial factors are:

Health/disability status: Ill-health is the most frequently cited reason for early exit, particularly for working-class men aged in their early fifties. The earlier the exit, the more likely it is to be caused by ill-health. Hence of those who are economically inactive in the UK and aged 50–69, the percentage who are sick and disabled is 53 per cent for the 50–54 age group, falling to 8 per cent for the 65–69 age group.[125] Nearly half of men on long-term sickness and disability benefits are aged 50–64. However, the complicating factor here is that ill-health often conceals joblessness and manifests itself as work-disability (the interaction of self-defined health status and labour market demand).[126] Many studies – especially those emanating from within government[127] – take health as entirely unproblematic, without considering the labour market effects, and for some years governmental strategies have been directed towards improving occupational health. Unfortunately, this will only have a limited impact unless there is significant employment growth. In addition, health status is strongly associated with social class, and income/class inequality continues to widen. The fact that those who work later in life tend to be healthier has resulted in official advice that 'working is good for one's health' – used as a justification for the labour market activation of older people and the raising of state pension ages. Inevitably, this simplistic message has been enthusiastically propagated by government

---

[124] The following section is based upon: Arthur, *Money, Choice and Control*; Phillipson and Smith, *Extending Working Life*; Loretto et al., *Older Workers*; Vickerstaff et al., *Encouraging Labour Market Activity*; Meadows, *Early Retirement and Income*; Meadows, *Retirement Ages*; Smeaton and Vegeris, *Older People*; Deborah Smeaton, Sandra Vegeris and Melahat Sahin-Dikmen, *Older Workers: Employment Preferences, Barriers and Solutions* (2009); Berry, *Future of Retirement*.

[125] DWP, *Older Workers 2013*, p. 14.

[126] John Macnicol, 'The History of Work-Disability', in Colin Lindsay and Donald Houston (eds.), *Disability Benefits, Welfare Reform and Employment Policy* (2013).

[127] For example, Ulrike Hotopp, 'The Ageing Workforce: A Health Issue?', *Economic and Labour Market Review*, 1, 2, Feb. 2007, pp. 30–35.

departments, neoliberal think-tanks and the popular media.[128] Hence *Fuller Working Lives* (2014) confidently declares that 'work is generally good for physical and mental health and well-being'.[129] However, this proposition is undemonstrable for the simple reason that those who work later in life tend to have better health status anyway – the problem of selection.[130] A related argument is that the abrupt 'cliff-edge' transition into retirement that (allegedly) pertained in the past was physically and psychologically damaging to individuals. In fact, there is no conclusive evidence that the cliff-edge transition is inevitably harmful.[131] Intuitively, there is a case for people having a clean break with past work, providing that they can adjust well to retirement and have the necessary financial resources. In any case, raising state pension ages will at best merely postpone the cliff-edge and not abolish it. For these and other reasons, examining the effects of retirement on health is methodologically challenging.

Occupational history/job quality/education and skill levels: After ill-health, redundancy or failure to get another job is the second most-cited reason for economic inactivity in later life. For example, when examining why those aged 50 to state pension age did not have a job, Smeaton *et al.* found that 'health reasons' explained 51 per cent of cases and redundancy 15 per cent.[132] Those individuals with the poorest educational and skill levels – and hence the worst-quality jobs – tend to retire earliest, while those with the highest educational qualifications tend to work past state pension age: for example, Whiting found that, of people between 50 and state pension age, 81 per cent of those with a degree were in employment, compared with only 52 per cent of those with no qualifications.[133] As has been argued earlier, self-employment and working part-time are associated with working later. There are also important sectoral divisions, with men aged 65+ being concentrated in manufacturing, construction and distribution and women more in service occupations.

[128] Gordon Waddell and A. Kim Burton, *Is Work Good for Your Health and Well-being?* (2006); Black, *Working*; Institute of Economic Affairs, *Work Longer, Live Healthier* (2013); Littlewood, 'Work on Into Your 70s'.
[129] DWP, *Fuller Working Lives – A Framework for Action*, p. 7.
[130] This obvious caveat has been known ever since health and ageing were first properly researched in the late nineteenth century, and was much discussed in the 1950s.
[131] David de Vaus, Yvonne Wells, Hal Kendig and Susan Quine, 'Does Gradual Retirement Have Better Outcomes than Abrupt Retirement? Results from an Australian Panel Study', *Ageing and Society*, 27, 5, Sept. 2007, pp. 667–682.
[132] Smeaton *et al.*, *Older Workers*, p. 53.
[133] Elizabeth Whiting, 'The Labour Market Participation of Older People', *Labour Market Trends*, 112, 6, July 2005, p. 288.

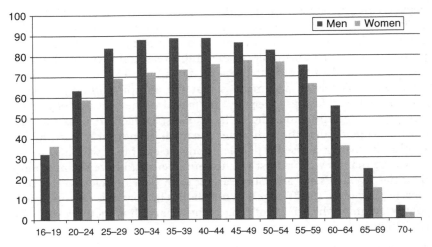

Figure 5.2 Employment rates, by sex and age, April to June 2012: United Kingdom, percentages.
Source: Office for National Statistics, *Pension Trends – Chapter 4*, p. 8.

Marital status/family responsibilities: The retirement of a spouse or partner can influence the other party in a marriage or partnership – what has been called 'synchronisation' of decisions[134] – as can the presence or absence of dependants in the home. The evidence does not appear to be clear-cut: on the one hand, Whiting argues that older people who are married or cohabiting are more likely to be in employment than those who are not; on the other, there is evidence that single people (presumably, living alone) may prefer to work later in life in order to enjoy the human contact of workplace colleagues.[135] Clearly, retirement can have a major effect on a relationship, both negative and positive.[136]

Age: There is a wide spread of employment rates by age and gender. As has been pointed out, 'unemployment' in middle age metamorphoses into 'early retirement', as can be seen in Figure 5.2.

Employment rates for men are highest in the 35–39 age group, and then start to fall from age 40, dropping more rapidly from age 50, after which the probability of labour market exit increases with every passing year. Attitudes towards returning to work vary according to when the

---

[134] Bardasi *et al.*, 'Retirement', p. 145.
[135] Whiting, 'Labour Market Participation', p. 291; Berry, *Future of Retirement*, p. 11.
[136] Helen Barnes and Jane Parry, 'Renegotiating Identity and Relationships: Men and Women's Adjustments to Retirement', *Ageing and Society*, 24, 2, March 2004, p. 224.

retirement takes place: unsurprisingly, those in their fifties expect to return to work; those in their sixties tend to be more accepting that they will not.

Gender: Historically, the experience of retirement has been highly gendered. For much of the past 130 years, the employment rates of married women were low and only began to rise from the 1950s onwards. Hence in 1931 the employment rate of married women was only c. 10 per cent, but by 1971 it was c. 40 per cent. The rate for women aged 65+ was 16 per cent in 1891, falling to 5 per cent in 1951 and then rising only slightly to 7 per cent by 2013. The result has been that discourses on retirement have hitherto been highly masculinist, examining the long fall in older men's employment from 1881 to 2001 (and then the slight rise). The traditional view was therefore that the concept of retirement from paid work hardly applied to women who, it was said, never retired from housework.[137]

Later life tends to be gender-differentiated: women on average retire earlier than do men, but are more likely than men to work past their (lower) state pension age, and for a greater duration; they also spend a longer period on state pensions.[138] Women tend to work part-time at later ages: 44 per cent of women aged 50–64 who still work do so part-time (as opposed to only 13 per cent of men), and of those still working past age 65 the part-time proportion is 80 per cent (57 per cent for men). The previous state pension age of 60 acted as more of a marker for women: as has been shown, a higher proportion retired at that age and fully 70 per cent of women aged 60–64 who are economically inactive today consider themselves 'retired', whereas at ages 55–59 the proportion is only 17 per cent.[139] Women on average live longer than do men, but have a higher incidence of recorded morbidity and disability in old age. As has been emphasised earlier in this book, women tend to be poorer than men in old age in a number of key aspects – pension income, earnings, housing wealth and savings. Women are also more likely to leave the labour market in late middle age because of caring duties.[140] As demonstrated in Chapter 1, women constitute two-thirds of state pensioners and there is a substantial feminisation of poverty in old age. There are also far more women than men in the 'oldest-old' population (aged 85+), and its numerical doubling over the next twenty years will increase health and social care expenditure. All in all, the raising

[137] Nesta Roberts, *Our Future Selves* (1970), p. 93.
[138] Phillipson and Smith, *Extending Working Life*, p. 31,
[139] DWP, *Older Workers 2013*, pp. 17–18.   [140] Loretto *et al.*, *Older Workers*, p. 42.

of state pension ages is likely to have a more damaging effect on women than on men.

Ethnic background: Explanatory theories of retirement tend to be very general, riding roughshod over the diversity of human experience that makes for a myriad of divisions in retirement. This is most true of the broad category 'ethnic minorities', which in the UK applies to an enormous variety of identities, economic situations and cultural experiences. This variety is determined by factors such as length of stay, educational attainment, social class and patterns of migration. There have been successive waves of immigration into the UK for centuries, and some areas (such as Cardiff, Bristol, Liverpool and the East End of London) have long had ethnic minority populations. The most recent arrivals (such as Somalis, or people from Turkey and Eastern Europe) are merely the latest iteration. Some ethnic groups, such as Gypsy, Roma and Traveller people, are officially classified as 'white' but experience substantial economic disadvantage and discrimination. Another complication is that ethnic categories are very broad, and have been rendered even more so in recent years by inter-marriage (for example, now one-half of African Caribbean men and one-third of African Caribbean women have a white partner). This raises a third issue: ethnic background is but one of several advantaging or disadvantaging factors. It is therefore necessary to examine the phenomenon of intersectionality[141] – the combining of different strands of advantage or disadvantage – in which social class rather than skin colour may well be the crucial factor: hence the family of a wealthy merchant from Gujarat will be very different from one from a Jamaican farmworking background. As has often been pointed out, there are wide inequalities within notionally precise ethnic categories.[142] The differences within the total ethnic minority population are noticeable in the hierarchy of school achievement, where Chinese girls achieve most and African Caribbean boys the least (although the latter have recently shown spectacular improvement). Another problem is therefore that there may be a great variation in the stock of cultural capital within ethnic minorities of notionally equal economic status (which can be attributable to their social class of origin in their mother country).

As emphasised below, an individual's economic and other circumstances in retirement are often the result of accumulated disadvantage across the lifecourse – a process which starts at birth. Here the 'ethnic penalty' is noticeable. Ethnic minority children suffer higher levels of

[141]   Helen Barnard and Claire Turner, *Poverty and Ethnicity: A Review of Evidence* (2011), p. 4.
[142]   Lucinda Platt, *Inequality Within Ethnic Groups* (2011).

poverty, partly because of their concentration in inner cities: hence an estimated 53 per cent of inner London children are in poverty, but the proportion is 72 per cent for Pakistani and Bangladeshi children and 55 per cent for African Caribbean children. Ethnic minorities experience lower earnings on average across a lifetime than indigenous 'white British'. They therefore have lower incomes in retirement, in terms of savings, private pension membership and even qualifying for the full basic state pension. Compared with white men aged 50–64, black British men of the same age are one-third more likely to be out of work, and Indian, Pakistani and Bangladeshi men are two-thirds more likely.[143] They tend to be concentrated in those employment sectors that are poorly paid: strikingly, 45 per cent of Bangladeshi men and 40 per cent of Chinese men work in the hotel and catering trade. In 2011, almost half of Bangladeshi and Pakistani workers earned less than £7 per hour.[144] In their collection of case histories, Helen Barnes and Rebecca Taylor found 'significant levels' of low-skilled, low-paid work in the work-histories of the sample of ethnic minorities that they interviewed.[145] The economic and other disadvantages experienced on average by ethnic minorities were eloquently recorded in a 2008 publication by the Equality and Human Rights Commission, which revealed their higher levels of self-employment, part-time working, low pay, unemployment, interrupted work-histories, reliance on means-tested benefits, and so on – all likely to render them an 'under-pensioned' group in the population.[146]

The average ages of different ethnic minorities vary but in most cases tend to be lower than the indigenous white British population: 53 per cent of people from ethnic minorities are aged under 30, and 85 per cent are aged under 50. For the white British population the respective proportions are 35 per cent and 64 per cent. Viewed another way, ethnic minorities constitute 15 per cent of the 25–49 age group but only 7 per cent of the 50–64 age group, and 4 per cent of people above state pension age.[147] However, this will change in the future as the large cohorts currently in early adulthood slowly age.

Ethnic minorities suffer higher levels of economic inactivity when aged 50–64 because on average they are more likely than the indigenous

[143] Phillipson and Smith, *Extending Working Life*, p. 67.
[144] Joseph Rowntree Foundation, *Tackling Poverty Across All Ethnicities in the UK* (2014), p. 3.
[145] Helen Barnes and Rebecca Taylor, *Work, Saving and Retirement Among Ethnic Minorities: A Qualitative Study* (2006), p. 32.
[146] Adam Steventon and Carlos Sanchez, *The Under-Pensioned: Disabled People and People from Ethnic Minorities* (2008).
[147] DWP, *Older Workers 2013*, p. 17; Steventon and Sanchez, *The Under-Pensioned*, p. 28.

white population to suffer from disadvantaging factors – notably precarious employment (including self-employment) and low skills. All in all, therefore, they are more likely to experience earlier withdrawal from the labour market and a more impoverished retirement.[148]

Region: As indicated earlier, there is a pronounced variation in rates of retirement by region, correlating closely with deindustrialisation. This is particularly the case with male early retirement. Whereas the overall UK employment rate for people aged 50–64 is 64.5 per cent, it is 70.2 per cent in the South East, 67.0 per cent in the South West, 66.8 per cent in the East – but only 62.4 per cent in the North West and Merseyside, 59.7 per cent in the North East and 58.3 per cent in Wales.[149] Indeed, one of the central problems in the UK economy is joblessness caused by the overlap of deindustrialisation, region, disability and age.

Financial resources and incentives: The prospect of financial security in retirement may encourage early exit; on the other hand, the more an individual has in the way of savings and private or occupational pensions, the more choice and control they possess and the later they remain in work. Clearly, there are two groups of financially advantaged people, who behave differently. Financial insecurity, on the other hand, inculcates a need to stay in work; but such impoverished individuals find it increasingly difficult to do so as they age.

Caring responsibilities: Informal caring is a factor causing labour market withdrawal and preventing a return to work. In 2003 Evandrou and Glaser found that 24 per cent of people aged 45 to 64 were caring for a sick, elderly or disabled person; Loretto, Vickerstaff and White cite findings that one in five people aged 50–59 are providing informal or unpaid care – duties that more affect women.[150] Above the age of 75, however, more men are carers – reflecting the predominance of women in that age group. A future increase in the numbers of the 'oldest-old' will mean more of a burden of caring.[151]

---

[148] Orla Gough and Rod Hick, 'Ethnic Minorities, Retirement Planning and Personal Accounts', *International Journal of Sociology and Social Policy*, 29, 9/10, 2009, pp. 489–490; Orla Gough and Roberta Adami, 'Saving for Retirement: A Review of Ethnic Minorities in the UK', *Social Policy and Society*, 12, 1, Jan. 2013, pp. 147–148.

[149] Department for Work and Pensions, *Older Workers Statistical Information Booklet. Quarter Two 2010* (2010), p. 12.

[150] Maria Evandrou and Karen Glaser, 'Combining Work and Family Life: The Pension Penalty of Caring', *Ageing and Society*, 23, 5, 2003, p. 583; Loretto *et al.*, *Older Workers*, pp. 42–44.

[151] Scales and Scase, *Fit and Fifty?*, p. 7.

Social class and early life factors: One difficulty in incentivising later-life working is that the impulses to earlier retirement originate near the beginning of life, in the form of structural inequalities that then accumulate into multiple disadvantage. By the time people are aged in their fifties and sixties, the dice are cast and changing outcomes is difficult, if not impossible. As Vickerstaff *et al.* comment, 'Financial security in retirement is typically the outcome of accumulated advantage through the working life and hence cannot easily be manufactured by planning in the immediate run up to retirement.'[152]

A report by Morten Blekesaune *et al.* shows this clearly: later entry into the labour market by middle-class people (most often, for middle-class people, caused by a longer period of education and training) tends to result in later retirement.[153] It is possible, of course, to interpret this as a deterministic, 'personal deficiency' explanation, which attributes later-life worklessness to early life failures (for example, in the education system). In other words, the focus is on the intrinsic qualities of people who end up in unstable, low-paid jobs, rather than the poor quality of those jobs. Nevertheless, the main lesson to be drawn is that inequalities in retirement mirror inequalities from birth to death. Policies focused on later life (notably, raising state pension ages) will therefore do little to change employment behaviour. In essence, people retire early because they choose the wrong parents.

Burn-out: There may have been an intensification of work in recent decades, which has led to higher rates of burn-out and therefore premature retirement. It is difficult to move beyond the anecdotal, since intensity of work is hard to measure. A counter-argument would be: if work has become more demanding and stressful in the last twenty years why then have the employment rates of older people risen? Certainly, the incidence of recorded mental and behavioural disorders has increased – they now make up 43 per cent of claims to long-term sickness and disability benefits, up from 15 per cent in the mid-1990s – as has the prescribing of anti-depressants. However, there is much debate over whether these recorded increases in incidence are 'real' (for example, caused by more competitive individualism) or 'artefactual' (for example, the product of astute marketing strategies by pharmaceutical companies, or the medicalisation of everyday life). Research by Sarah Vickerstaff and colleagues certainly revealed high levels of burn-out and work stress

[152] Vickerstaff *et al.*, *Encouraging Labour Market Activity*, p. 11.
[153] Morten Blekesaune, Mark Bryan and Mark Taylor, *Life-course Events and Later-life Employment* (2008).

among interview subjects, many of whom had long working histories.[154] This was identified by them as a major obstacle to extending working lives.

Personality/community networks/social capital: Finally, one sociological imponderable unamenable to precise quantification is that individuals have different attitudes towards work and leisure. For some, retirement can be a liberation from drudgery and stress; for others, it is most unwelcome, representing what George Bernard Shaw called 'the horror of the perpetual holiday'. The cliff-edge into retirement therefore varies greatly in its impact.[155] To some extent, this is determined by the quality and remuneration of a job – and therefore social class – but it can also vary by random, personality-based factors (such as the existence of hobbies and leisure interests outside work). Hence Thompson, Itzin and Abendstern found in their interview-based study that class and income differences in retirement mattered a lot, but so also did personality: 'Since later life is a time of sharp changes, it demands a special responsiveness and imaginative adaptability. Those who make or seize their new chances are most likely to flourish in their purposefulness; those who cannot find meaning to their lives, to fade altogether.'[156] Community responsibilities and involvement can be quantified, and have been interestingly identified as important by Phillipson and Smith, who observe that 'decisions about work and retirement must also be located in the wider social networks within which personal ties are embedded'.[157]

Can this heterogeneity within the retired population be captured? One useful attempt is Pamela Meadows's sixfold classification of the early retired.[158] In abbreviated form, this is: 1. those who are encouraged to leave their jobs and draw a pension, as part of organisational restructuring; 2. those who choose to retire early and draw an actuarially reduced pension; 3. those who become unemployed over the age of 50 and drift into inactivity; 4. those who develop health problems that make it difficult for them to work; 5. those (mainly women) who give up work to become carers; 6. those who have given up work because a spouse or partner has retired.

All in all, therefore, it is clear that the personal/circumstantial factors determining the timing and impact of retirement are embedded in,

[154] Vickerstaff et al., *Encouraging Labour Market Activity*, pp. 31, 33, 41.
[155] Hirsch, *Crossroads*, p. 29.
[156] Paul Thompson, Catherine Itzin and Michelle Abendstern, *I Don't Feel Old: The Experience of Later Life* (1990), p. 244.
[157] Phillipson and Smith, *Extending Working Life*, p. 65.
[158] Meadows, *Early Retirement and Income*, p. 2.

and react with, socio-economic inequalities and sectoral labour market demand. The greatest choice and control with regard to the timing of retirement is possessed by those who are best endowed in terms of social class, income, job quality, financial means, health and social networks; those least well endowed have very little choice and control.

What is new about the 'new' retirement?

At this point, it is worth discussing whether or not the detailed survey-based research of the past fifteen years validates those 'postmodern' theories of ageing mentioned in Chapter 1 that – particularly in the work of Anthony Giddens – have been indirectly used to justify labour market activation for older people. The question raises enormous issues regarding how we distinguish between continuity and change when examining historical trends and collective experiences; it can only be answered briefly.

There is no doubt that, by the 1980s, the spread of male early retirement was engendering a lively debate on the emergence of a new 'Third Age' at the end of the lifecourse and its significance for social analysis. As Martin Kohli put it, in a famous and wide-ranging article, 'Given that social life is structured around work and its organisation, how can we theoretically cope with a situation in which a large (and still growing) part of the population has left the domain of formally organised gainful work, and left it for good?'[159] As has been noted, similar questions had been posed in the 1950s but by the 1980s and 1990s they had an added urgency. Indeed, they were often expressed in over-apocalyptic assertions about the 'radical transformation' of retirement that had taken place,[160] accompanied by sweeping and unjustified assertions of the new prosperity of retirees.

Has retirement become more 'deinstitutionalised' or 'detraditionalised' in the last twenty years? The reasoning here is that, in the past, there existed a more clear-cut, crisp division between the three stages of the old lifecourse (education, work, retirement); this older 'institutionalised' or 'bureaucratised' lifecourse is said to be one in which particular life events occurred at a predictable time. Hence retirement is said to have become 'consolidated' in the 1950s and 1960s as a social norm. From the 1980s onwards, however, a 'fragmentation' is said to have occurred,

---

[159] Martin Kohli, 'Ageing as a Challenge for Sociological Theory', *Ageing and Society*, 8, 4, December 1988, p. 371.

[160] For example, John Goodwin and Henrietta O'Connor, 'Notions of Fantasy and Reality in the Adjustment to Retirement', *Ageing and Society*, 34, 4, April 2014, p. 1.

with the spread of early exit and more complex pathways into retirement. The traditional three-stage lifecourse model is said to have metamorphosed into one in which transitions from middle age into retirement became more variegated and open to negotiation, driven by increasingly complex preretirement life-histories characterised by new factors such as divorce, part-time working and changes of job. Finally, in the 1990s and 2000s, average ages of retirement rose with the employment boom and governments in industrialised societies introduced policies to encourage later-life working; the concept of retirement is said to have changed once again.

This has some validity as a broad explanatory narrative. However, some of the detailed component parts are less convincing. First, it is suggested that there are now more gradual transitions into complete retirement from a career job, via part-time working in a bridge job; there is said to be less of a cliff-edge abruptness. Yet as has been shown, part-time bridge jobs are nothing new. In the past, the process of lifecycle deskilling meant that working-class men and women often moved to less physically demanding jobs when aged in their fifties, sixties and seventies. In times of recession (most notably, the 1930s) older unskilled urban workers did everything they could to continue working at any job, including very low-grade, casualised, menial occupations (the last resort being night watchman, caretaker, street vendor, charwoman, cleaner and so on). This was out of desperate necessity rather than choice. Hence David Caradog Jones's 1934 survey of Merseyside found that overall male earnings fell by an average of 15s0d (75p) per week after age 65, with most male workers having to downshift to lighter or part-time jobs. For workers aged in their late sixties there were no clear boundaries between categories like 'employed', 'unemployed', 'retired', 'part-time' and 'fulltime'.[161] Again, in 1935–1936, Seebohm Rowntree discovered that, of those working-class men aged 65+ who were still in the labour market, about one-quarter were working part-time ('jobbing') and one-third were self-employed.[162] As mentioned above, now 57 per cent of UK men aged 65+ still in the labour market work part-time and 43 per cent are self-employed; for equivalent women aged 65+, the respective proportions are 80 per cent and 22 per cent.[163] There probably has been some increase in part-time bridge jobs, but it may only reflect the wider increase in the UK economy generally (from 831,000 part-time jobs in 1951 to 8,000,000 now). In other words, the phenomenon of more part-time working is not exclusive to later life. The cliff-edge metaphor

[161] Macnicol, *The Politics of Retirement*, pp. 269–271.
[162] Nuffield Foundation, *Old People*, p. 85.   [163] DWP, *Older Workers*, p. 17.

therefore only applies with any accuracy to the peak of fordist capitalism in the twenty-five years after the Second World War, and to those most securely employed within it.[164]

Are transitions into retirement now 'more negotiated' than in the past – by which is presumably meant 'more voluntary'? It is unlikely. Surveys from the 1950s to the present reveal early retirement to be mainly involuntary, occurring earliest for those with least skills, savings, health status and so on.[165] As has been argued at the beginning of the chapter, only one in eight people aged 50–64 classify themselves as 'retired'. If retirement is now more of a preference, one would need to explain why, over the past twenty years, more older people have apparently preferred to remain at work. As has been shown, the ability to negotiate one's retirement is the prerogative of only a privileged minority at the top.

Another novel feature is said to be the shorter period spent at work and the longer period spent in fulltime education before work and in retirement after it, with lengthening life expectancy at later ages and a long-run fall in the average age of permanent labour market exit. In other words, within the three-stage model of the lifecourse, the first and third stages have become elongated, and the middle stage truncated (see Figure 5.3).

This tends to be accepted uncritically.[166] As is shown above, it only applies to the male lifecourse – but this is often forgotten. Hence by a process of elision Nicholas Barr argues that, 'In 1950, a typical person left school at 15 and started work – a 50-year working life for a man, given pensionable age of 65. Today most people do not start work till 18, and many not until 21, and many retire earlier than 65. On any reckoning, the average working life is shorter'.[167] In fact, the argument is incorrect. Since life expectancy gains at age 65 have been relatively modest, improved survival to 65 plus the increased number of women in the labour market has meant that a baby born in, say, 1980 is likely to contribute, by the time they have died, more years of work to the UK economy than a baby born in 1930. It is probable, therefore, that people are now working *more*.[168]

---

[164] Interestingly, there is evidence that bridge jobs were quite common in the USA in the 1970s. See Joseph F. Quinn and Michael Kozy, 'The Role of Bridge Jobs in the Retirement Transition: Gender, Race and Ethnicity', *The Gerontologist*, 36, 3, 1996, pp. 364–365.

[165] For example, Cabinet Office, *Winning the Generation Game*, p. 22.

[166] For example, Barrell *et al.*, *Macroeconomic Impact*, p. 4.

[167] Nicholas Barr, 'Pensions: Challenges and Choices: What Next?', 17 Jan. 2005, www .econ.lse.ac.uk/staff

[168] Macnicol, *Age Discrimination*, pp. 86–87.

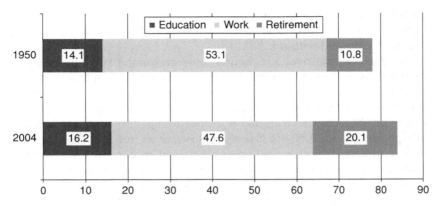

Figure 5.3 Lifecourse, men retiring in 1950 and 2004.
Source: Nicholas Barr, 'Retirement Age – a Good News Story', British Politics
and Policy at LSE (12 Mar 2010), blogs.lse.ac.uk.

Is there now a wider spread of retirement ages? This is also a difficult
question to answer. As has been shown, before the 1940s, labour force
participation by men started to fall from early middle age onwards. It
is therefore not self-evident that this variability has increased – but a
definitive answer must await more detailed and sophisticated empirical
investigation than can be offered here. Transitions into retirement may
now be more complex – but, again, this is an intuitive, commonsense
observation that is difficult to demonstrate, as is the contention that
the stages of the lifecourse have become more 'blurred'. Certainly, the
proportion of retirees who have been divorced has steadily increased,
and there are more old people living alone.[169] Again, this only reflects a
wider societal change – the growth of single-person households – and is
not exclusive to old age.

Finally, an undeniably novel feature is that retirement from work now
affects women much more than it did in the past. As argued earlier in this
chapter, past models of retirement tended to be masculinist, based on
the assumption that self-identity came through paid employment, thereby
ignoring the retirement experience of women (whose labour force participation was historically lower than men's). Where women's retirement
was researched, the general verdict was that women adjusted to it better
than did men since they did not feel the loss of paid work so acutely. As
two commentators put it in 1991, regarding women: 'Their experience
in weaving together different strands, their experience in coping with

[169] Scales and Scase, *Fit and Fifty?*, pp. 5, 9, 13.

transitions between different statuses, their experience in shaping their identities from a variety of models rather than so much from one – are all conducive to making the best of a way of life after retirement that does not differ so much from their lives before.'[170] The gender-differentiated impact of retirement is only beginning to be explored,[171] and will be the subject of much research in the future. However, one thing that has not changed is that women never retire from their role as carers.

Conclusion

This chapter has traced the evolution of retirement in the UK, with some USA comparisons, and has examined the factors determining retirement today. The evidence shows clearly that the principal historic cause has been long-run economic restructuring and the consequent decline in the demand for the labour of older men, which is a trend experienced by all industrialised societies. Supply-side factors, based largely upon human volition, have played some part – but only in a minor and contributory way. Yet since the 1970s, under neoliberalism's influence, exactly the opposite verdict has become dominant, and retirement is seen as largely caused by supply-side factors – of which, the alleged incentive effect of state pensions (the UK) and Social Security (the USA) is said to be of prime importance. From this follows the proposition that retirement can be delayed by a withdrawal of benefits through raising state pension ages. History has been rewritten in order to justify this policy outcome.

[170] Young and Schuller, *Life After Work*, p. 127.
[171] Barnes and Parry, 'Renegotiating Identity', pp. 213–233.

6   Intergenerational equity

What obligations do different generations have towards each other? Should there be consistent treatment across generations? How should public expenditure be allocated between generations? These and other related questions have always been central to the study of ageing and old age, but they have assumed renewed importance of late with the re-emergence of a debate on intergenerational equity – put simply, the question of whether each generation should receive a fair allocation of resources, compared with those generations that have gone before and will follow. Immediately, of course, problems arise – most notably, how one might define a generation, what constitutes 'fairness' or exactly how any reallocation would take place. These and other issues will be discussed in the pages that follow. It will be argued that, although generational analysis is important, the revival of intergenerational equity concerns is a symptom of the neoliberalisation of old age that is the central theme of this book. It has made up one of the justifications for cutting back welfare support to retired people and forcing them to work later in life.

The recent debate

It has taken an economic recession, massive cuts in public expenditure and a notional change in the political culture to breathe new life into a debate that appeared some thirty years ago in the USA during the neoconservative hegemony. Social policy in the UK has recently appeared to favour older people over younger, and questions have been asked about the fairness of this. Intergenerational equity has been much discussed in the UK media, with nearly every announcement of public expenditure cuts being accompanied by a crude generational impact statement. Concerns that today's children may end up worse off than their parents are emblematic of wider twenty-first-century fears that, for western societies, economic growth may have stalled and post-Enlightenment narratives of progress may no longer apply in an increasingly dystopian future.[1] Intergenerational equity has been explored in several populist books,[2] more seriously by research funding bodies like the Equality and Human Rights Commission and the Leverhulme Trust, and by new pressure groups: in the UK, the Intergenerational Foundation; in the USA, Americans for Generational Equity; in Germany, the Foundation for the Rights of Future Generations. It has also been the subject of much press discussion. The idea that our current economic woes have in part been caused by 'over-generous' redistribution to older people has become an integral part of prevailing political discourses, intruding into many debates – from the 2011 'granny tax' to the right of wealthy pensioners to receive the winter fuel allowance and Freedom Pass and whether or not Chancellor George Osborne's economic policies in 2012–2014 have been intergenerationally fair.[3] A striking example was Niall Ferguson's first Reith Lecture of 2012, when Ferguson declared that 'the biggest challenge facing mature democracies is how to restore the social contract between the generations'. He observed that it was 'perhaps not surprising that a majority of current voters should support policies of intergenerational inequity, especially when older voters are so much more likely to vote than younger voters. But what if the net result of passing the bill for baby boomers' profligacy is not just unfair to the young but economically deleterious for everyone?' Having blamed older people for the UK's debt crisis, Ferguson then went on to declare, with deliciously unconscious irony, that 'as our economic difficulties have worsened, we voters have struggled to find the appropriate scapegoat'.[4]

On the face of it, the intergenerational equity debate has been fuelled by the undeniable and acute plight of young people, who are suffering high unemployment, rising university tuition fees, over-inflated house prices, falling living standards, stagnating wages and a seeming end to upward social mobility.[5] In the UK, the number of 16–24 year-olds not in education, employment or training was 955,000 in mid-2014 (a jobless rate of 13.3 per cent). In some countries of Europe (notably, Spain)

[1] Harry R. Moody, 'Justice Between Generations: The Recent History of an Idea' (unpublished paper, n.d.), p. 3.

[2] David Willetts, *The Pinch: How the Baby Boomers Took Their Children's Future – and Why They Should Give it Back* (2010); Francis Beckett, *What Did the Baby Boomers Ever Do for Us?* (2010); Ed Howker and Shiv Malik, *Jilted Generation: How Britain Has Bankrupted Its Youth* (2010).

[3] For example: Sam Fleming, 'Pensioners "Better off than Most" as Working Parents Take Brunt of Cuts', 23 Mar. 2012, *The Times*.

[4] Niall Ferguson, 'The Rule of Law and its Enemies', The Reith Lectures, BBC Radio 4, broadcast 19 June 2012, www.bbc.co.uk/programmes. Ferguson did not seem to be aware that older voters are more likely to vote Conservative.

[5] Philip Inman, 'Debt and Housing Costs Make Young Worse Off than Past Generations', *Guardian*, 5 Aug. 2014, www.theguardian.com

it is well over 50 per cent. Young people have also become the main victims of the UK's obsessive need to keep house prices buoyant. It was an over-inflated housing market that provided the collateral for the long, debt-fuelled boom that ran from the early 1990s to 2008, and the political and fiscal consequences of a collapse in house prices, with widespread foreclosures and evictions, is something UK governments dare not contemplate. In London – the great engine of the UK's new economy, and with a more febrile housing market than anywhere else – mortgage-funded home ownership has become the privilege of a minority: it has been calculated that, by the year 2020, the average deposit required from first-time buyers in London will be over £100,000.[6] By late 2013, house prices in the UK were rising by 16 per cent per annum on average, and the average price of a property in London (£544,232) was well out of reach of the majority of its citizens. There was considerable apprehension over yet another unsustainable 'housing bubble' and a consequent house-price crash. The result has been that nearly half of European people aged 18 to 30 are still living with their parents[7] – earning themselves the unfortunate nickname of 'generation rent' and raising the extraordinary possibility of a trend back to the multi-generation extended family living communally.

Again, rising university tuition fees are likely to impose debts of at least £25,000 per person on graduates at the start of their careers.[8] A graduate couple, setting up home together, will therefore start out with a combined debt of c. £50,000 – hardly good news for future birth rates, and therefore the 'demographic timebomb', or for their prospects of ever owning a home. Many university graduates have found themselves forced to work for long periods of time in unpaid internships or voluntary work, just to get a foothold in the job market. Yet another warning that today's young people may be worse off than their parents was sounded by a report from the Social Mobility and Child Poverty Commission, chaired by the former Labour MP, Alan Milburn, which also suggested that wealthier pensioners should have some benefits means-tested.[9] The political responses to the evident plight of the young have in some quarters been hostile, with the two main political parties outbidding each other with

---

[6] Jonathan Prynn, '£100,000 Deposit to Buy a First Home', *Evening Standard*, 24 Jan. 2013.

[7] Shiv Malik, 'The Dependent Generation: Half Young European Adults Live With Their Parents', *Guardian*, 24 March 2014, www.theguardian.com

[8] Tom de Castella, 'Have Young People Never Had it So Bad?', *BBC News Magazine*, 6 Feb. 2013, www.bbc.co.uk

[9] 'Alan Milburn Says Child Poverty "No Longer Problem of the Workless and Work-shy"', BBC News, 17 Oct. 2013, www.bbc.co.uk

'tough love' proposals. In his speech to the October 2013 Conservative Party annual conference, the Prime Minister, David Cameron, suggested that young people aged 16 to 24 could lose their automatic entitlement to housing and other benefits unless they were in work, training or education: it was too easy to 'opt for a life on benefits'.[10] Not to be outdone, the Labour leader, Ed Miliband, announced in June 2014 that a future Labour government would remove entitlement to Job Seeker's Allowance from low-skilled jobless 18–21 year-olds if they did not find work or improve their qualifications.[11] Finally, younger generations face years of public expenditure cuts (only one-quarter of which have currently been implemented) and welfare state contraction. The plight of this young 'lost generation' will increasingly become a major electoral issue.

By contrast, older people appear on the face of it to have suffered much less. Their employment rates have held up in the recession. Pensioner poverty has been reduced significantly since the mid-1990s but child poverty has been reduced by less, while that of working-age adults has risen slightly: using the relative poverty line of 60 per cent of median net disposable income, 16 per cent of pensioners were in poverty before housing costs (BHC) and 13 per cent after housing costs (AHC) in 2012/13. In that year 17 per cent of children were in relative poverty BHC and 27 per cent AHC; the respective figures for working-age adults in 2012/13 were 15 per cent BHC and 21 per cent AHC.[12] Again, the value of the state pension is now maintained by the 'triple lock' outlined in Chapter 3, home ownership among pensioners is at an all-time high and projections indicate that retired people will be prioritised in the future allocation of public expenditure.[13]

A selfish generation?

Pitting one generation against another in a kind of zero-sum game has become an easy and simplistic response to the UK's current economic woes, whereas in many ways the real culprit has been the economic forces unleashed by thirty-five years of neoliberalism. For example, the fact that youth unemployment is a Europe-wide phenomenon refutes

[10] 'David Cameron Suggests Cutting Benefits for under-25s', BBC News, 2 Oct. 2013, www.bbc.co.uk

[11] Andrew Grice, 'Miliband: Young Jobseekers Must Train or Lose Their Benefits', Independent, 18 June 2014, www.independent.co.uk

[12] Department for Work and Pensions, Households Below Average Income: An Analysis of the Income Distribution 1994/5 –2012/13 (2014), p. 9.

[13] Toby Helm, 'Osborne's Cuts Shape the Economy and the Future Role of the State Too', Guardian, 23 June 2013, www.theguardian.com

allegations that it has somehow been 'caused' by a UK-specific older generation. The very same newspaper report that bemoaned the plight of young first-time buyers in London also admitted that the problem had been caused by 'foreign investors and City professionals' buying property as an investment – a clear result of the financialisation of the economy and the associated widening income inequality producing a fabulously wealthy 'super-rich' at the top end of the London housing market. Keeping house prices buoyant has been deliberate government policy – as in the recent Help to Buy scheme – and may be only a short-termist, politically irresponsible postponement of an inevitable housing slump. The aforementioned UK's 'social mobility tsar', Alan Milburn, was a senior member of the Labour government that introduced and then raised university tuition fees. Again, youth unemployment was as high in the 1980s, indicating that it is the first casualty of major economic restructuring. The fact that children and working-age adults have fared worse than pensioners in the experience of poverty since the 1990s is much more a tribute to factors like unemployment and an expansion of low-paid jobs than deliberate governmental policy to favour old people.

Retired people face difficulties, too – below-inflation returns on savings, the collapse of most final-salary pension schemes, a switch in the annual uprating of private or occupational pensions from the Retail Price Index to the lower Consumer Price Index, low annuity values, a raising of state pension ages now and in the future and so on. Quantitative easing has compounded the problem of low interest rates by reducing the yield from gilts and bonds, further eroding the value of defined benefit pensions and annuities. Twenty years ago, a man aged 65 retiring with a £100,000 pension fund would have been able to obtain a guaranteed annuity income of over £15,000 per annum; now it would be less than £6,000 per annum. The very same low interest rates that are continuing to fuel a housing boom, to the great disadvantage of young people, have also eroded pensioner incomes. Warnings have been sounded that today's retirees may also experience lower standards of living than did their parents in retirement – indeed, that successive generations will have to endure this fate. Unless they enjoy inherited wealth, cohorts born in the 1960s and 1970s are likely to be less well off in retirement than those born in the 1940s.[14] As will be argued later, a proper generational accounting exercise, examining gains and losses by age group, would have to be detailed and complex: most of the allegations recently made have been simplistic and based upon selective evidence. Such allegations

[14] Andrew Hood and Robert Joyce, *The Economic Circumstances of Cohorts Born between the 1940s and the 1970s* (2013).

also depend on an instantaneous, cross-sectional view, ignoring the fact that current retirees may have spent decades paying off mortgages, raising families and enjoying living standards lower on average than those of today.

Nevertheless, there has been no shortage of commentators arguing that the baby boomers have somehow been allocated too great a share of public resources, that intergenerational tensions have risen and that remedial action should be taken to rectify this injustice. In essence, a new age-based identity politics is being fashioned in order to obscure class issues. Talk of 'generations at war' diverts attention from the widening socio-economic inequalities that have occurred in the last forty years. As Lester Thurow approvingly observed nearly twenty years ago, in a famous passage, 'In the years ahead, class warfare is apt to be redefined as the young against the old, rather than the poor against the rich.'[15] Another commentator at that time sternly declared that 'There is little to be gained any more in studying the welfare states simply as battlegrounds between rich and poor, employer and employee, and our other synonyms and apologies for class.'[16] Hence recent popular movements by young 'Facebook activists' have been presented as age conflicts rather than class conflicts – as in the student protests in the UK against higher tuition fees and the slow privatisation of higher education, or the Arab Spring movements for regime change that spread rapidly across many youthful Middle Eastern countries in 2010–2012.

What has caused this alleged generational imbalance in the allocation of public resources? One explanation is that it happened by chance, without anyone noticing until it suddenly became apparent – history as a chapter of accidents. Another is that one particularly selfish 'welfare generation' has been able to manipulate the public policy agenda to its own advantage – covertly, concertedly and conspiratorially. It is a human agency explanation *reductio ad absurdum*, with little cognisance taken of structural economic factors and meagre supporting evidence from case studies in the policy process. The most striking past example was the analysis by the social historian, David Thomson, who maintained that New Zealand's welfare state had been youth-oriented in the 1950s and 1960s, when members of an alleged 'welfare generation' were young and raising families, but changed in the 1980s, as they approached retirement, and became more fiscally oriented towards retirees – moving from

[15] Lester Thurow, 'The Birth of a Revolutionary Class', *New York Times Magazine*, 19 May 1996, p. 47.

[16] David Thomson, 'The Welfare State and Generation Conflict: Winners and Losers', in Paul Johnson, Christoph Conrad and David Thomson (eds.), *Workers Versus Pensioners: Intergenerational Justice in an Ageing World* (1989), p. 34.

a 'youth state' to an 'elder state'. Unfortunately, Thomson's thesis rested more on allusion and speculation than on thoroughly researched case studies.[17] Many of the examples he cited, in throwaway fashion – such as reductions in employment protection, or the easing of exchange controls – were quite obviously products of neoliberalism rather than generational self-interest. The spread of male early retirement was viewed by Thomson as an unalloyed blessing that the pampered older generations had bestowed upon themselves: it was 'in large part a voluntary response to the enhanced income and leisure that now go with aging'.[18] Conspicuously absent from his list of examples was the Thatcher government's attack on state pensions in the UK. Even more puzzling was the fact that elsewhere Thomson had argued that state support to older people had *declined* since early Victorian times.[19] Nevertheless, these and other empirical shortcomings have not inhibited suggestions that, in the interests of intergenerational justice, a redistribution of public resources should take place in favour of the young.

Three lifecourse perspectives

Much analysis of alleged intergenerational inequity depends upon an instantaneous, cross-sectional view of resource allocation between age groups. However, a proper investigation needs to adopt a lifecourse perspective, recording all positive and negative experiences over a completed life. Analytically, it is helpful to draw a distinction between three such approaches.[20]

First there is the 'cohort effect'. Until now, every generation has been (on average) wealthier, healthier, better housed, more educated, and so on, than the ones preceding it. This is a consequence of rising living standards and hitherto the assumption has been that it will always continue. The implicit generational contract is based upon the view that today's old people helped to bring about the rising prosperity enjoyed by the non-old – and therefore the non-old should support them. Those concerned with intergenerational equity argue that progress is now being halted:

---

[17] David Thomson, *Selfish Generations? How Welfare States Grow Old* (1996). See also, Thomson, 'The Welfare State'.

[18] David W. Thomson, 'A Lifetime of Privilege? Aging and Generations at Century's End', in Bengtson and Achenbaum, *Changing Contract*, pp. 228, 229.

[19] David Thomson, 'The Decline of Social Welfare: Falling State Support for the Elderly since Early Victorian Times', *Ageing and Society*, 4, 4, Dec. 1984, pp. 451–482.

[20] Section by the author, in David Piachaud, John Macnicol and Jane Lewis, *A Think Piece on Intergenerational Equity* (2009), pp. 10–11.

living standards will henceforth stagnate or even fall, since all industri-alised societies face a very serious fiscal perfect storm made up of several toxic elements – an economic recession (the likely duration of which is uncertain), the need to reshape economies to reverse global warming, the growing challenge from developing countries like India and China and the public expenditure consequences of future ageing populations.

Second, the paradox is that, at any one time, old people appear to con-sume a disproportionately large amount of social security and health care resources. In the UK, the proportion of National Health Service expendi-ture allocated to those aged 65+ has risen steadily since 1948, to over 40 per cent today. As has been outlined in Chapter 4, the great success story of recent decades has been the conquest of death in childhood, youth and middle age. On the face of it, therefore, a cross-sectional, instantaneous view would seem to reveal substantial generational inequity in the distri-bution of public resources in favour of the old. Hitherto this age bias in resource allocation has been deemed acceptable because pensioners are 'our future selves' and have paid taxes in the past, as well as supporting their own children. They have therefore contributed to the rising living standards of the non-old. The implicit welfare contract is that we are, in essence, redistributing resources to our future selves.

Third is the controversial claim that the baby boomers form a uniquely selfish 'welfare generation' that has gone through life at every stage absorbing a disproportionate share of public resources, and has ended up in old age with 'over-generous' provision (particularly in regard to state pensions). However, complaints of this nature were not made when the baby boomers were younger. For example, as children they were not seen as responsible for the enormous strains put on the UK's educa-tion system through sheer numbers of pupils in the 1950s and 1960s.[21] Those who believe that intergenerational inequity in resource allocation has taken place are really combining the most pessimistic interpretations of all three lifecourse perspectives.

A recent revival

The current intergenerational equity debate is essentially a revival of long-standing concerns that have been articulated before – albeit in a more muted form – with quite different generations as villains and victims. In essence, the USA has witnessed three iterations: the first, and least significant, was in the late 1930s and early 1940s, during and immediately

---

[21] In the UK, there were 5,100,000 fulltime pupils in schools in 1946/7, 7,200,000 in 1964/5 and 9,300,000 in 1975/6.

after the passage of Social Security. Some concern was expressed that retirees might form a powerful, single-issue political lobby that could distort the democratic process by demanding improvements in services that only benefited older people.[22] These fears have always existed as a sub-text in grey politics: most notably, that insightful observer of changes in gerontology, Bernice Neugarten, warned gently in 1979 that allocating resources on the basis of age rather than need ('the greying of the budget') might create divisiveness in society.[23] The second was in the Reaganite 1980s when there were many-pronged attacks on the US welfare state and calls to privatise Social Security. The economic and geopolitical traumas of that decade led to a mood of pessimism and insecurity about America's ability to dominate the world economically and engendered exaggerated fears about structural flaws in the US economy – low levels of aggregate savings and investment, stagnating living standards for many blue-collar Americans, poor productivity and the budget deficit (which seemed to be passing on a bitter legacy to future generations). Finally, in recent years the Social Security privatisation agenda has resurfaced, to which has been added environmentalist concerns about which generations should be responsible for the costs of climate change. A constant feature of each wave of concern has been that working-age 'producers' have been crudely and simplistically pitted against passive, retired, burdensome 'consumers'. For example, in the UK the 1954 Report of the Phillips Committee asserted that 'the burden of old age involves the transfer to the elderly of income currently derived from the exertions of others. To the extent that such transfers take place, the elderly are a burden on the rest of the community.'[24]

It was in the neoconservative, Reaganite 1980s that the debate really took off in the USA (but not in other western nations) and predictions of 'age wars' became quite common. The year 1984 is often seen as the starting-point, when the demographer Samuel Preston raised the issue in his Presidential Address to the Population Association of America, and the pressure group Americans for Generational Equity (AGE) was first founded. Ostensibly, this was because of post-1970s concerns over sluggish economic performance, public expenditure constraints, apprehension over a future ageing population and uncertainty over the long-term fiscal sustainability of Social Security. Much was made of the fact that poverty rates for American children had not fallen as fast as those for old

---

[22] Macnicol, *Age Discrimination*, pp. 50–51; Longman, *Born to Pay*, p. 32.

[23] Bernice Neugarten, 'The Young-Old and the Age-Irrelevant Society' (1979), in Dail A. Neugarten (ed.), *The Meanings of Age: Selected Papers of Bernice L. Neugarten* (1996), p. 53.

[24] *Report of the Committee on the Economic and Financial Problems*, p. 33.

people. There was growing concern about the 'feminisation of poverty' in families headed by a young female, and this was an integral part of the anti-welfare attacks on single mothers in the Reagan years. (The fact that there was a substantial feminisation and racialisation of poverty in old age, such that an old African American woman was five times more likely to be poor than an old white man, aroused little comment.)[25] In 1980s America, a child on average was much more likely to be poor than was an old person. Hence in 1984, 22.0 per cent of Americans aged under 16 were in poverty, compared with 12.4 per cent aged 65+ (this having fallen from 35.2 per cent in 1959 and 24.6 per cent in 1970).[26] In Daniel Patrick Moynihan's characteristically grandiose words, America had become 'the first society in history in which a person is more likely to be poor if young rather than old'.[27] However, as Meredith Minkler pointed out, children are poor primarily because their parents are poor, and labour market restructuring over the previous two decades had led to job losses and falling real wages: this, and not the political power of retirees, was the reason for child poverty.[28]

From a cross-sectional viewpoint, resource allocation appeared generationally unfair. Only 12 per cent of the US population was aged 65+ in the mid-1980s, yet that age group allegedly absorbed 56 per cent of all federal spending.[29] (The fact that this is a feature of all modern welfare states was ignored.) Even more controversial were the claims that retirees were taking out much more in benefits than they had paid in via contributions and taxes: three times,[30] or perhaps 'even five to ten times' more.[31] It was alleged that the US Social Security system contained a corrupting and eventually unsustainable bias towards ever-inflating costs. Each successive generation had a vested interest in expanding it, since they themselves would eventually be beneficiaries: it was therefore a dishonest Ponzi scheme, akin to pyramid selling or a chain letter.

Many who worked with older people were appalled and angered by these kinds of allegations, believing them to be suffused with a savage ageism in which crude human capital criteria were being used to devalue older people – as in Samuel Preston's assertion that 'Expenditure on

[25] John Macnicol, 'Ageing and Justice', Labour History Review, 55, 1, Spring 1990, p. 79.
[26] U.S. Bureau of the Census, Statistical Abstract of the United States: 1986 (1985), p. 1985.
[27] Daniel Patrick Moynihan, Family and Nation (1986), p. 112.
[28] Meredith Minkler, 'Scapegoating the Elderly: New Voices, Old Theme', Journal of Public Health Policy, 18, 1, 1997, pp. 9–10.
[29] Peter G. Peterson, 'The Morning After', The Atlantic Monthly, October 1987, www .theatlantic.com
[30] Philip Longman, 'Justice Between Generations', Atlantic Monthly, 1 June 1985, www .theatlantic.com
[31] Peterson, 'The Morning After'.

the elderly is almost exclusively consumption expenditure, in the sense that it does not appreciably affect the future productive capacity of the economy. Most types of expenditure on children are both consumption and investment.'[32] The intergenerational equity debate was therefore sharply polarised, with very strong feelings on both sides. Those working in gerontology believed that it would, unless strenuously opposed, undermine the strong moral claim by old people to enjoy a poverty-free retirement. Old age would lose its status as a specially protected stage of life. For gerontologists, the debate became, in Martin Kohli's words, 'a common rallying point for repudiation and indignation, and an easy target for claiming the scientific and moral high ground'.[33] All in all, it was, in Harry R. Moody's apt phrase, 'a policy nightmare for gerontology'.[34]

On a deeper level, therefore, the whole debate symbolised a major political realignment and an attempt to restructure welfare states by establishing what neoconservatives in the 1980s quite openly called a 'new generational contract' – one that was more individualistic, in which benefits to retired people would be cut as part of a wider undermining of the solidaristic basis for postwar welfare states. It was necessary 'to lower the overall income expectations of the aged, or to change patterns of work', as three commentators euphemistically put it.[35] In effect, old age would be privatised and neoliberalised: apart from a basic safety net, provision for retirement would have to come from individuals themselves via the private market in financial products. As Alan Walker put it, 'Stripped of all its euphemisms the newly emerging contract between age cohorts in some western countries consists of cuts in social security for both current and future pensioners and reductions in rights of access to health care.'[36]

The main lobbying groups in the 1980s and early 1990s – AGE and the Concord Coalition (founded in 1992) – campaigned for a rebalancing of public resources towards the young and popularised the idea that a grossly unfair intergenerational inequity in the allocation of resources had

[32] Samuel Preston, 'Children and the Elderly: Divergent Paths for America's Dependents', *Demography*, 21, 4, Nov. 1984, p. 452.

[33] Martin Kohli, 'Generational Equity: Concepts and Attitudes', in Camila Arza and Martin Kohli (eds.), *Pension Reform in Europe: Politics, Policies and Outcomes* (2008), p. 211.

[34] Moody, 'Justice Between Generations', p. 1.

[35] Paul Johnson, Christoph Conrad and David Thomson, 'Introduction', in Johnson *et al.* (eds.), *Workers Versus Pensioners*, p. 9.

[36] Alan Walker, 'Intergenerational Relations and the Provision of Welfare', in Alan Walker (ed.), *The New Generational Contract: Intergenerational Relations, Old Age and Welfare* (1996), pp. 11, 16.

taken place.[37] Such concerns were to an extent held across the political spectrum, but they were undoubtedly more common on the political right and inextricably linked to the privatisation of Social Security, Medicare and Medicaid.[38] At a populist level, there was much discussion in a compliant media of how the selfish generation of retired 'greedy geezers' had demanded far too much.

The campaign of the 1980s and early 1990s was a well-orchestrated one, munificently bankrolled by business money and part of a wider strategy by the big American corporations after the 1970s to change the socio-political agenda in Washington. After something of a lull in the late 1990s and early 2000s as the US budget deficit was reduced, the campaign has resurfaced again in the aftermath of the 2008 recession. Funding organisations and individuals tend to be from those sections of the financial services industry that would benefit directly from a privatised Social Security and health care system. They have extensive links with neoconservative think-tanks and the Republican Party.

No individual illustrates this better than Peter G. Peterson (b. 1926), who has had a long career as a wealthy Wall Street banker and company executive, strongly loyal to the Republican Party. Peterson was CEO of Bell and Howell, 1963–1971, among several business activities, and served in the Nixon administration, notably as U.S. Secretary of Commerce from 1972. In the 1970s and 1980s, he was CEO of Lehman Brothers and its successor, Lehman Brothers, Kuhn, Loeb Inc., before going on to found the private investment firm, the Blackstone Group, in 1985. He was thus at the heart of the very banking sector that caused the 2008 fiscal debt crisis, although he does not appear to have predicted it. In 2007 – a year before the crisis broke – Peterson and his business partner sold the Blackstone Group for $4billion – of which Peterson's share was nearly £2billion.[39] By 2013, Peterson had net assets of $1.5billion, placing him 352nd in the Forbes List of top 400 wealthy individuals in the USA.[40]

Peterson was a co-founder of the Concord Coalition in 1992 and now he decided to use $1billion of his newly acquired fortune to fund more lobbying organisations that would campaign for reductions in the federal deficit. He set up the Peter G. Peterson Foundation in 2008, as

---

[37] For a good account, see Jill Quadagno, 'Generational Equity and the Politics of the Welfare State', *Politics and Society*, 17, 3, 1989, pp. 353–376.

[38] Laurence Kotlikoff and Jeffrey Sachs, 'Privatizing Social Security: It's High Time to Privatize', *The Brookings Review*, Summer 1997.

[39] 'Peter G. Peterson', 2014, pgpf.org/board/peter-g-peterson; 'Blackstone Group', 2014, www.sourcewatch.org

[40] 'Forbes 400', 2013, www.forbes.com

well as channelling money into neoconservative bodies like the Heritage Foundation, the American Enterprise Institute and his own Fix the Debt (supported by an initial donation from him of $5million). Between 2009 and 2012, the Peterson Foundation gave a total of $6,036,060 to the Concord Coalition.

Since the 1980s, Peterson has argued in favour of cutbacks in Social Security, Medicare and Medicaid, often deploying intergenerational equity as a justifying argument. Hence in 1987 he declared that 'We have witnessed a widening split between the elderly, among whom poverty is still declining, and children and young families, among whom poverty rates have exploded – a development with dire implications for our future productivity.' He warned of worsening dependency ratios, low savings levels, unsustainable cost-of-living increases in Social Security benefits, the Reagan administration's inability to cut entitlement programmes and so on. (He was one of those deficit hawks who ended up deeply disillusioned with Reagan's fiscal policies.) The answer was to impose major cuts on Social Security – including raising the eligibility age.[41] Peterson has written prolifically on the topic, authoring many populist articles and books, notably *Will America Grow Up Before it Grows Old: How the Coming Social Security Crisis Threatens You, Your Family, and Your Country* (1996) and *Gray Dawn: How the Coming Age Wave Will Transform America – and the World* (1999).

An intriguing aspect of Peterson's hostility towards the fiscally 'over-privileged' older generations was the involvement of his very own Blackstone Group in Southern Cross, the UK's largest provider of care homes in the early 2000s, with 31,000 old people as residents. Southern Cross was founded in 1996, and prospered in the then-lucrative care home market (the economic good times being fuelled by rising property values and local authorities being relatively wealthy – thus able to fund care home places). In September 2004, Blackstone bought a large (£162,000,000) share in Southern Cross, as part of a second management buy-out, as well as purchasing other UK care homes. Blackstone prepared Southern Cross for flotation on the Stock Exchange on a sale-and-leaseback arrangement, and this was duly completed in mid-2006, netting Blackstone some £648,000,000 – four times its original investment. Earlier in 2006, Blackstone had made £1billion through selling 294 Southern Cross care homes to the Royal Bank of Scotland. (By contrast, many of the care home staff earned little more than the minimum wage, and their residents were relatively defenceless and vulnerable.)

---

[41] Peterson, 'The Morning After'.

Blackstone then exited. Thereafter, cuts in funding to local authorities rendered them less able to supply the same number of needy older people, thus cutting care home incomes, and property values stopped rising, reducing the paper value of the care homes. In the summer of 2011 a crisis occurred: Southern Cross was in a desperate financial situation, with a pre-tax loss of £311,000,000, and announced that it would have to withhold 30 per cent of its rental payments while it restructured itself. Blackstone denied that it had left Southern Cross with unsustainably high rents to pay (an annual rent bill of £250,000,000), and said it was not to blame.[42] Nevertheless, many observers believed that Blackstone's ruthless asset-stripping was the cause: the verdict of the *Daily Mail* (a newspaper normally sympathetic to the financial services industry) was that the Southern Cross scandal had laid bare 'the full extent of US private equity firm Blackstone's profiteering at the expense of the elderly and the vulnerable'.[43] For the purpose of this study, the significant irony is that clearly Peter Peterson viewed old people as both a fiscal disaster *and* an enormously profitable investment opportunity.

A 2007 Mission Statement of the reconstituted AGE is interesting. It warns that, for the first time in US history, future generations of workers could experience 'falling levels of non-health consumption', and continues: 'Averting this outcome will require our leaders to do more than simply raise taxes or cut benefits. They must also create a sustainable generational contract – and, in so doing, change the expectations of every age group with respect to patterns of work, saving and retirement.' The existing generational contract must therefore be revised and the budget deficit cut by reducing the scope of Medicare, Medicaid and Social Security (partly to disincentivise retirement), encouraging more saving and adjusting taxes in favour of the young. Labour supply concerns are central, and this imperative is clothed in the language of intergenerational justice:

Demographic projections suggest that older workers must play a greater role in the labour force if desired levels of economic growth are to be maintained. Reforms that raised taxes on working-age populations to fund promised retirement benefits could have the unintended effect of making retirement more attractive. In order to preserve current work incentives, reforms must maintain parity in the living standards of workers and retirees.

---

[42] Alex Hawkes, 'Blackstone Denies Blame for Southern Cross's Plight', *Guardian*, 2 June 2011, www.theguardian.com
[43] Simon Neville, '£1bn Gamble of the Care Home Sharks Revealed: Southern Cross Predators Sold Off almost 300 homes to RBS', *Daily Mail*, 4 June 2011, www.dailymail .co.uk. See also, Simon Goodley, 'Southern Cross Care Fiasco Sheds Light on Secretive World of Private Equity', *Guardian*, 3 June 2011, www.theguardian.com

The economic rationality behind these social justice concerns is very striking. The AGE Mission Statement reiterates those long-standing neo-classical apprehensions over high levels of social spending resulting in low levels of private saving, and this in turn impeding the process of capital accumulation: 'savings rates will need to rise if we are to limit the growing dependence of retirees on generational transfers'. 'Strengthening incentives to save' is therefore a key aim.[44] As noted, there is a major conflict of interest here, in that the funders of AGE would benefit directly from higher private savings: presumably they could be trusted to invest these savings wisely and safely.

A fascinating sub-text in this neoliberal message is that the domestic problem of population ageing is placed in the context of much bigger geopolitical concerns related to US foreign policy, the interests of globalised finance capital and energy sources. It has to be remembered that energy companies exert an enormous influence on the American political process: companies like Exxon Mobil fund much research denying climate change, advocating deregulation in energy policy and the economy generally, and attacking federal social policy as unaffordable. The overlap between several themes in this book is interesting.[45] The oil-producing countries of the Middle East are very youthful, with as much as 60 per cent of their populations aged under 30, and this could create a politically volatile situation, ripe for permeation by Islamic extremism. Writing in 2004, at the height of the second Gulf War and well before the youth-led Arab Spring movements, Michael Klare perceptively observed that demographic and socio-economic factors made Saudi Arabia (America's closest oil-producing ally) potentially unstable:

Such a high concentration of young people would pose a significant social and economic problem for any developing country, but was particularly troublesome in Saudi Arabia because per capita income had dropped from $28,600 in 1981 (when it was roughly equivalent to that of the United States) to a mere $6,800 in 2001. This plunge was exacerbated by a sharp rise in unemployment among young, college-educated Saudi men, from almost zero a decade earlier to more than 30 per cent. The result, inevitably, was a surplus of well-educated,

---

[44] Americans for Generational Equity, 'Mission Statement and Plan of Action' (c. 2007), www.americanbenefitscouncil.org

[45] Perhaps personified by Michael J. Boskin. He has written on retirement, presenting it as a rational choice, driven by benefit incentives. He is a Professor of Economics at Stanford University and a Fellow of the neoconservative think-tank, the Hoover Institution, based there, a research associate of the NBER, Chair of the President Ford's Council of Economic Advisers between 1989 and 1993 and a member of the Board of Directors of Exxon Mobil.

ambitious and often alienated young men with high expectations and few economic opportunities – perfect fodder for political or religious extremists.[46]

The intriguing connection between domestic social problems and America's world role is revealed in a policy statement by AGE:

The boomers will be retiring in a world that is fast being transformed by economic competition from low-wage emerging economies, rising fiscal pressures throughout the developed world, nuclear proliferation, the spread of anti-western values in conflict-ridden youthful societies, and even global warming. These developments carry with them a heightened risk of economic disruption that, if realised, could adversely affect domestic living standards.[47]

The interests of globalised finance capital are very evident in the anticipated concerns that Japan and Europe, with their ageing populations, face even greater demographic challenges than does the USA and will also build up budget deficits unless action is taken there. Without such action, 'The diversion of capital from more productive uses could slow growth everywhere – and potentially unleash social tensions in emerging markets, where global trade and investment play an important stabilising role.'[48]

The value of generational analysis

The fact that the intergenerational equity debate has become highly politicised in recent years should not blind us to the fact that generational analysis can be very valuable, and has inspired some interesting work by sociologists. It forces us to examine social stratification by age – along with the more common divisions of class, gender and ethnicity – adding an extra dimension to social analysis. The question of what should be a 'just' distribution across generations has been central to all human relations and societal organisations – from the Biblical injunction to 'honour thy father and thy mother: that thy days may be long'[49] to today's debate about caring responsibilities within the family. Prehistoric tribal societies observed complex rules of reciprocity and obligation across the generations, such as food-sharing practices[50] – something that survived well

---

[46] Michael T. Klare, *Blood and Oil: The Dangers and Consequences of America's Growing Petroleum Dependency* (2004), p. 87.
[47] Americans for Generational Equity, 'Mission Statement'.   [48] *Ibid.*
[49] Vern Bengtson, 'Will "Generational Accounting" Doom the Welfare State?', *The Gerontologist*, 33, 6, 1993, p. 813.
[50] John B. Williamson and Diane M. Watts-Roy, 'Framing the Generational Equity Debate', in John B. Williamson, Diane M. Watts-Roy and Eric R. Kingson (eds.), *The Generational Equity Debate* (1999), pp. 4–5.

into the twentieth century in impoverished British working-class families, where for commonsense human capital reasons the adult male breadwinner would have been the first to be fed. (Income distribution within the working-class household by age and gender remained for a long time completely hidden from the gaze of social investigators.) Again, the division of labour in agricultural societies was based much less on skill or gender than on age and physical strength (the two often overlapping).[51] Intergenerational tensions and conflicts over such issues as land allocation have always existed.[52] Some societies were ruled by powerful gerontocracies; by contrast, others practised parricide against old people who had become a burden. In short, preindustrial societies displayed as complex and ambiguous attitudes towards old age as do ours today. At a populist level, the young have always been perceived as mildly threatening to the staid cultural practices of the middle aged – from the flappers of the 1920s, to the jitterbugs of the 1930s, to the youth gangs of the 1950s and the counter-cultural hippies of the 1960s. So intergenerational tensions are not exactly new.

Generational conflicts of a low-level kind and shared generational identity are an integral part of family life, forming the basis of age stratifications and assigned roles within the extended family. They also figure prominently in popular culture (for example, in the way that the film *Mama Mia!* celebrated the triumph of the middle-aged woman) and fiction. As Jane Pilcher has observed, the term 'generation' is widely used in everyday life, yet remains insufficiently explored in sociology.[53] Common usage would include 'generation gap', 'generation in limbo', 'my generation', Angry Young Men or the Beat Generation.[54] It has also become an historical shorthand: for example, there long survived the myth of a 'lost generation' of political leaders in the UK – those killed in the trenches of the First World War. (The fact that emigration was greatly reduced in 1914–1918 invalidates this.) Another popular but implausible thesis was that the over-liberal child-rearing practices advocated by Dr Benjamin Spock in the 1940s and 1950s had somehow produced the licentious, rebellious young adults of the 1960s. More recently, Tom Brokaw's book on *The Greatest Generation* (1998) of young American men who fought in

---

[51] Macnicol, *Politics of Retirement*, pp. 28–29.
[52] Nancy Foner, *Ages in Conflict: A Cross-Cultural Perspective on Inequality Between Old and Young* (1984); Richard Wall, 'Intergenerational Relationships Past and Present', in Walker, *New Generational Contract*, pp. 37–55.
[53] Jane Pilcher, 'Mannheim's Sociology of Generations: An Undervalued Legacy', *British Journal of Sociology*, 45, 3, September 1994, p. 481.
[54] Gene Feldman and Max Gartenberg (eds.), *Protest: The Beat Generation and the Angry Young Men* (1958).

the Second World War and established the postwar peace settlement is an exotic example of history as collective human agency. Demographers have always used cohort-based analysis, and have at times tried to identify the shared experiences of one particular collection of birth cohorts – for example, the appallingly high mortality rates among Russian men who fought in the Second World War, or the later-life health effects of poverty among UK babies born in the depressed areas in the 1930s.[55]

The study of generations should therefore be central to social science and gerontology. As has been outlined in Chapter 1, the ageing process involves the interaction between different conceptions of time or age. How generational units position themselves in time and across time – involving a dialectic between biographical time and historical time – is therefore crucial, as is the question of shared identity and consciousness.[56] The most celebrated early exposition was Karl Mannheim's dense and rather opaque essay – a sociological exploration, rather than an empirical one, and perhaps more cited than actually read – on 'The Problem of Generations' (1923). Mannheim explored the nature of a generation as a temporal unit, speculating on its role as an agent of change against the structural forces that formed the historical background. He believed that experiences in childhood and youth played an important part in determining adult consciousness, and was intrigued by the extent to which these experiences might be shared by members of the same birth cohort and carried forward into adulthood, such as to influence events. Mannheim acknowledged the divisions that existed within a generation, but recognised that it could still possess a collective identity. However, mere similarity of historical location or chronological contemporaneity was not enough; members of a generation had to experience the same concrete historical problems.[57]

Academic interest in the sociology of generations grew after the Second World War. The discipline of sociology in the 1950s tended to be dominated by structural-functionalism, one concern of which was how values conducive to social order (or disorder) were transmitted down the generations.[58] Again, in the late 1950s juvenile delinquency was the focus of much research (arguably, this was a major impetus behind the

[55] D. J. P. Barker, *Mothers, Babies and Health in Later Life* (1994).

[56] For useful discussions, see Gunhild Hammarstrom, 'The Constructions of Generation and Cohort in Sociological Studies of Ageing: Theoretical Conceptualisations and Some Empirical Implications', in Britt-Marie Oberg et al. (eds.), *Changing Worlds and the Ageing Subject* (2004), pp. 41–64; Pilcher, 'Mannheim's Sociology', pp. 481–495.

[57] Karl Mannheim, 'The Problem of Generations', in Mannheim, *Essays on the Sociology of Knowledge: Collected Works Volume Five*, edited by Paul Kecskemeti (1957), pp. 276–320.

[58] Vern L. Bengtson, 'Generation and Family Effects in Value Socialisation', *American Sociological Review*, 40, 3, June 1975, pp. 358–371.

American War on Poverty) – the most famous example being Richard Cloward and Lloyd Ohlin's *Delinquency and Opportunity* (1960). Student protest against the Viet Nam War and the wider counter-cultural and civil rights movements of the 1960s led to much examination of how and why one generation rebelled against another.[59]

In the 1970s and 1980s, the discipline of gerontology increasingly adopted a lifecourse perspective, viewing ageing as a long process and analysing the myriad interactions between the ageing self and background structural factors. The analytical distinction between 'age', 'cohort' and 'generation' became ever more important,[60] as did the intergenerational reciprocities and obligations within the extended family and society at large. One gerontologist who has perhaps done more than anyone to explore these issues has been Vern Bengtson, who has observed that the problem of generations is 'how to deal with the periods of dependency and independence dictated by the course of individual development and ageing. This we do by means of lifecourse and generational reciprocities, receiving, giving and receiving over time, at both the family and macrosocial level.'[61]

Social policy researchers have always shown an interest in resource allocation by age – though generally in a cautious way, perhaps because to go too far might undermine the solidaristic basis for modern welfare states. Conducting an empirical assessment of each generation's gains and losses through the welfare state would be interesting, if highly challenging.[62] Nevertheless, the transmission of advantage or disadvantage across the generations has often been investigated, from the eugenic pedigree charts of the 1930s to the transmitted deprivation research of the 1970s and recent social mobility studies. In addition, longitudinal surveys (such as the National Child Development Study or the 1970 British Cohort Study) have traced the fortunes of one particular birth cohort across the lifecourse, recording the interaction between intrinsic and extrinsic factors.

Generational analysis is thus central to social science itself. By contrast, moral philosophers have been slow to consider both age as a social division and the problem of distributional justice between age cohorts,

[59] Vern L. Bengtson, Michael J. Furlong and Robert S. Laufer, 'Time Aging, and the Continuity of Social Structure: Themes and Issues in Generational Analysis', *Journal of Social Issues*, 50, 2, 1974, pp. 3–13, 18.

[60] Judith Burnett, *Generations: The Time Machine in Theory and Practice* (2010), p. 3.

[61] Bengtson, '"Generational Accounting"', p. 813.

[62] For a useful preliminary exploration, see John Hills, 'Does Britain Have a Welfare Generation?', in Walker, *New Generational Contract*, ch. 3.

tending instead to assume fixed populations over short time periods.[63]
It is striking that, although Rawls perceptively discussed justice between
generations in this seminal text,[64] and a few others followed him,[65] subsequent political theorists have tended to ignore inequalities of age. For
example, three recently published comprehensive texts consider inequalities of gender, race/ethnicity, class and disability, but say little or nothing
about age.[66]

Allegations of intergenerational inequity thus lack a clear theoretical
underpinning. There is, of course, one interesting irony: the recent intergenerational equity debate has been associated with neoliberalism, yet
neoliberalism would normally disavow the use of explicit (and especially
post-Rawlsian) theories of distributional justice, believing instead that
only the market should distribute rewards.

Finally, there is no doubt that one recent, positive and important application of intergenerational equity has been in the area of climate change:
what obligation do current generations have towards their children to
leave them an ecologically sustainable world?[67] It is a truism that children
are one of the few groups in society who cannot campaign for themselves:
their interests have to be held in trust by adults. Even more intriguing
is the question of protecting generations as yet unborn. In the case of
global warming, the conduct of present generations can have irreversible
and potentially catastrophic consequences in the future.[68]

This issue has a long history, going back at least to Thomas Malthus.
Some political theorists did occasionally consider humankind's ethical
duties towards the future, and whether abstract rights should be enjoyed
by both present and future generations. For example, Henry Sidgwick,
in *The Methods of Ethics* (1907), stated that 'the interests of posterity
must concern a Utilitarian as much as those of his contemporaries'.[69]
It became even more important after 1973: as well as changing the
social policy agenda, the oil crisis raised the whole question of future

---

[63] Peter Laslett and James S. Fishkin, 'Introduction: Processional Justice', in Laslett and
Fishkin (eds.), *Justice Between Age Groups and Generations* (1992), p. 1.

[64] John Rawls, *A Theory of Justice* (1971), pp. 284–293.

[65] For example, Bruce A. Ackerman, *Social Justice in the Liberal State* (1980); Laslett and
Fishkin (eds.), *Justice Between Age Groups.*

[66] Will Kymlicka, *Contemporary Political Philosophy: An Introduction* (2002); John S. Dryzek,
Bonnie Honig and Anne Phillips (eds.), *The Oxford Handbook of Political Theory* (2006);
Lesley A. Jacobs, *Pursuing Equal Opportunities: The Theory and Practice of Egalitarian
Justice* (2004).

[67] Piachaud *et al.*, *A Think Piece*, pp. 68–72.

[68] Emilio Padilla, 'Intergenerational Equity and Sustainability', *Ecological Economics*, 41,
2002, pp. 72–73.

[69] Quoted in William R. Zame, 'Can Intergenerational Equity be Operationalised?', *Theoretical Economics*, 2, 2007, p. 187.

energy supplies – particularly, whether a 'peak oil' situation would soon be reached. Would sufficient resources be left for future generations?[70] It has gained importance as, in the second decade of the twenty-first century, western nations consider whether they should move to no-growth economies.

Some analytical issues

The debate on intergenerational equity over the past thirty years has raised many issues, the most important of which will now be considered.

The concept of a generation

What exactly is a 'generation'? Classically, the term has referred to a fifteen- to thirty-year age group, with most definitions suggesting twenty-five years. However, it is arguable that it could be applied to smaller birth cohorts, occupying between one and five years. Sober analysis of the term has been hampered by today's tendency to impose it on a series of opportunistically chosen one-year birth cohorts. Within the family, the meaning of 'generation' refers to biological divisions between children, parents, grandparents and (possibly) great-grandparents. One intriguing meaning is that a generation represents the time it takes for a newborn baby to replace its parents' role. Yet these nuclear family-based definitions are less sustainable now with increasing family diversity: repartnering and step-children create complications, aunts and uncles may be younger than nephews and nieces, and the time between generations can be attenuated (where there are teenage births) or age-gapped (with delayed child-bearing producing the multi-generation, 'beanpole' family).[71]

There has been much discussion in sociology of how the boundaries of one generation should be set.[72] If Mannheim's criterion is to be followed, a generation must have shared values via its historical location, and this (as argued below) is problematic. To be sure, major life events – such as the birth of one's first offspring – have varied by generation and have

---

[70] Robert M. Solow, 'On the Intergenerational Allocation of Natural Resources', *Scandinavian Journal of Economics*, 88, 1986, pp. 141–143.

[71] For a much more detailed discussion, see Vern L. Bengtson, 'Is the "Contract Across Generations" Changing? Effects of Population Aging on Obligations and Expectations Across Age Groups', in Bengtson and Achenbaum, *Changing Contract*, ch. 1.

[72] Bennett M. Berger, 'How Long Is a Generation?', *British Journal of Sociology*, 11, 1, Mar. 1960, pp. 10–23; Alan B. Spitzer, 'The Historical Problem of Generations', *American Historical Review*, 78, 1973, pp. 1355–1357.

bestowed a measure of generational identity: in 1961 the average age of a mother at first birth was 24.7, and now it is 28.1. Youth has become increasingly 'stretched' over the last hundred years (in the late nineteenth century, most children in the UK left school at 10 or 11 and went to work, at that age becoming, in effect, little adults).

However, a significant problem is that the start- and end-point boundaries of any generation do not necessarily possess any demographic or cultural significance – and that is particularly true of the baby boomers. Demographically, the UK definition is conventionally taken to be those born between 1941 (when the birth rate began to rise from its historic low-point in the 1930s) and 1970. The US definition is slightly different, encapsulating the 76,000,000 Americans born between 1946 and 1965 (with 'Generation X' born 1965–1981). However, as shown in Chapter 4, in both countries annual birth rates varied within this time-span. By Mannheim's criterion, a legitimate question to ask is whether in the year 1971 a 1-year-old baby boomer had a shared cultural location with a 30-year-old one born in 1941.

Remarkably, many who were involved in the intergenerational equity debate of the 1980s were pointing the accusatory finger at the *pre* boomers, born in the 1920s, for having commandeered too much in the way of public resources. On this account, the baby boomers were innocent victims. The two most popular texts of the time, Paul Light's *Baby Boomers* (1988) and Phillip Longman's *Born to Pay* (1987), uttered dire warnings. As Longman put it elsewhere, the baby boomers faced 'a disastrous retirement' unless a number of fundamental socio-economic trends were reversed.[73] He saw the rise of grey power as a cumulative trend that had been at work for many decades, steadily redistributing public expenditure to the retired in an unsustainable way. The baby boomers thus faced 'abandonment in old age. For it is they, along with their children, who will inherit the consequences of this spendthrift era.'[74] Light commented that 'Under Reagan the baby boomers' real income has declined, their housing ownership has lagged, their savings rate is nil, and their promotion prospects are lousy.'[75]

Laurence Kotlikoff's 1992 exploration of how generational accounting might be applied to fiscal policy derived in part from concerns that the baby boomers would be the prime victims of the growing budget deficit: implicitly, it was the preboomers that were to blame for

---

[73] Longman, 'Justice Between Generations'.   [74] Longman, *Born to Pay*, pp. 32–34.
[75] Paul Light, *Baby Boomers* (1988), pp. 45–46.

allowing the deficit to build up.[76] David Thomson also identified the 'welfare generation' as the preboomers born in the 1920s, 1930s and early 1940s. These were 'the big winners' whose contributions would 'cover only a fraction of their gains'. They had been treated 'uniquely generously through life by the modern state, relative to their successors'.[77] As a baby boomer himself, Thomson (b. 1953) wistfully complained of 'witnessing the declining prospects of my contemporaries and successors as they sought careers, families and homes in deteriorating circumstances and in the face of increasingly unsympathetic governments'.[78] Some working in gerontology shared these concerns: in 1989, Thomas Cole commented that the baby boom generation 'today finds itself the first in American history that cannot count on surpassing its parents' station in life. Prohibitive housing prices, high interest rates, sluggish economic growth, and glutted job markets have turned confident expectations of upward mobility into a gloomy view of the future.'[79] Academic responses in the 1980s accordingly tried to assess whether the preboomers had gained too much at the expense of the subsequent boomers. Hence a thoughtful and meticulous analysis by Richard Easterlin *et al.* in 1993 empirically tested the 'common perception' that, compared with their predecessors at the same age, 'the economic status of the baby boom generation (their material level of living) has declined, both absolutely and relative to older generations; that their retirement prospects have correspondingly diminished; and that tensions across age groups have risen'.[80] It is striking that identical 'selfish generation' arguments were used in condemnation of the preboomers in the 1980s as are used against the baby boomers now.

Intragenerational divisions

A frequent allegation is that the baby boomers have such a strong collective shared identity that they have kept their '1960s values' as they have aged, carrying them intact into old age and refashioning retirement into a paradise of hedonistic self-actualisation – a curious kind of cultural determinism. This narrative of course views the baby boomers as demographically and culturally monolithic. There is an interesting sub-text here, reflecting a neoconservative dislike of the 1960s as the

---

[76] Laurence J. Kotlikoff, *Generational Accounting: Knowing Who Pays, and When, for What We Spend* (1992), esp. p. 53.

[77] Thomson, *Selfish Generations?*, p. 1; Thomson, 'A Lifetime of Privilege?, p. 220.

[78] Thomson, *Selfish Generations?*, p. 6.   [79] Cole, 'Generational Equity', p. 377.

[80] Richard A. Easterlin, Diane J. Macunovich and Eileen M. Crimmins, 'Economic Status of the Young and Old in the Working-Age Population, 1964 and 1987', in Bengtson and Achenbaum, *Changing Contract*, ch. 4, p. 67 (quote).

time when there allegedly occurred the fatal liberalisation of culture and an expansion of welfare that set in motion all the dysfunctional economic trends that have beset America ever since. The implication is also that one generation has uniquely shared values and, in terms of beliefs, is hermetically sealed off from generations that went before and those that follow.[81] Once again, it is a behavioural and attitudinal explanation for economic change.

In fact, there is within one generation considerable heterogeneity and many inequalities – of class, gender, ethnicity, age, income, wealth, health status, educational attainment, religion, location and so on. There are even differences in age structure. For example, most ethnic minorities in the UK possess a youthful age structure, implying that they should be excluded from blame; by contrast, the 'white Irish' are relatively old. Attitudinally, there is also great variation – for example, in voting behaviour. In the May 2010 UK general election, the voting behaviour of 55–64 year-olds (the core of the first wave boomers) was: Conservative, 38 per cent; Labour, 28 per cent; Liberal Democrat, 23 per cent.[82] As Robert Hudson succinctly puts it, 'Despite their iconic demographic standing, the boomers by no means all look the same, and equally important, they also very much resemble people from other generations in obvious ways . . . the world of the boomers is marked by both intracohort differences and intercohort similarities.'[83] Another interesting caveat relates to location: in a geographically large and culturally diverse country like the USA, can a generation really be said to possess shared values?[84] It is therefore difficult to see how one particular generation could have overcome all its internal divisions and acted in concert to monopolise public resources.

This brings one to a related question: should one consider *collective* resource consumption by the whole generation, or average *individual* per capita consumption? Clearly, the former would be flawed, since it would be primarily a function of total numbers. Bizarrely, the locus of blame would need to be placed on the generation that preceded the baby boomers, for it was they who decided to have large families. If, on the other hand, the argument is that individual baby boomers have been over-resourced then we come up against the aforementioned problem that there are enormous intragenerational inequalities. How would we

---

[81] For a study that rather implies this, see Kenneth Howse, 'Updating the Debate on Intergenerational Fairness in Pension Reform', *Social Policy and Administration*, 41, 1, 2007, pp. 50–64.

[82] Ipsos MORI, 'How Britain Voted in 2010', 2010, www.ipsos-mori.com

[83] Robert Hudson, 'Preface' in Hudson, *Boomer Bust Vol. II*, p. vii.

[84] Hammarstrom, 'The Constructions of Generation and Cohort', p. 60.

decide exactly which individuals have been over-resourced and which under-resourced?

Equity or equality?

'Each generation should pay its own way' declares the UK's newly formed Intergenerational Foundation.[85] But what exactly does this mean – intergenerational equity or intergenerational equality? 'Equity' implies fairness, which is an arbitrary and contentious notion. Arguably it has always been the basis for the implicit risk-pooling that underpins the British welfare state. Manual workers die prematurely and have shorter survival in retirement. They are therefore much less likely to claim the state pension and live long on it. The higher social classes on average live longer and have higher lifetime earnings; they pay more into the National Health Service, but have lower levels of recorded sickness. A 'postcode lottery' means that where one lives can determine access to new, expensive pharmaceuticals. People who remain childless pay for state education. Healthy people support those with disabilities. The lines of redistribution are complex and cross-cutting – by age, class, gender, ethnicity, income, health status, region and so on – but have hitherto not been subject to popular challenge. We know relatively little about how ordinary citizens internalise this implicit intergenerational contract, but we do know that opinion surveys have consistently shown strong public support for welfare policies that protect older people – although the post-2008 recession has caused attitudes to harden somewhat. Hence the 2012 British Social Attitudes Survey found that the proportion surveyed who wished to see more government spending on retired people was 73 per cent in 1998, 74 per cent in 2004 and 57 per cent in 2011.[86] Likewise, Martin Kohli has provided cross-national survey evidence to show that there is still strong support for the traditional generational contract, in which retired people's benefits are protected.[87]

On the other hand, 'equality' implies each generation receiving identical amounts of resource allocation, via a generational accounting exercise, to produce 'a situation in which future generations face the same fiscal

---

[85] 'Intergenerational Foundation', 2014, www.intergenerational.org.uk

[86] A. Park, E. Clery, J. Curtice, M. Phillips and D. Utting, *British Social Attitudes 29 2012 Edition* (2012), p. vi.

[87] Martin Kohli, 'Ageing and Justice', in Robert H. Binstock and Linda K. George (eds.), *Handbook of Aging and the Social Sciences*, 6th edn. (2006), pp. 456–478; Kohli, 'Generational Equity'.

burdens as do current generations when adjusted for growth'.[88] Quite how this would be done – adjusting for changes in GDP and inflation, for example – is difficult to envisage. Complex formulae have been constructed with this aim – generally focusing on fiscal transfers without examining experiential factors[89] – but the legitimacy and practicality of this whole approach must be questionable. In essence, it involves calculating certain future liabilities with regard to social security and health care costs and labelling these the 'debt' that will fall on the shoulders of future generations, while ignoring other possible items of expenditure (for example, foreign wars), the ability of governments to raise taxes and the possibility of economically positive outcomes that would reduce future levels of public debt.[90] In addition, future social security liabilities tend to be presented as 'unfunded', ignoring the future income from contributions. The greatest difficulty – alluded to below – would be identifying the 'over-resourced' and the 'under-resourced', and then effecting a fair redistribution. To take but one example, women on average live longer than men, have higher levels of sickness and disability and form a majority of those on state pensions and/or means-tested social assistance in old age. On the face of it, rectifying alleged intergenerational inequality would involve punishing women; but counterbalancing this would be a host of factors that disadvantage women. Put succinctly, women are poorer than men in old age, and accordingly receive more from the welfare state: are they therefore 'winners' or 'losers'?

Concerns about intergenerational equity and the suggested remedy of lifecourse accounting usually focus on public transfers – in particular, social security and health care costs. However, private transfers between generations within an extended family, via inheritance of financial capital or cultural capital, are also 'unfair' in that they are a major generator of socio-economic inequality. Where it has been researched, income distribution within the extended family has been shown to be common.[91] There seems to be growing evidence of intergenerational transfers from grandparents and parents to children: 40 per cent of those expecting to retire in 2013 provided financial support to younger dependants, paying out an average of £240 per month; similarly, grandparents are predicted

[88] Roberto Cardarelli, James Sefton and Laurence J. Kotlikoff, 'Generational Accounting in the UK', *Economic Journal*, 110, 467, Nov. 2000, pp. 547–548.

[89] For example, Kotlikoff, *Generational Accounting*.

[90] For the opposed view, see James K. Galbraith, L. Randall Wray and Warren Mosler, *The Case Against Intergenerational Accounting: The Accounting Campaign Against Social Security and Medicare* (2009).

[91] For example, Dorothy Jerrome, 'Ties That Bind' in Walker, *New Generational Contract*, ch. 4.

to provide increasing support for their grandchildren's university education over the next ten years.[92] Older relatives also provide much informal care within the extended family, thereby enabling younger generations to engage in paid employment. They therefore contribute indirectly to economic growth. All in all, what is striking about extended families is the amount of intergenerational reciprocity that exists.[93]

If it were to produce accurate results, any generational accounting exercise would therefore have to list *all* experiential variables across the lifecourse, and then attribute causality. Total well-being would have to include 'the amount of leisure time one has, the extent of one's privacy or independence, the pleasure derived from work, and the number and well-being of other family members, including both one's offspring and parental and older generations'.[94] Relatively few attempts at this have been made: one, by Francoise Cribier, examined two birth cohorts of Parisians; another, by Paul Light, balanced out all the experiences of the baby boom generation, rightly emphasising the divisions within it.[95]

Even at the level of averages, a quick glance at the baby boomers shows that their path through life has not been all gain. The first wave boomers were born into austerity but reached maturity in times of relative prosperity; with the second wave boomers, it was the reverse.[96] Just taking those born at the peak of births, in the late 1940s, we can see that they experienced higher infant mortality, lower average family incomes, large class sizes in school and much poorer results in public examinations compared with schoolchildren today. Only 5 per cent of this birth cohort went to university. These peak boomers were becoming established in the labour market in the late 1960s, when unemployment was low, but they then experienced rising unemployment and inflation in the 1970s, when membership of occupational pension coverage was beginning to decline. They are now entering retirement at a point when returns from savings are lower than inflation: little wonder that increasing numbers of them have had to postpone retirement. All in all, they do not seem to have been very adept at manipulating the public policy agenda in their

---

[92] Prudential press release, '2 in 5 Retirees Support Their Families Financially', Apr. 2013, www.prudential.co.uk; 'Grandparents Will Pay More to Fund Grandchildren's University Education, Says New Study', *UCU News*, 9 Oct. 2013, www.ucu.org.uk

[93] Anne Foner, 'Age Integration or Age Conflict as Society Ages?', *The Gerontologist*, 40, 3, 2000, pp. 272–276.

[94] Easterlin *et al.*, 'Economic Status', p. 68.

[95] Francoise Cribier, 'Changes in Life Course and Retirement in Recent Years: The Example of Two Cohorts of Parisians', in Johnson *et al.*, *Workers versus Pensioners*, ch. 10; Light, *Baby Boomers*.

[96] Maria Evandrou, 'Introduction', in Evandrou, *Baby Boomers*, pp. 9–10; Burnett, *Generations*, chs. 5 and 6.

own favour. In short, it would be very difficult to give weightings to all of these experiential factors, in order to decide which birth cohorts were 'winners' and which were 'losers'.

Corrective justice

Most intergenerational equity narratives founder on the question of agency: how far has one generation been able to act as collective agents of change? Interestingly, Samuel Preston's early discussion did not blame any one generation: instead, he identified the causal factors as rising extra-marital births and family break-up (contributing, he claimed, about 45 per cent of the increase in child poverty between 1970 and 1982), stagnating average real incomes for young people (caused by the difficulty of absorbing the baby boomers into the labour force and by slow economic growth), cuts in Aid to Families with Dependent Children and increases in Social Security for retirees (a result of universal self-interest: the adult population wanted good benefits when old, whereas children lacked that constituency of support). Preston's solutions therefore included a universal child allowance scheme and a better education system.[97]

However, other accounts strongly imply that one selfish 'welfare generation' has acted in its own interests, although (as mentioned above) detailed empirical evidence from the policy process is not exactly forthcoming. Accordingly, it is often suggested that remedial action should be taken via a process of confiscation from 'over-resourced' retirees. Exactly how this would be done is rarely made explicit. New, punitive inheritance taxes are not suggested. One early proposal from the Intergenerational Foundation was that older people with excess housing space should take in a young lodger who was experiencing difficulty in finding rented accommodation – a suggestion that aroused some derision. The sound and fury of outrage has mostly been over those fiscal concessions to older people – such as free or subsidised public transport, or the winter fuel allowance – which cost relatively little (for example, the winter fuel allowance constitutes less than 2 per cent of all benefit expenditure to pensioners).

Four serious problems immediately suggest themselves. First, as was shown in Chapter 1, most retired households in the UK are income-poor, living on average at about half the living standard of non-retired households, and there is a marked gap between the top quintile and the rest. In addition, the table of pensioner household original incomes

---

[97] Alan Atkisson, 'Equity Between Generations: An Interview with Sam Preston', *Caring for Families*, Spring 1989, www.context.org

cited in Chapter 1 showed clearly that there is very high reliance on cash benefits on the part of the poorest 60 per cent of retired households, ranging from 79 per cent of gross income for the bottom quintile, to 74 per cent for the second-bottom and 67 per cent for the middle; by contrast, the top quintile received only 26 per cent of its gross income from cash benefits.[98] It is difficult to see how there is much scope for redistribution to younger households, other than from the richest 10 per cent or 20 per cent of retired households – and such a step would be politically unacceptable.

Second, any confiscation would hit hardest at those who had the self-restraint and foresight to save for their old age. It would be the classic 'penalty on thrift' – a major problem with all means-tested state pension schemes. Third, on a philosophical level there is the interesting question of whether such corrective justice really requires collective human agency to be demonstrated (just as, in law, intent is everything): arguably, a generation can only be 'punished' for monopolising a disproportionate share of public resources if it has acted deliberately and concertedly. If, on the other hand, unequal generational outcomes have been caused by structural economic factors over which human beings have had relatively little control then remedial action would be morally unjustified.

Finally, even if collective human agency could be proved, the problem is that corrective justice could only be applied at the very end of a lifecourse, and by then it would be too late. Can one really envisage an 80-year-old baby boomer having his or her accumulated savings confiscated by the state on the grounds that he or she was a member of a generation that had been 'over-resourced' in the past? Apart from anything else, this would only deny a younger generation its rightful inheritance. It would be spectacularly counter-productive.

A view from history

As noted above, intergenerational equity concerns imply either that one particular generation has determined policy outcomes to its own advantage or that over time social policy has become too biased in favour of the retired – either by design (via a 'welfare generation') or by accident. The precise causal mechanisms are generally left unexplored, and therefore it is worth quickly gazing backwards at the history of social policy in the UK to test the evidence.

Intergenerational equity concerns can be detected, but they were not exactly abundant and rarely articulated explicitly. Age divisions did figure

---

[98] Office for National Statistics, *The Effects of Taxes and Benefits, 2012/13* (2014), p. 15.

in nineteenth-century social discourses, which were permeated by class, gender and age distancing.[99] For example, the first modern advocate of contributory state old age pensions, Canon William Blackley, frequently displayed strong hostility towards the fearsome, vibrant masculinity of the improvident young male who would not save for old age – 'the really ignorant, sensual, unenlightened *boys* of our nation', with 'their waste, their sensuality, their ignorance and their selfishness'.[100] Again, the moral economy of the Poor Law was based upon hierarchies of deservingness derived from labour market value: the most deserving (given relatively lenient treatment) were the 'impotent poor' (the aged, the widows and orphans, the mentally and physically handicapped) who had marginal economic utility; the least deserving were young, able-bodied males and lone mothers, who had greatest labour market relevance. This was for rational economic reasons, rather than generational favouritism.

The movement to lift the aged off the Poor Law, via a system of state pensions, was in part directed at making it more deterrent against the able-bodied young male. It was a paradoxical strategy, in which youth and old age were interconnected. Interestingly, the proportion of Poor Law expenditure absorbed by the aged increased over the second half of the nineteenth century, as the conditions for outdoor relief to other categories of claimant were gradually tightened.[101] However, this shift in age allocation was seen as a success.

An interesting example of generational concerns is to be found in the nineteenth-century British friendly societies, which ran contributory sickness benefit schemes for the skilled working class. The age distribution of morbidity meant that older friendly society members always had higher rates of sickness. It was therefore essential for the societies that they recruit a steady supply of new, young members who paid in more than they cost in benefits. Older workers who wished to join a friendly society might be charged higher entrance fees and contributions. Generation-specific societies became increasingly common, especially in rural areas where the pool of members would be smaller.[102] Over the course of the nineteenth century, older friendly society members experienced progressively higher levels of recorded morbidity and therefore sickness benefit claims. The causes of this have been much debated, as has the question of how far it contributed to an alleged insolvency crisis among the

---

[99] For an interesting discussion, see Harry Hendrick, *Images of Youth: Age, Class and the Male Youth Problem, 1880–1920* (1990).
[100] William Lewery Blackley, 'National Insurance: A Cheap, Practical, and Popular Means of Abolishing Poor Rates', *Nineteenth Century*, 4, November 1878, pp. 854, 838.
[101] Macnicol, *Politics of Retirement*, pp. 39–40.
[102] Simon Cordery, *British Friendly Societies, 1750–1914* (2003), pp. 70–71, 128–133.

societies.[103] The net effect was that, by the early twentieth century, older friendly society members were being increasingly subsidised by younger ones. On a cross-sectional view, this appeared to be intergenerationally unjust. However, from a lifecourse perspective, it was part of the implicit intergenerational contract that was to become a feature of the welfare state.

The campaign for state old age pensions raised some intergenerational equity issues. Advocates of contributory, insurance-based schemes, like William Blackley and Joseph Chamberlain, took a very individualist view and argued that citizens should only receive their 'own' savings back in retirement without any intergenerational redistribution at the collective level. By contrast, those who advocated non-contributory, tax-funded schemes (notably, Charles Booth) believed that contributory schemes were inherently impractical, since they would do nothing for those who needed state pensions most in old age (the low-paid, and women).

One of the few explicit considerations of intergenerational equity was Booth's very brief discussion, in *Old Age Pensions and the Aged Poor* (1899), of whether it was right to impose a large funding burden on the young in order to finance a tax-funded, non-contributory universal pension scheme. In a remarkably prescient passage Booth stated:

It has also been objected that the young would pay for the old; but as it is felt that they will in their turn grow old, the form of this objection has been changed and has taken the shape, that those who never reach pension age pay, but receive nothing, however poor they may be. To this the answer is that the burthen of the old falls *now* mainly on the young or middle aged. A pension system readjusts this burthen against the rich and in favour of the poor, but leaves the relation between young and old practically untouched. The taxes which a young man pays to help support the old of his day justify his claim to like consideration if he live to be old, and if he do not live, it is the nature of an insurance – he takes his chance and at least benefits by the knowledge that old age, if it comes, is safeguarded.[104]

Non-contributory, tax-funded state pensions were introduced by the 1908 Old Age Pensions Act at a rate of 5s0d (25p) per week for all aged 70+, subject to a sliding scale income test and certain eligibility conditions. The new pension proved very popular: it redistributed from young and middle-aged to old, from rich to poor and from men to women – in other words, much more than simple generational redistribution. In practice – largely because of the age limit and means-testing – it was

---

[103] Usefully discussed in Bernard Harris, Martin Gorsky, Aravinda Guntupalli and Andrew Hind, 'Sickness Insurance and Welfare Reform in England and Wales, 1870–1914', in Bernard Harris (ed.), *Welfare and Old Age in Europe and North America: The Development of Social Insurance* (2012).

[104] Charles Booth, *Old Age Pensions and the Aged Poor* (1899), p. 63.

selective in coverage: in 1909, 42.1 per cent of the population aged 70+ received old age pensions; by 1920 this had risen to 56.1 per cent, and by 1926 it was 65.5 per cent.[105] On the face of it, the beneficiaries of the 1908 Act were a clear example of a 'welfare generation' enjoying benefits that they had never paid for in prior taxes. However, they played little or no part in bringing the Act about, and the channels of redistribution were much more than age-based.

The period after the 1908 Act was characterised by increasingly militant pensioner activism via the National Conference on Old Age Pensions, which sought universal pensions (with no means-tests) of £1 per week paid from the age of 60. This would have cost over twelve times more than the existing scheme. The National Conference was primarily a product of the increasingly militant labour movement, but its emergence does mark the first appearance of a 'grey power' pressure group in the UK.[106]

What is clear is that, by the second decade of the twentieth century, there was general acceptance of the principle that the working-aged should support the poorest old people. In that sense, an implicit 'welfare contract' had been established, underpinned by a right to retirement. The labour movement continued to press its demand for state pensions at age 65 or even 60, with no means-testing, as a reward for the 'veterans of industry' who had performed a lifetime of service in the labour market or for women who had raised families. Faced with these demands, the Treasury began working on an alternative contributory scheme: the mechanics of contributory insurance could be used to hold down benefits and contain costs. The Treasury's concern was not about intergenerational inequity, but about cost containment. As noted in Chapter 1, a secondary aim was the encouragement of retirement at a time of high unemployment in order to redistribute jobs to younger unemployed men.

The 1925 Widows', Orphans' and Old Age Contributory Pensions Act effected a partial shift to contributory insurance funding, thereby establishing more of a lifecourse redistribution. However, the need to make the Act politically attractive meant that initially it had a large 'pay-as-you-go' funding element (so that it could mature quickly). It therefore was generationally redistributive at the outset, full funding only being achieved after some eighty years of operation. As has been shown, those concerned with intergenerational inequity often argue that contributory

---

[105] Helen Fisher Hohman, *The Development of Social Insurance and Minimum Wage Legislation in Great Britain* (1933), p. 52.

[106] Andrew Blaikie, 'The Emerging Political Power of the Elderly in Britain 1908–1948', *Ageing and Society*, 10, 1, March 1990, pp. 22–23.

insurance funding is a kind of unsustainable Ponzi scheme, involving an unfair redistribution from working-age citizens to current pensioners (particularly problematic if a population is ageing). However, the Conservative government of 1924–1929 believed that contributory insurance would gradually shift the funding onto a basis more intergenerationally fair than tax funding (and much less redistributive from rich to poor). During the passage of the Act, Winston Churchill (Chancellor of the Exchequer) warned that the number claiming pensions would double in thirty years. The country 'would have to support them with an active population little larger than it is today'. Without the automatic safeguards of contributory insurance funding, there would be 'an overburdened Treasury, fettered Parliaments, and a dependent people . . . Are we justified in laying these charges upon posterity?'[107]

The view that social policy became increasingly biased towards retirees is not borne out by the events of the fifteen years after the 1925 Act. There was much discussion of attaching a retirement condition to receipt of the state pension, as a means of redistributing jobs to the young unemployed[108] – a proposal that encouraged the view that older workers were industrially obsolescent. In some quarters, they were almost blamed for the recession, since they tended to be concentrated in the economically depressed areas of heavy industry.[109] Again, by the mid-1930s the long decline in the birth rate was giving rise to concerns over the likely consequences of an ageing population: a decreasing supply of new workers, higher taxes to pay for pensions and other services to older people, a rising fiscal burden on those of working age, democracy paralysed by an increasingly sclerotic political process and a loss of economic 'enterprise'.[110] In the 1930s, the majority of old people suffered poor health care provision: eligibility for National Health Insurance ceased at age 65 and geriatric medicine was relatively undeveloped.

The late 1930s was a time of renewed pensioner activism with the formation of the very militant National Federation of Old Age Pensions Associations and the National Spinsters' Pensions Association. There was strong political pressure for a large rise in the basic state pension, culminating in the summer of 1939. (This episode, though ignored by most social policy historians, was perceptively commented on by W. G. Runciman, in his classic *Relative Deprivation and Social Justice* (1966)).[111]

[107] House of Commons Debates, 5s, 183, 28 April 1925, Cols.77–79.
[108] Ernest Bevin, *My Plan for 2,000,000 Workless* (1933); Political and Economic Planning, *The Exit from Industry* (1935).
[109] Macnicol, *Politics of Retirement*, p. 255.
[110] Richard and Kathleen Titmuss, *Parents Revolt* (1942).
[111] W. G. Runciman, *Relative Deprivation and Social Justice* (1972), pp. 80–81.

The only concessions made were a lowering of the women's pension age to 60 and supplementary allowances, paid by the Assistance Board, introduced for those pensioners who could prove themselves in need.

These policy responses (introduced by the 1940 Old Age and Widows' Pensions Act) represented a grudging concession to the needs of old people. However, social conditions in wartime were most hazardous for them (bombing, evacuation, rationing, hospital closures, the blackout, chaotic public transport and so on).[112] As Richard Titmuss observed, subconscious human capital considerations meant that in wartime the needs of the young took priority over those of the old.[113] Wars are highly gendered, but they are also generational in impact.

The Beveridge Report of 1942 is often viewed as a progressive and liberal public document. In fact, retired people were accorded a very low priority in the Report, which was littered with linguistic hostility towards old people, influenced by Beveridge's concerns about the fiscal effects of a future ageing population. Although the wartime coalition government set the new pension at more generous levels, roughly one-quarter of British pensioners in the early 1950s had to have their state pensions supplemented by means-tested National Assistance.

It is very difficult to arrive at a simplistic 'gain' or 'loss' verdict regarding the relative status of old people in the postwar welfare state. They gained enormously from the founding of the National Health Service (for the first time, geriatric medicine developed significantly). There was also a large volume of research conducted into retirement, age discrimination and the problems of older workers generally. However, as already noted, concerns over the increasing 'burden' of an ageing population featured prominently in the reports of the Royal Commission on Population (1949) and the Phillips Committee (1954). By the mid-1960s, unemployment was beginning to rise, and from the late 1970s onwards official policy (supported by a tripartite partnership of governments, employers and trades unionists) encouraged early retirement as a means of redistributing available jobs to the younger unemployed. This was assisted by a number of policies, notably the Job Release Scheme of 1977–1988 – rightly described as 'the most explicit policy of generational substitution yet seen on the statute book'[114] – under which older workers were permitted to retire early, on condition that their jobs were filled by unemployed

---

[112] Well discussed in Robin Means and Randall Smith, *The Development of Welfare Services for Elderly People* (1985), chs. 1, 2 and 3.

[113] R. M. Titmuss, *Problems of Social Policy* (1950), pp. 334, 500, 559.

[114] Philip Taylor and Alan Walker, 'Intergenerational Relations in the Labour Market: The Attitudes of Employers and Older Workers', in Walker, *New Generational Contract*, p. 162.

school leavers. In addition, as outlined earlier in this book, in the 1980s there were governmental moves to reduce old age protection – most notably, via the falling relative value of the state pension. Social and economic policies of the late 1970s and 1980s were therefore biased *against* older people. Indeed, by the 1990s there was growing concern that older workers were suffering high levels of age discrimination in employment – a somewhat erroneous explanation for the economic restructuring that had deindustrialised older men.

Conclusion

The analysis of society by age and generation can be enormously useful and intergenerational equity certainly raises some legitimate issues with regard to justice between generations – the most important of which, for the present and the future, is climate change. However, there are big problems in any generational accounting exercise – most notably, the diversity that exists within any one notional generation, deciding what policies and social experiences should be included, and the fact that an accurate assessment can only be made at the end of a completed life – at which point remedial action is too late. The recently revived concerns over intergenerational inequity first articulated in the 1980s, and blaming an entirely different 'welfare generation', have been used to justify a neoliberal political strategy of raising state pension ages, forcing people to work later in life and expanding labour supply. The strong implication (never fully spelled out) is that the baby boomers have conspiratorially manipulated economic and social policies in their own favour and have ended up as unfairly over-resourced. This simplistic narrative is essentially a prelude to a more individualist view of welfare entitlement, in which the risk-pooling, solidaristic principles underpinning existing welfare states will be eroded. Put under detailed forensic scrutiny, however, the arguments alleging generational misallocation of resources are revealed as unconvincing and ahistorical.

7   Towards age equality?

To what extent are people discriminated against on grounds of age? This is a question that has been central to the discipline of gerontology ever since its first, hesitant beginnings over 100 years ago. Gerontologists have long argued that older people tend to be devalued in advanced industrial societies, for reasons that may be psychological, social, cultural or economic. They maintain that ageism is as virulent, corrosive and socially damaging as racism or sexism – and all the more so because it manifests itself in ways that are subtle or disguised. Anti-ageism has thus been an integral part of the growth of a rights-based, anti-discrimination culture in western societies since the 1960s, which in turn is associated with the emergence of new social movements and a distinct kind of identity politics. In the UK, age discrimination in employment was broadly made illegal under the 2006 Employment Equality (Age) Regulations and mandatory retirement has been effectively abolished (unless 'objectively justified'). Politically, the culmination of this growing interest to date has perhaps been the assigning of the year 2012 as the European Union 'Year of Active Ageing and Solidarity Between Generations'. It would seem that the rights of older people are finally being recognised.

Combating ageism raises the issue that is central to this book: the tension between, on the one hand, the ideal of an 'ageless' society, in which age would not be used as a basis for social judgements, and, on the other, the need to defend old age as a specially protected stage of life. An integral part of the social democratic compromise with neoliberalism – best represented by New Labour when in government between 1997 and 2010 – has been the strategy of removing the 'discriminatory' barriers to active labour market participation and redefining economic and labour market problems as cultural, attitudinal and prejudice-based. Anti-ageism has therefore been a legitimating principle behind the labour market activation of older people. It has formed part of a portfolio of justifying arguments – demographic pressures, fiscal constraints, improved health and longevity, social justice – in support of raising state pension ages. Hence legislation against age discrimination in employment was seen by the Turner Commission as an essential part of the strategy of raising state pension ages.[1] More recently, in September 2010 the pensions minister Steve Webb declared that the state pension system had to be made 'sustainable' in the face of increasing longevity, and that where older workers wanted to continue working, 'they don't find themselves pushed out of the workplace or experience age discrimination'.[2]

The new 'equality agenda'

The arrival of a New Labour government in May 1997 led to an overhaul and expansion of the UK's anti-discrimination laws, after the benign neglect shown by Conservative governments between 1979 and 1997. Most notably, following the 2006 Equality Act there was established a new Equality and Human Rights Commission (EHRC) to supersede previous bodies – the Equal Opportunities Commission, the Commission for Racial Equality and the Disability Rights Commission. The EHRC enforces equality legislation on age, disability, gender, ethnicity, religion or belief, sexual orientation and transgender status, and encourages compliance with the 1998 Human Rights Act. The UK's 2010 Equality Act has brought together nine existing pieces of anti-discrimination legislation and identifies the protected characteristics of age, gender, race/ethnicity, religion and belief, sexual orientation, marriage and civil partnership, pregnancy and maternity, and gender reassignment. With regard to age, both direct and indirect discrimination are covered, and age discrimination in the distribution of goods, facilities and services is outlawed for all aged 18+ in public and private sectors. It is an ambitious piece of legislation.

This new 'equality strategy' was central to New Labour's overall economic and social policy agenda, and at times some very grandiose – if not puzzling – claims were made for it, such as the promise of 'ending inequalities for older people'.[3] The implication of this would seem to be that all inequalities in old age – of income, savings, health status, disability, housing, gender, ethnicity and so on – would abruptly be ended. The same strategy has been continued – albeit in muted form, and with less than total enthusiasm – by the Conservative/LibDem coalition. There were rumours that the EHRC would be abolished after the 2010 general election, but it narrowly survived – for the time being. A possible pointer

[1] Pensions Commission, *First Report*, p. 42.
[2] Quoted in Inman, 'Retirements to Spike'.
[3] Office of the Deputy Prime Minister. Social Exclusion Unit, *A Sure Start to Later Life: Ending Inequalities for Older People. A Social Exclusion Unit Final Report* (2006).

to the future was the Conservatives' announcement in October 2014 that a future Conservative government would seek to opt out of rulings by the European Court of Human Rights.[4] It is certainly the case that a legalistic anti-discrimination strategy is not popular in the UK Conservative Party, compared with the laissez-faire view that the market should be left free to distribute rewards on the basis of merit and performance. Nevertheless, all three main political parties in the UK remain committed to the pursuit of 'social justice' – a rather nebulous concept that can mean many things.

The context for all of this has been labour market activation. New Labour's 'rights' agenda (which balanced the 'responsibility' to get a job) comprised policies such as the National Minimum Wage, help with job search via 'personal advisers' (under the New Deals), extended child care, employment credits and legislation against employment discrimination. The aim was to remove the 'discriminatory barriers' that face workless people, and this goal was presented in the beguiling language of 'empowerment' (drawing inspiration from both the social model of disability and anti-ageism): as the DWP put it, 'We have introduced the National Minimum Wage and family-friendly employment legislation, and have strengthened protection against all forms of discrimination.'[5] However, this apparent enhancement of rights was balanced by the 'responsibility' to get a job, at any wage and of any quality, enforced by cutbacks in benefits and greater conditionality. This was the ideological and policy context in which age discrimination in employment was problematised.

Essentially, while in government New Labour appropriated the emancipatory, liberationist arguments of the post-1960s civil rights movements (with regard to race/ethnicity, gender, disability, sexual preference and age), and turned them into a justification for expanding labour supply. By this process, 'active ageing' became 'labour market activation'. That this strategy had a strong underlying economic aim is perhaps revealed by the fact that it received no clear philosophical or political justification. The goal of equal treatment was seen as axiomatically good, on purely *a priori* grounds. Certainly, equal treatment has become a central foundational principle underpinning much post-Rawlsian liberal political theory. It may also be that this would be the strategy that a majority of the population would choose from behind a veil of ignorance. On the other hand, conservatives might take the Nozickian position that the only rights that exist are those over one's labour and property; and many on

---

[4] Owen Bowcott, 'Conservatives Pledge Powers to Ignore European Court of Human Rights Rulings', *Guardian*, 3 Oct. 2014, www.theguardian.com

[5] DWP, *A New Deal*, p. 15.

the left would argue that enhancing basic equality of opportunity must be accompanied by a reduction of inequalities of outcome to an 'acceptable' level via a redistribution of income. These and other issues will be explored later in this chapter.

Varieties of ageism

Ageism and age discrimination are complex and challenging concepts that have engendered much debate,[6] but heuristically it is useful to make a threefold distinction.

(a) *Ageism in social relations and attitudes* refers to those beliefs, actions and vocabularies that serve to accord people a diminished social status solely or mainly by reference to their age. To pass judgement on individuals, and thereby define their social worth, on the basis of a morally irrelevant characteristic such as age is held to be an affront to natural justice. Ageism can of course apply at any age, although it is generally held to be most objectionable when directed at older people. It operates at different levels – linguistic, attitudinal, interpersonal, cultural, economic, institutional – and may be so finely woven into prevailing assumptions, popular consciousness and the culture of organisations (as 'institutional ageism') that it is extremely difficult to 'prove' and therefore eradicate.[7] Ageism is manifest in everyday linguistic expression, cognitive processes, discourses, jokes, visual imagery, advertising, fashion, patterns of thinking, popular culture and so on. It can be subtle and disguised – for example, the 'compassionate ageism' (patronising praise) that infantilises older people. As one wide-ranging survey has commented, ageism 'can take many forms, from bureaucratic regulation to physical aggression. It may be written, verbal or expressed through subtle body language or gesture. It may be unambiguous or complex. It may be directed at an individual or at older people collectively. It may be articulated by one individual or expressed collectively by an organisation.'[8]

Ageism is often presented as a relatively new phenomenon, dating from Robert Butler's celebrated article of 1969,[9] and therefore a product of the modern civil rights movement. This may be true of the

---

[6] For examples, see Bill Bytheway, *Ageism* (1995); Todd Nelson (ed.), *Ageism: Stereotyping and Prejudice Against Older Persons* (2002); Macnicol, *Age Discrimination*; Malcolm Sargeant (ed.), *Age Discrimination and Diversity* (2011). The most famous work, Erdman Palmore, *Ageism: Negative and Positive* (1990) is very one-dimensional in its analysis.

[7] Tessa Harding, *Rights at Risk: Older People and Human Rights* (2005).

[8] Bill Bytheway, Richard Ward, Caroline Holland and Sheila Peace, *Too Old: Older People's Accounts of Discrimination, Exclusion and Rejection* (2007), p. 6.

[9] Robert N. Butler, 'Age-Ism: Another Form of Bigotry', *The Gerontologist*, 9, 4, 1, Winter 1969, pp. 243–246.

term, but not of the broad idea. Psychologists have long researched 'prejudice' against older people: for example, one American study published in 1953 explored the negative attitudes displayed by young people towards the old, commenting that 'In our culture, with its emphasis on youth and speed, old people are expected to play a decreasingly active role in our social and industrial life. These cultural expectations encourage the formation of misconceptions and stereotypes about old age.'[10] We may therefore merely be attaching a new name to a very old problem.

(b) *Age discrimination in employment* basically involves the use of crude age-based judgements in personnel decisions relating to hiring, firing, remuneration, promotion, demotion, mandatory retirement and so on. This is held to be inherently ageist because age is by itself not an accurate indicator of productivity. A basic truism in gerontology is that heterogeneity in health status and cognitive ability increases as cohorts age, rendering the use of such age proxies morally dubious and economically dysfunctional. It is argued that employers should move towards more enlightened 'age management' personnel policies that would bring the best out of each individual employee, regardless of their age. Most notably, mandatory retirement should be replaced by 'flexible' or 'phased' retirement, whereby older workers could gradually taper off their working activity (perhaps supplemented by an occupational pension). Arguably, ageism more affects women, whom society 'allows' to age less gracefully than men; by contrast, age discrimination appears more to affect older men, since their employment rates have historically fallen.

Age discrimination in employment has a long history, having been the subject of debate for decades. The main point at issue has always been whether the labour market problems of older workers are caused primarily by discrimination per se, or by economic restructuring (with discrimination as a minor contributory cause).[11] Organisations like the U.S. Department of Labor and the International Labour Office researched the problems of older workers in the 1930s, including the discrimination they appeared to face. There was also a lively debate in the UK in the 1950s, with government policy directed at raising the employment rates of older people and investigating the possible discriminatory attitudes of employers. As one official publication put it, 'Workers are wanted almost everywhere and this demand seems certain to increase . . . the

---

[10] Jacob Tuckman and Irving Lorge, 'Attitudes Toward Old People', *Journal of Social Psychology*, 37, May 1953, p. 249.
[11] Macnicol, *Age Discrimination*, pp. 36–37.

encouragement of the employment of the elderly is a pressing necessity; we cannot afford that the willing and able worker should stand idle.'[12]

It is important to note that, at certain points in recent history, economic inactivity among older people has *not* been regarded as a problem and allegations of discrimination have been muted. Over the last eighty years there have been pronounced swings in official policy towards older workers between retention and early exit, depending upon the state of the economy. In times of recession and restructuring, such as the 1930s and 1970s/80s, the emphasis has been on the encouragement of early exit. By contrast, in times of stable economic growth, such as the 1950s/60s and 1992–2008, the emphasis has been on retention. It is significant that interest in age discrimination reappeared in the UK and across Europe just at that point in the 1990s when the employment rates of older workers started to rise and, on the face of it, the problem of age discrimination therefore appeared to be diminishing. If the current recovery from recession falters, there may be a swing back to early exit policies and less discussion of age discrimination, with young people being seen as more deserving of the available jobs. It is a process that the American legal academic Howard Eglit in 1974 called 'the shifting of the problem of insufficient jobs from one age group to another'.[13]

(c) *Age discrimination in the distribution of goods and services* is the third and most recent aspect of ageism. It has long been discussed by campaigners, but is only now being addressed in the UK by the 2010 Equality Act. Perhaps the most egregious examples are to be found in health and social care – particularly the informal, institutional ageism that permeates medical cultures and is so difficult to eradicate by official directive. The evidence on ageism in health care tends to be anecdotal, but is cumulatively powerful.[14] In addition, older people have long faced many everyday, practical obstacles in obtaining travel or motor insurance, credit or other goods and services.[15] They can find insurance premiums suddenly rising when they reach the age of 65, 70 or 75, regardless of their individual claim record or risk profile.

---

[12] Ministry of Labour and National Service, *Employment of Older Men and Women* (1952), pp. 2, 4.

[13] Quoted in Timothy S. Kaye, 'Divided by a Common Language: Why the British Adoption of the American Anti-Discrimination Model Did Not Lead to an Identical Approach to Age Discrimination Law', *Journal of International Aging, Law and Policy*, 4, 2009, p. 84.

[14] There has been a spate of convincing press reports on this problem in the UK in recent years.

[15] Age Concern and Help the Aged, *Insurance and Age: Exploring Behaviour, Attitudes and Discrimination* (2007); Age Concern, *Age of Equality? Outlawing Age Discrimination Beyond the Workplace* (2007).

There are, of course, major problems in trying to create age-neutral access to goods and services. For example, much age-based targeting in health care (such as routine screening) can be said to be reasonable, given the incidence of morbidity by age. Its justification is an impersonal cost–benefit analysis. Restrictions on treatment to older people may have a rational, clinical basis (such as likely post-operative outcomes, or the existence of comorbidities) rather than an irrational, prejudicial one. It would be challenging, to say the least, to infer ageism from a comparison between health resource input and health outcomes by age, controlling for all the variables such as class, gender, ethnic background, lifestyle, individual genetic predisposition and locality. How would one decide what should be the 'correct' resource allocation by age, or the 'correct' age of death? Again, travel and motor insurance premiums tend to reflect average age-based risk, with younger drivers also paying high premiums. Concessions to older people (such as free public transport) have an adverse impact on younger age groups, and could therefore be held to be indirectly discriminatory. These examples illustrate the key question in all discussions of the rights and wrongs of ageism: exactly when is the use of an age proxy reasonable, and when is it unreasonable?

The origins of ageism

Where does ageism originate? A number of possible sources have been suggested, of which three principal ones should be considered. First, it is possible that there are psychological, sociobiological or human capital origins, triggered by our deeply internalised fears of our own ageing, decrepitude and death, which we transfer onto others. In a famous passage, Robert Butler appeared to support this interpretation: 'Age-ism reflects a deep seated uneasiness on the part of the young and middle-aged – a personal revulsion to and distaste for growing old, disease and disability; and fear of powerlessness, "uselessness", and death.'[16]

A sociobiological perspective would lead to the conclusion that prevailing images of beauty are biased towards the young not because of ageism per se, but because in all societies youth is associated with energy, strength, resilience, fertility and other qualities necessary for the survival of humanity. Of course, the problem here is that, if we are psychologically hard-wired in this way, we can no more eliminate ageism than we can eliminate bodily decline and death. A recent survey of public perceptions of ageism in Europe, very much from a psychological perspective, states at the outset that 'Our framework for investigating discrimination

---

[16] Butler, 'Age-Ism', p. 243.

assumes that it is not necessarily deliberate and does not always result from malign intentions or motives. It can be a product simply of the way people perceive and categorise one another.' And a few pages later this is reinforced: age is 'a primary dimension of categorisation . . . and is also an important social marker, determining social roles, status, power and responsibility to people of different ages'.[17] If age has become a categorisation over the course of human history, then both it and the resultant ageism are not likely to be easily eradicated.

A second set of explanations might be cultural, based upon an alleged marginalisation of older people since preindustrial times – sometimes controversially expressed as the 'veneration to degradation' thesis.[18] The problem here is that social historians cannot agree on whether the status transition of old age, from the preindustrial to the postmodern, has been negative or positive. For example, in the preindustrial past there were plenty of examples of gerontocide, parricide and institutionalised hostility towards tribal elders. How do we compare these to the animosity currently being shown to older people in today's intergenerational equity debate? As has been shown in Chapter 6, age conflicts are as old as human history itself.

Third, one could argue that economic explanations hold the key, and that the spread of male retirement over the past 130 years has been accompanied by a more negative perception of the economic value of older people. If only one in eight UK males aged 65+ is now economically active (in the conventional sense), then the status of that group will fall in a social context in which citizenship is defined by labour market value. Despite being materially better off than previous generations of old people, today's retirees are, it would be argued, spiritually devalued. As Thomas Cole has observed:

We must acknowledge that our great progress in the material and physical conditions of life has been achieved at a high spiritual and ethical price. Social Security has not enhanced ontological security or dignity in old age. The elderly continue to occupy an inferior status in the moral community – marginalised by an economy and culture committed to the scientific management of growth without limit.[19]

The central irony is that, on a lifecourse perspective, age discrimination is self-inflicted. We are in effect discriminating against our future selves.

---

[17] Dominic Abrams, Pascale Sophieke Russell, Christin Melanie Vauclair and Hannah Swift, *Ageism in Europe: Findings from the European Social Survey* (2011), pp. 6, 14. See also, Age UK, *A Snapshot of Ageism in the UK and Across Europe* (2011).

[18] Macnicol, *Politics of Retirement*, pp. 13–14.   [19] Cole, *The Journey*, p. 237.

Why the revival?

If there is a long tradition of psychologists, sociologists, historians and anthropologists researching age-based 'prejudice', age stratifications and age conflicts, why then has age discrimination experienced a resurgence of interest in the last twenty years?

The answer is that combating it has been inextricably linked to all the wider economic concerns and associated strategies explored in this book. The most obvious causal factor has been the fall in the economic activity rates of older men (aged 50+) that has occurred in all advanced industrial societies, with particular intensity since the early 1970s (discussed in Chapter 5). The average age of permanent labour market exit has risen since the early 1990s and the current recession has had surprisingly little impact on older people's employment. However, there is still apprehension over a possible long-run trend to labour market withdrawal at progressively lower ages. This would be exacerbated by changes in the age structure of the population: Government Actuary projections in 2002 suggested that by 2022 there will be 1,000,000 fewer working-age people under 50 and 3,000,000 more aged 50+.[20]

There are also concerns over the ageing of the UK population after the second decade of this century (discussed in Chapter 4, and shown to be exaggerated). The argument is that action against age discrimination is needed in order to extend working lives, maximise human capital, stimulate economic growth and defuse the demographic timebomb. The UK government's position has always been that early retirement represents a significant amount of lost GDP: *Winning the Generation Game* (2000) calculated this as £16billion per annum, plus between £3billion and £5billion in additional benefit expenditure.[21] However, as noted in Chapter 4, a recent report (commissioned by the DWP and therefore wholly and uncritically supportive of raising state pension ages) put the proportionate loss of GDP caused by early retirement at a mere 1 per cent, since it affected only 1.5 per cent of the working-age population.[22] It would seem, therefore, that economic concerns over the cost of early retirement have been inflated.

A third concern (least often mentioned) has been the human tragedy of older jobless men who may never work again – it is a gendered problem – and who are concentrated in areas of severe deindustrialisation where suitable replacement jobs are scarce. In the UK, 45 per cent of people aged 50–64 who are unemployed have been unemployed for over a year.

---

[20] Whiting, 'Labour Market Participation', p. 287.
[21] Cabinet Office, *Winning the Generation Game*, p. 30.
[22] Barrell *et al.*, *Macroeconomic Impact*, pp. 2, 17.

Of those claiming disability or long-term sickness benefits, 59 per cent are aged 45–64. As has been shown, those who permanently leave work earliest are the least skilled, lowest-paid manual workers with little or no occupational pension provision. They represent a 'forgotten army' of impoverished, older unemployed.

The final reason is the theme of this book: raising the employment rates of older people has been part of a broader macro-economic strategy, which particularly operated between the early 1990s and 2008, of achieving non-inflationary economic growth by expanding labour supply and driving down wages. As one UK government publication revealingly declared, 'Increasing the number of people effectively competing for jobs actually *increases* the number of jobs in the economy... More people competing for jobs means that people are less keen to demand wage increases.'[23] Combating age discrimination in employment has therefore been integral to the overall strategy of labour market activation and the raising of state pension ages. Activation has driven the revival of interest in age discrimination in employment, which in turn has dragged the other two aspects of ageism into policy prominence.

Interpretative problems

Ageism is arguably more complex and nuanced than other forms of discrimination. Considerable debate has raged over its inherent dilemmas and contradictions, only a few of which will be considered here. An immediate difficulty is whether ageism is like sexism or racism,[24] and therefore whether it can be successfully combated by equal opportunities legislation. Race and sex are often said to be immutable or unchanging characteristics, whereas age is a relative characteristic: it is arguably much more difficult to define victim and perpetrator in the case of the latter than the former. This is a particular problem if age discrimination laws apply at any age, since all citizens will be in the protected group. Again, age discrimination in employment is often viewed as essentially irrational and prejudice-driven, perhaps stemming from employers' deep-seated fears of their own ageing, decrepitude and death, or the fact that they suffer from 'structural lag' in holding erroneous views about older workers' negative characteristics (absenteeism, slowness, skills deficiencies, unfamiliarity with new technology and so on). However, many apparently ageist personnel policies may have a rational basis, such as the higher salary costs of older employees or the fewer potential years of

---

[23] Cabinet Office, *Winning the Generation Game*, p. 39.
[24] Erdman B. Palmore and Kenneth Manton, 'Ageism Compared to Racism and Sexism', *Journal of Gerontology*, 28, 3, 1973, pp. 363–369.

work that they can offer a firm.[25] The use of age proxies in personnel decisions may also be cheaper, more convenient and less controversial than individual performance appraisal, just as mandatory retirement at a certain age treats every employee similarly, via a kind of rough justice (although this can be unfair on an individual level).[26]

A difficult problem is that there is a balance of positive and negative discriminations across the lifecourse, and at any point in the lifecourse. Much depends upon whether one takes a 'synchronic', instantaneous perspective or a 'diachronic', lifespan one.[27] Health care allocation is a good example. There are many justified allegations that old people suffer negative discrimination in health care, as in the recent debate in the UK about the rationing of early-stage Alzheimer's drugs like Aricept. However, it must also be recognised that, over the past fifty years, the proportion of health care spent on old people has steadily risen in all western societies. Illness management regimes (notably, through pharmaceuticals) have been so successful at lowering mortality and controlling morbidity in the young and middle-aged that all medicine is increasingly becoming geriatric medicine. It is possible to argue, therefore, that old people enjoy substantial *positive* discrimination in health and social care resource allocation.

Finally, there is no doubt that certain age restrictions are widely supported and approved – for example, concessions to older people (such as free or subsidised public transport), laws that protect the young, age-based school curricula, mandatory retirement ages for occupations where public safety may be at risk and so on. Essentially, a major conceptual difficulty in analysing age discrimination is deciding exactly at what point our strongly internalised and widely accepted notions of 'age-appropriate' behaviours (for example, in choosing friends and partners) become discriminatory. Certain age divisions and age-targeted policies are considered reasonable, and therefore widely accepted.

Dilemmas of discrimination

At this stage, it is worth briefly considering the dualistic and potentially contradictory meanings of discrimination. This may appear to be a slight digression, but it is necessary because the analysis of ageism involves

---

[25] Martin Lyon Levine, *Age Discrimination and the Mandatory Retirement Controversy* (1988), ch. 19.

[26] Erdman B. Palmore, 'Compulsory Versus Flexible Retirement: Issues and Facts', *The Gerontologist*, 12, 4, Winter 1972, pp. 343–348.

[27] Norman Daniels, 'Justice and Transfers Between Generations', in Paul Johnson, Christoph Conrad and David Thomson (eds.), *Workers Versus Pensioners: Intergenerational Justice in an Ageing World* (1989).

examining in microcosm some of the problems inherent in the broader concept of discrimination.

Of course, hair-splitting debates on the nature of human rights can appear very much a privileged, Eurocentric luxury. In many Third World societies, the taken-for-granted rights enjoyed in the developed world are absent. Establishing a basic minimum of human rights is a desperate necessity. As defined by indicators such as the United Nations Human Development Index, such rights would include access to clean drinking water, basic shelter, a minimum subsistence diet, a target life expectancy at birth, political participation, the right to free speech, a minimum number of years of schooling, high adult literacy rates, freedom from torture and slavery and so on.[28] Nevertheless, it is the rights of older people in developed societies that are under consideration here, in the context of the debate over the contentious nature of human rights and social justice that has grown in the past century, and particularly since the first publication of John Rawls's *A Theory of Justice* in 1971.

It is a basic principle of any modern, liberal democratic society that its citizens should not suffer harmful discrimination on the arbitrary and morally irrelevant grounds of race/ethnicity, gender, age, disability, religion or sexual orientation. Equality of citizenship requires that the state should create what several moral philosophers have termed an 'egalitarian plateau' for all.[29] Discrimination is viewed as a violation of the principle of equality of opportunity and selection by merit, and a denial of the intrinsic worth or 'personhood' of each individual. In the celebrated words of the United Nations *Universal Declaration of Human Rights*, 'All human beings are born free and equal in dignity and rights. They are endowed with reason and conscience and should act towards one another in a spirit of brotherhood.'[30] Another verdict is that 'The antidiscrimination project represents a claim of enormous moral power: the demand that society recognize the human worth of all its members, that no person arbitrarily be despised or devalued.'[31] Much progress has undoubtedly been made. Overt discrimination was quite legal in the UK in the 1950s and 1960s. Landlords could display public notices saying 'flat to let – no Irish, no coloureds', yet such blatant discrimination went unpunished by law. There is certainly some way to go – for example, recent years have seen increases in random racist attacks and hate crimes

---

[28] United Nations Development Programme, *Human Development Index* (2014), hdr.undp.org
[29] Kymlicka, *Contemporary Political Philosophy*, pp. 3–4.
[30] Article 1, *The Universal Declaration of Human Rights* (1948), www.un.org./en/docuuments/udhr
[31] Andrew Koppelman, *Antidiscrimination Law and Social Equality* (1996), p. 10.

against disabled people – but the social landscape of the UK has been transformed over the last fifty years.

All discrimination involves the application of assumed group characteristics to an individual, regardless of that individual's actual personal characteristics. Group generalisations are of course a useful cognitive tool. They are a necessary way of making sense of the world and may have a rough heuristic accuracy, but they overlook the diversity and difference that exist at an individual level. (Much of the literature on ageism condemns the use of ageist 'stereotypes' but fails to distinguish between these and 'generalisations'.) This is the basis for many objections to anti-discrimination legislation by market liberals: they argue that society is composed of individuals, each of whom possesses a unique set of characteristics. Assumed group characteristics are therefore erroneous and possibly mischievous.[32] Clearly, much depends upon the accuracy of the generalisation or proxy used.

Legislative action against employment discrimination is always built upon the contradictory foundations of social justice and economic efficiency. Political theorists prefer to consider the former; however, the timing of legislation's appearance is better explained by the latter, as are its functions. On the one hand, selection by merit, without regard to the productivity-irrelevant characteristics of race/ethnicity, gender, age, religion, sexuality or disability status, enhances individual rights, combats the exclusion of disadvantaged groups and contributes to social integration. On the other hand, application of the merit principle is a more efficient (and ruthless) method of employee selection: the best candidate gets the job. Most definitions of employment discrimination therefore maintain that true discrimination occurs when a personnel decision is made on grounds *other than* productivity: 'Discrimination at work involves treating some people less favourably than others on the basis of characteristics that are irrelevant to their ability to do the job in question.'[33] In law, discrimination is 'rational', 'justified' or 'fair' if a personnel decision can be proved to be productivity-related (fulfilling the criterion of 'business necessity', having a 'proportionate' aim or with an 'objective justification'). In such cases, the likelihood of discrimination diminishes considerably and, in legal process, the burden of proof falls on the plaintiff. Anti-discrimination laws thus allow an employer to discriminate *more*, but on the 'rational' grounds of productivity. In the final analysis, such laws may primarily benefit employers by

---

[32] Nicholas Capaldi, 'Affirmative Action: Con', in Albert G. Mosley and Nicholas Capaldi, *Affirmative Action: Social Justice or Unfair Preference?* (1996), pp. 73–74.

[33] Linda Clarke, *Discrimination* (1995), p. 1.

maximizing workforce productivity.[34] Indeed, the pursuit of greater economic efficiency may clash with the enhancement of rights (if, for example, 'efficiency' meant eroding working conditions, employment protection and remuneration).

Disturbingly, some campaigners against ageism appear to be untroubled by this. For example, Erdman Palmore has suggested that a major objection to mandatory retirement is that it is an inefficient way of distinguishing between productive and unproductive workers. It should therefore be replaced by more 'rational' personnel procedures: 'Seniority or tenure rules could be waived, or open competition for promotions regardless of age could be used, or periodic reviews of productivity, etc., could be undertaken to weed out those with diminished abilities.'[35] In Palmore's eyes, less productive workers must be seen as 'weeds' in the labour market garden, and the abolition of mandatory retirement will facilitate their removal. In fact, this would only create new victims of an equally unjust form of discrimination (against those with sub-optimal productivity).

Economic efficiency criteria mean that there is always a powerful business case for anti-discrimination diversity policies: they enlarge the pool of customers and potential markets, enhance a firm's image, improve staff loyalty and acknowledge an increasingly multicultural society based upon cultural heterogeneity.[36] As one UK government publication put it,

Treating staff fairly and recognising individual talents and needs is not just the thing to do, but makes good business sense as well. Employers who recruit from the widest pool of possible applicants are able to choose the very best candidates. This has a positive impact on productivity... Fairness and productivity go hand in hand. Tackling discrimination helps to attract, motivate and retain staff. It helps employers make the best use of skills and experience. It can lead to a more diverse workforce, new ideas, and access to wider markets.[37]

Again, in 2008 the then-Chair of the Equality and Human Rights Commission, Trevor Phillips, said of the proposed new Equality Bill:

Critically this bill must help the private sector do a better job. Statistics prove many businesses that champion diversity have bigger profit margins because they understand their customers better. Sensitive positive action measures can actually help businesses that take diversity seriously. Positive action is not and

---

[34] Lynn Turgeon, *State and Discrimination: The Other Side of the Cold War* (1989), pp. 18–19.

[35] Erdman Palmore, 'Is Age Discrimination Bad?', *The Gerontologist*, 46, 6, 2006, p. 848.

[36] Barbara Bagilhole, *Understanding Equal Opportunities and Diversity* (2009), p. 30.

[37] Department of Trade and Industry, *Age Legislation Fact Sheet No. 1* (2006).

should never be a charter for incompetency. What we want to see is a green light for employers to get the best out of a diverse workforce.[38]

The World Bank has recently constructed a 'Human Opportunity Index' as a more precise definition of equality of opportunity globally: this includes indicators such as clean water, basic education, health services, minimum nutrition and citizenship rights. The Bank has stressed that this is necessary for economic growth and political stability.[39]

There is a case for saying that the merit principle usefully purges personnel decisions of moral judgements: all that matters is a person's ability to do the job. Proponents of the social justice case also argue that, even if anti-discrimination legislation is initially motivated by economic efficiency aims, it can nevertheless change the way people think by making it expensive for them to discriminate. Forcing a change in employment practices can cause language, discourses and patterns of thinking to change in response. As such, they tend to support 'positive' or 'affirmative' action, based upon several justifications.

The first of these is quite straightforward: it is that socio-economic inequalities are so deeply embedded in society that only by treating people *unequally* through positive action can a true level playing field be established. As Judith Squires has argued, 'treating citizens as equals does not entail treating them equally'.[40] Recognising difference means favouring certain groups. In the case of old age, we should acknowledge that it tends to be an especially vulnerable time of life, in terms of income, savings, health status, access to the labour market and so on, and therefore deserving of special treatment.[41]

Second, the 'corrective justice' case maintains that positive action is morally necessary in order to right past wrongs. In the USA, there has been much heated discussion of whether slavery in the past should be used as a justification for affirmative action in favour of African Americans. Inconclusive and somewhat fruitless debates have taken place over issues such as whether or not the slave trade in the long run improved the material conditions of the descendants of its victims (today's African Americans) compared with the descendants of those left behind in Africa (who on average enjoy a lower standard of living), or whether today's

---

[38] Equality and Human Rights Commission, 'Commission Welcomes Outlawing of Age Discrimination', 2008, www.equalityhumanrights.com

[39] World Bank, *How Far Are We from Ensuring Opportunities for All? The Human Opportunity Index*, 2012, www.worldbank.org; World Bank, *Inequality of Opportunity Hampers Development*, 28 June 2012, www.worldbank.org

[40] Judith Squires, 'Equality and Difference', in Dryzek *et al.*, *Oxford Handbook*, p. 478.

[41] Colin Duncan, 'The Dangers and Limitations of Equality Agendas as a Means for Tackling Old-Age Prejudice', *Ageing and Society*, 28, 8, Nov. 2008, pp. 1133–1158.

generation of white people should suffer punishment (via restricted job opportunities) for the misdeeds of earlier generations (the slave traders), and therefore whether corrective justice is warranted. In the case of age, the 'past wrongs' argument can be even more problematic. As has often been argued, the twentieth-century debate on age discrimination is not exactly a story of murders, lynchings, 'freedom rides' or marches on Washington: older people have not suffered a history of purposeful unequal treatment (although their suffering may have been hidden from history).[42] There is also the slightly facetious argument that, on a life-course perspective, today's old people must have been guilty of discriminating against older generations in the past, when they themselves were young: if they are both victims and perpetrators, are we then justified in allocating them preferential treatment?

The third justification for affirmative action is powerful. This, the 'social utility' or 'social harmony' argument, maintains that operating a hiring preference educates society, and changes the way that people think. If discriminated-against groups are elevated into high-profile public positions, they will act as role models and more will follow, thus enlarging the potential pool of applicants (particularly since a significant proportion of hiring is word-of-mouth). In the long run, this can lead to greater economic efficiency since hiring decisions will increasingly be made on grounds of merit. School desegregation in the USA was based upon this principle, and it can be applied to age discrimination. For example, there is no logical reason why a 75-year-old woman could not work in a shop selling heavy metal music CDs, providing she had the necessary expertise. The main obstacle is societal prejudice, and this can be dispelled over time by her (and others like her) doing such a job. Slowly, attitudes will change. On the utilitarian principle, the community as a whole will eventually gain, even if some individuals who are excluded from the benefits of affirmative action will suffer.[43]

If, therefore, we argue that older people are substantially disadvantaged by socio-economic forces outside their control (most notably, a long-run decline in employment opportunities caused by contracting sectoral labour market demand), then we would argue that they should be treated *unequally* and favourably. Most notably, the public policy concessions they currently enjoy would be extended to include age-sensitive employment policies to offset their increasing labour market vulnerability and really 'make work pay' – reduced income tax liabilities, a citizen's

[42] Macnicol, *Age Discrimination*, p. 24.
[43] Ronald Dworkin, *Taking Rights Seriously* (1977), pp. 227–232.

income for all aged 60+, in-work benefits, or even age-based employment quotas. However, such radical suggestions have not been forthcoming.

Historical evolution of the concept of discrimination

The changing meaning of the word 'discrimination' is associated with the slow transition to liberal democratic capitalist societies that has occurred since the nineteenth century, accompanied by an increasing emphasis on individual rights and the development of the concept of citizenship.[44] In the mid-nineteenth century it therefore had a neutral meaning – to 'differentiate' or to 'distinguish' – reflecting the UK's quasi-feudal social structure, in which there were wide disparities of wealth and income, limited social mobility, inequality before the law (for example, with regard to women) and voting rights restricted to a few adult males (the franchise being based upon economic interests, rather than individuals). Entry to the great independent schools was almost automatic for those with the right social background. Hence Winston Churchill's entrance examination for Harrow School was 'no more than a formality', since the headmaster of the school 'had no intention of rejecting the son of so distinguished a parent as Lord Randolph'.[45] When the young William Temple received the news of his First Class Honours degree result at Oxford in 1904, 'several offers of work arrived by telegram, and two dozen more reached him within forty-eight hours'.[46] Selection to the middle-class professions was largely by patronage, or what would now be called 'word-of-mouth' hiring, and many skilled working-class apprenticeships were distributed on the basis of family connection. There was widespread affirmative action, but it applied to the socially advantaged (who certainly did not consider themselves harmed in the process). Even after competitive entry was formally and slowly introduced into the professions, much informal affirmative action via patronage remained.[47] The class structure reproduced itself effortlessly. Discrimination was widely accepted, and the idea of individual rights was therefore undeveloped.

However, the spread of democracy and changes in the occupational structure over the past hundred years have solidified individual rights and

---

[44] T. H. Marshall, 'Citizenship and Social Class', in Marshall, *Sociology at the Crossroads and Other Essays* (1963), pp. 104–122.

[45] Henry Pelling, *Winston Churchill* (1974), p. 32.

[46] F. A. Iremonger, *William Temple. Archbishop of Canterbury. His Life and Letters* (1948), p. 60.

[47] Koppelman points out that in the USA there have been many historical examples of formal affirmative action policies that have aroused little controversy, such as veterans' preference in civil service hiring. Koppelman, *Antidiscrimination Law*, p. 35,

transformed our conceptualisation of discrimination. The term has taken on normative meanings, both negative and positive. Negative discrimination implies harm done by one individual to another, via a restriction of their rights, or 'a social pattern of aggregate behaviour' inflicted by one group upon another.[48] Positive discrimination, on the other hand, can encompass strategies such as positive action, preferential treatment or other versions of affirmative action (most notably, employment quotas), or concessions to any one particular group (for example, free or subsidised public transport). Discrimination has been divided into *direct* (open and obvious to all) and *indirect* (involving a denial of intent to discriminate, but nevertheless having an adverse or disparate impact on one particular group via 'processes that are fair in form but discriminatory in operation').[49] Indirect discrimination may be more pervasive yet harder to prove, being deeply embedded in a group culture and manifesting itself in institutional discrimination;[50] it may be revealed only through statistical discrimination tests of unequal outcomes. The essential principle – established by the classic *Griggs versus the Duke Power Company* case in the USA in 1971 – is that conduct or outcome matters more than intent or state of mind. A final complication is that discrimination can be 'multiple', 'compounded' or 'intersectional', involving a combination of disadvantaging factors. For example, older women are often said to suffer a 'double' or 'triple' jeopardy by age, sex and/or ethnicity[51] – but even this categorisation may be too simplistic. There can also be 'discrimination by association' and 'hierarchies of discrimination' (for example, different ethnic minorities may experience varying intensities of discrimination). Clearly, discrimination is by no means a straightforward, unproblematic concept, and presents several intriguing analytical issues that need to be explored.

Defining the protected groups

The first point to note is that legislative action against discrimination still tends to apply only to the public sphere – in areas such as employment, education, housing, access to public spaces, selection for public office and the distribution of goods and services. In our private worlds, we still enjoy considerable freedom to discriminate by making choices based upon our preferences or even prejudices – for example, in selecting

---

[48] Michael P. Banton, *Discrimination* (1994), p. 5.
[49] Quoted in Kaye, 'Divided', p. 21.
[50] An example would be trying to change a racist 'canteen culture' in a police force.
[51] Susan Sontag, 'The Double Standard of Aging', in Vida Carver and Penny Liddiard (eds.), *An Ageing Population: A Reader and Sourcebook* (1978), pp. 72–80.

friends or an area in which to live. Again, prohibited grounds for discrimination are generally defined in law. It may therefore be permissible to discriminate on other, whimsical grounds (for example, sartorial style or eye colour) – though not if these were shown to have an adverse impact on a protected group: for example, a prejudice against bow ties might discriminate indirectly against members of the Nation of Islam. However, it is undoubtedly the case that everyone experiences some form of discrimination, even if they are not always aware of it. As Michael Banton puts it, 'discrimination is a general feature of social life'.[52]

Although most discrimination is 'top-down' (inflicted by relatively advantaged individuals or groups against relatively disadvantaged ones), it can also apply the other way. In addition, prejudice can operate within disadvantaged and discriminated-against groups (for example, racism between ethnic minorities). Indeed, the meanings of discrimination are now becoming so complex and multi-layered that there is a danger that different strands may at times be in conflict with each other. The initial working of the 2010 Equality Act has shown that rights can be in conflict – for example, sexuality rights versus religious rights. But which rights should trump others? In late 2013, a legal decision by the Supreme Court in the UK elevated Scientology to the status of a formal religion, raising the question of what exactly is a religion – or, indeed, what is a 'belief'.[53]

There is also a danger that the possible disadvantaging factors may be enlarged too greatly. For example, ethnic categories have become much more complex in the last fifteen years, and the rise of mental and behavioural disorders will pose increasing problems in the future: would a borderline, fluctuating bipolar condition be considered so disabling that its sufferers would be placed in a protected group? If discrimination of all kinds is widespread, and multi-directional, then outlawing its most egregious forms involves making a value judgement with regard to which discriminations are unacceptable and which are acceptable. Why not, for example, broaden the definition of protected groups to include everyone, and outlaw *all* 'word-of-mouth' hiring?

Discrimination versus other causes

A second difficulty is that discrimination is but one of several causes of disadvantage. Only when the others have been considered and eliminated

---

[52] Banton, *Discrimination*, p. 3.
[53] John Bingham, 'Scientology is a Religion, Rules Supreme Court', *Telegraph*, 11 Dec. 2013, www.telegraph.co.uk

can discrimination be identified as the principal cause.[54] This can be problematic, since discrimination is usually subtly intertwined with, and reinforced by, other factors. Discrimination will therefore tend to act as an accelerator of existing socio-economic disadvantage: precisely what role it plays is difficult to determine.

There has been considerable debate across the political spectrum regarding the actual causes of unequal outcomes. 'Discrimination' as an explanation tends to be supported by centrist social democrats. Interestingly, both free market liberals and those on the political left are somewhat critical of it. The former tend to dismiss discrimination per se, and identify cultures, tastes and preferences, cognitive deficiencies, genetic factors, market distortions by vested interests and so on.[55] Personal deficiencies of an intrinsic and unalterable kind figure strongly in this analysis, as in Gary Becker's assertion that 'Perhaps more than half the total differences between the earnings and abilities of Negroes in the United States results from deficiencies brought to the market place, rather than from market discrimination itself. . . These deficiencies include poor health, low morale and motivation and limited information about opportunities. The most pervasive force, however, is insufficient and inferior education and training.'[56]

Hence for many American market liberals the economic disadvantages experienced by African Americans are not attributable to discrimination per se, but to an allegedly self-destructive black culture, or cognitive deficiencies, or even rational choices.[57] Interestingly, 'culture' is frequently used by market liberals to explain why Third World societies do not experience rapid economic development.[58] This analysis assumes that culture is fixed, intrinsic and immalleable, rather than the product of structural economic factors and therefore ever-changing. For example, Charles Murray's statement that 'something in black culture tolerates or encourages birth out of wedlock at higher rates than apply to white culture in any given year'[59] ignores the fact that, for much of the twentieth century, the African American marriage rate was actually higher than the white one: it only began to fall from the 1950s, in response to declining

[54] Banton, *Discrimination*, p. 5.
[55] See, for example: Thomas Sowell, *Markets and Minorities* (1981); Peter Saunders, *The Rise of the Equalities Industry* (2011).
[56] Gary S. Becker, 'Discrimination, Economic', in David L. Sills (ed.), *International Encyclopedia of the Social Sciences, Vol. IV* (1968), p. 209.
[57] Capaldi, 'Affirmative Action: Con'.
[58] Vic George, *Wealth, Poverty and Starvation: A World Perspective* (1988), pp. 10–11. As an example, see Edward Banfield, *The Moral Basis of a Backward Society* (1958).
[59] Charles Murray, 'Does Welfare Bring More Babies?', *The Public Interest*, 115, Spring 1994, p. 22.

job opportunities for less skilled young black males. The view that culture is all-powerful sits uneasily alongside the other neoliberal view that 'cultural change' can be quite easily achieved by altering behavioural incentives.

Free market liberals even argue that discrimination would be logically impossible in a truly capitalist economy. The cash nexus is said to be blind to differences of age, ethnicity, gender, religion and so on. In conditions of perfect market competition, it is argued, an employer will always behave rationally, and it would be economically irrational to select an employee on productivity-irrelevant qualities such as gender, ethnicity, religion or age: an employer's profits would suffer in consequence.[60] Discrimination is inefficient, and therefore costly – an impediment to what should be a free market in labour. (It is a position not unlike Adam Smith's famous critique of slavery in *The Wealth of Nations* (1776).[61]) Of course, in the real world as opposed to the hypothetical abstractions of pure market economics, an employer may indeed be willing to suffer some drop in profits in order to indulge his or her prejudices or 'taste for discrimination' – quite how much of a drop is the key question.[62]

Supporters of free market, individualistic capitalism are therefore highly critical of anything other than formal equality – that is, basic equality of opportunity, or procedural fairness, with no attempt to reduce inequalities of outcome. Excessive interference in individual liberty, via legislation countering discrimination, is viewed as harmful, since it distorts the market and imposes an 'unfair' burden on employers. Only the market should distribute economic rewards. Accordingly, many American market liberals approve of the very limited notion of rights enshrined in the 1964 Civil Rights Act, aimed at improving economic efficiency by facilitating better employee selection on the criterion of merit and removing the 'artificial' restrictions on personal freedom (including quasi-legal racial discrimination) that had previously characterised American society. However, neoliberals have tended to oppose the subsequent strategy of affirmative action: it is seen as 'reverse discrimination' based upon criteria of race, sex, religion and so on, and therefore, they argue, illegal under the 1964 Act.[63]

By contrast, those on the political left are also critical of 'discrimination' as an explanation, arguing that socio-economic inequalities are more important: for example, much of what appears to be race-specific

---

[60] Epstein, *Forbidden Grounds*, pp. 445, 452.
[61] Adam Smith, *The Wealth of Nations* (1961, edited by Edwin Cannan), p. 90.
[62] Gary S. Becker, *The Economics of Discrimination* (1957), p. 6.
[63] Robert K. Fullinwider, *The Reverse Discrimination Controversy: A Moral and Legal Analysis* (1980).

disadvantage is actually class-specific. The left's analysis would also stress personal deficiencies, but would contend that these have socio-economic causes and are to some extent remediable. For example, the 'cohort effect' – whereby each generation tends on average to be better educated than the one preceding it – may explain some of the labour market disadvantages of older workers: it would be argued that these disadvantages can be offset by more investment in lifelong learning and reskilling (always assuming that there are available jobs).[64]

Those on the political left would also argue that many inequalities originate very early in life and become so deeply embedded that they can only be countered by policies that are radically redistributive: anti-discrimination legislation is therefore too little, too late.[65] Inherited wealth, family environment, transmitted social capital, genetic predisposition and so on are seen to be much more likely causes of inequality.[66] For example, children are highly unequal in reading ability even before they start attending school at the age of 5.[67] Thereafter, socio-economic status probably determines between 70 and 75 per cent of educational outcomes, and the 'school effect' determines less than 12 per cent.[68] As has been shown in Chapter 5, the socio-economic inequalities that produce early retirement are cumulative, and originate very early in life. 'Discrimination' is therefore something of a red herring – a plausible but basically erroneous explanation that it is tempting to embrace as easily understood, and one which will tend to obscure the fact that structural economic inequalities are the real problem.

From this critical perspective, 'discrimination' as an explanation for unequal outcomes is misleading not only in analysis but also in prescription, transforming economic causes into attitudinal and cultural ones and therefore suggesting remedies based on the latter analysis. Such a focus shifts attention from causal factors such as flows of capital nationally and globally, the behaviour of multinational corporations and the massive growth of low-grade service jobs requiring casualised, 'flexible' and non-unionised workforces. All that is being established is an equal opportunity to participate in a market economy that will then produce highly *unequal* outcomes, and thereby legitimate them. As Nick

---

[64] Smeaton and Vegeris, *Older People*, ch. 5.
[65] David Piachaud, 'Social Justice and Public Policy: A Social Policy Perspective', in Gary Craig, Tania Burchardt and David Gordon (eds.), *Social Justice and Public Policy: Seeking Fairness in Diverse Societies* (2008), pp. 47–48.
[66] White, *Equality* (2007), p. 61.
[67] John Hills *et al.*, *An Anatomy of Economic Inequality in the UK: Report of the National Equality Panel* (2010), pp. 330–331.
[68] Anne West and Hazel Pennell, *Underachievement in Schools* (2003), p. 145.

Johns has commented, 'Equal opportunities is inherently conservative in nature... It was designed to justify economic and social inequalities... it is about equalising opportunities to become unequal.'[69] A pure meritocratic approach is thus perfectly compatible with wide disparities of income and status, in which, as Judith Squires puts it, 'a talented elite dominate while the disadvantaged are deemed to have failed as a result of their own personal deficiencies'.[70] This very limited version of equality of opportunity was the one propagated by the New Labour government when in power between 1997 and 2010, and has continued thereafter. As Tony Blair famously defined it, 'true equality' was 'not equal incomes... [but] equal worth, an equal chance of fulfilment, equal access to knowledge and opportunity'.[71] More recent official guidance on the new equality strategy declares that 'The government's equality strategy sets out our vision for a strong, modern and fair Britain. It is built on two principles of equality – equal treatment and equal opportunity.'[72]

The question of timing

A final intriguing issue is the temporal coincidence, briefly noted above, between the growth of individual rights and the transition to meritocratic, free market societies from static, quasi-feudal ones where social relations are calcified by time. One striking example of this is the way that the black civil rights movement in the USA during the 1950s and 1960s coincided with, and arguably was caused by, the economic modernisation of the South and northwards migration of millions of African Americans. The Deep South slowly moved from a quasi-feudal social structure, characterised by an oppressive racism and the sharecropping system, to a more fluid capitalist economy with 'freer' social relations.[73] Here it is worth considering an argument often deployed by market liberals. They maintain that discrimination has naturally lessened as capitalism has evolved, inexorably sweeping away the cobwebs of this outdated feudal relic. In the words of Milton Friedman:

---

[69] Nick Johns, book review, *Social Policy and Administration*, 44, 5, Oct. 2010, p. 643.
[70] Squires, 'Equality and Difference' in Dryzek *et al.*, *Oxford Handbook*, p. 474. See also Alex Callinicos, *Equality* (2000), pp. 38–39; White, *Equality*, p. 71; Andrew Mason, *Levelling the Playing Field: The Idea of Equal Opportunity and its Place in Egalitarian Thought* (2006).
[71] Tony Blair, 'Speech to Labour Party Conference', 1 Oct. 1999, http://news.bbc.co.uk
[72] Government Equalities Office, 'Policy Paper: Equality Strategy', 2010, www.gov.uk/government/publications/equality-strategy-7
[73] Nicholas Lemann, *The Promised Land: The Great Black Migration and How it Changed America* (1991).

It is a striking historical fact that the development of capitalism has been accompanied by a major reduction in the extent to which particular religious, racial, or social groups have operated under special handicaps in respect of their economic activities; have, as the saying goes, been discriminated against . . . discrimination against groups of particular colour or religion is least in those areas where there is the greatest freedom of competition.[74]

However, this argument can instructively be turned on its head. A more convincing analytical narrative is that state policies against employment discrimination have been, and continue to be, an essential part of the transition to a more competitive free market economy with highly unequal outcomes. In support of this, it is interesting that, in the UK (as in the USA), *effective* laws against employment discrimination have been largely a post-1960s phenomenon (most notably, the 1970 Equal Pay Act, the 1975 Sex Discrimination Act and the 1976 Race Relations Act). There was legislation on disability discrimination (largely a response to the plight of disabled veterans of the Second World War), but it was too limited in scope to be effective. For example, the 1944 Disabled Persons (Employment) Act (amended in 1958) set a quota of 3 per cent disabled people in the workforces of firms employing more than twenty workers, but made little difference. Likewise, racial discrimination was tentatively countered by the 1965 and 1968 Race Relations Acts. As any student of the subject knows, improving the effectiveness of UK legislation against disability, race and gender discrimination was a long process from the 1950s to the present.[75] Private members' bills seeking to outlaw racial discrimination were introduced into the House of Commons regularly from 1951 onwards, but failed to gather enough support.[76]

On the face of it, the appearance of effective legislation against employment discrimination coincided with the emergence of a civil rights movement in the UK (and even more so in the USA). However, structure and agency interacted: legislative change also occurred precisely at that time when there began the move away from a manufacturing-based economy and towards a more service and white-collar employment base with more unstable, insecure, 'flexible' jobs and a culture of competitive individualism that has characterised western economies ever since. These economies were undergoing considerable modernisation, technological innovation and restructuring in the 1960s and 1970s, and there were calls for a more efficient use of human capital. Since the early 1970s they

---

[74] Milton Friedman, *Capitalism and Freedom* (1962), pp. 108–109.
[75] Bagilhole, *Understanding Equal Opportunities*, chs. 4 and 5; Linda Dickens, 'The Road is Long: Thirty Years of Equality Legislation in Britain', *British Journal of Industrial Relations*, 45, 3, Sept. 2007, pp. 463–494.
[76] Kaye, 'Divided', p. 11.

have experienced an acceleration in the growth of part-time jobs and low-grade service jobs. Arguably, anti-discrimination laws have been the midwife of this transition, facilitating a freer movement of labour and, more recently, legitimating coercive activation policies. Interestingly, laws against the unfairness of employment discrimination have coincided with a widening of income and wealth inequality and a massive erosion of human rights via increasing electronic surveillance.

Measuring discrimination

A final analytical problem is that the 'true' level of discrimination in any society is impossible to assess: it may be greater or lesser than any survey can reveal. On the one hand, much discrimination goes unnoticed (particularly at the hiring stage); on the other, the introduction of new laws can make a population too 'discrimination conscious'. In its comprehensive analysis of the etymological history of the words 'discrimination' and 'discriminate', the *Oxford English Dictionary* points one to an intriguing observation of UK life in 1968 by the Trinidadian Albert Gomes that encapsulates this problem: 'If you move around for ever with the expectation of being discriminated against, the chances are you won't ever be disappointed.'[77]

This can be strikingly illustrated in the case of age. Experience of the American Age Discrimination in Employment Act of 1967 shows that reported cases (particularly those that reach the law courts) are only the tip of the iceberg, and that litigants face many personal, financial and legal obstacles.[78] On the other hand, conservative opponents of the Act accuse it of encouraging frivolous litigation. Indirect age discrimination is notoriously difficult to prove in the case of age: for example, the age profile of a firm will reflect factors other than discrimination, and different levels of health spending between age groups reflect clinical need more than discrimination. Statistical discrimination tests – inferring intent from outcome – are therefore highly problematic, as are opinion surveys.

Anti-ageism campaigners argue that 'Britain is today a profoundly ageist society', and 'in denial about ageism'.[79] Ageism may therefore be so widespread, deep-seated and finely woven into prevailing assumptions and popular consciousness that it is extremely difficult to 'prove'

---

[77] Albert Maria Gomes, 'I Am an Immigrant', *The Listener*, 80, 2062, 3 Oct. 1968, p. 427.
[78] Raymond F. Gregory, *Age Discrimination in the American Workplace: Old at a Young Age* (2001).
[79] Age Concern, *Age of Equality?*, p. 7.

and therefore eradicate:[80] 'Ageism has a dramatic, detrimental effect on older people but this is often not acknowledged . . . Ageism is not obvious. You may not be aware it's happening, but it may result in you receiving different treatment.'[81] Likewise, a wide-ranging research study commissioned by the Equality and Human Rights Commission declares that ageism 'permeates the fabric of our society', and that ageist practices are manifest 'in all aspects of later life – for example, public spaces, consumer marketplace, expectations for personal appearance, sexuality, household decision-making and public services'.[82]

Supporting evidence is often in the form of public opinion or focus group surveys, in which ordinary citizens are asked to report their personal experiences of discrimination. For example, a 2005 survey sponsored by Age Concern (now Age UK) – adopting a psychological perspective – concluded that ageism was a 'bigger problem than racism or sexism', according to one of its authors: 28 per cent of respondents reported that they had been treated unfairly because of their age in the past year.[83] Interestingly, young people frequently report experiencing more ageism than do old[84] – an earlier survey found that the highest levels of ageism were experienced by the 16–24 age group, and the lowest by those aged in their seventies.[85] Another survey found that 49 per cent of respondents experienced some kind of prejudice in the past year: of these responses, ageism was the most frequently cited (37 per cent), followed by sexism (34 per cent) and racism (22 per cent). Again, respondents aged 70+ were less likely to say that they had been victims of prejudice.[86] More recently, a Europe-wide survey (commissioned by Age UK) found that 64 per cent of respondents in the UK perceived age discrimination to be a 'quite serious' or 'very serious' problem. There was an extraordinary variation between countries, even between those with similar cultures: in France, 68 per cent of respondents considered age discrimination to be a 'quite serious' or 'very serious' problem, yet the proportion in Turkey was a mere 17 per cent; in Sweden, it was 51 per cent, but in neighbouring Denmark only 22 per cent. No explanation was offered for these wide

[80] Harding, *Rights at Risk.*
[81] Age Scotland, *What is Ageism?* n.d., www.ageuk.org.uk/scotland
[82] Smeaton and Vegeris, *Older People*, pp. 2, 3.
[83] Steve Connor, 'Ageism "Bigger Problem Than Racism or Sexism"', *Independent*, 7 Sept. 2005 www.independent.co.uk
[84] Sujata Ray, Ellen Sharp and Dominic Abrams, *Ageism: A Benchmark of Public Attitudes in Britain* (2006), pp. 46–48.
[85] Age Concern England, *How Ageist is Britain?* (2005), p. 15.
[86] Dominic Abrams and Diane M. Houston, *Equality, Diversity and Prejudice in Britain* (2006), pp. 36–37.

variations – most notably, whether they reflected differences in culture or in perception.[87]

However, it is well known that subjective responses can be unreliable: one would not base a public health strategy on self-reported health, for example; again, the fact that surveys show that nearly 80 per cent of Americans believe in the existence of angels does not necessarily prove that angels exist.[88] The authors of a recent study demonstrating widespread age discrimination, and based upon interviews with (self-defined) older people, candidly admit that 'We therefore decided to relax our definition and maintain open minds as to what constitutes age discrimination. Essentially, age discrimination is what older people make of it... there is a difference between "real" experiences and "hard" evidence... a request for the latter imposes limitations on what can be recounted.'[89]

This may be technically correct, in that only those who experience discrimination can adequately describe it. Minor episodes of discrimination can accumulate into something major and significant.[90] Again, ageism may be so deeply embedded and 'natural' that it is impossible to demonstrate other than by personal testimony. The problem is that *any* negative experience encountered by an older person can be internally processed as discrimination, erroneously attributed to ageism and cited as proof of its existence. These same authors do acknowledge that certain aspects of the design and management of public places affect life for older people (for example, the provision of public toilets), but that 'it is hard to state conclusively that this is the result of age discrimination'. Other examples, like the 'pensioners' hairdo' are very borderline indeed.[91] Elsewhere, two of the authors thoughtfully observe that teasing apart the cumulative and synergistic elements of multiple discrimination can be very challenging, particularly when ordinary citizens may define racism or ageism in very different ways.[92]

A key interpretative difficulty not confronted by such studies is how to distinguish widely accepted notions of 'age-appropriate' behaviours (for example, in choosing friends and partners, or in occupying public spaces) from outright ageism normalised as 'everyday discrimination'

---

[87] Abrams *et al.*, *Ageism in Europe*, esp. p. 32.
[88] Jennifer Agiesta, 'Angels: Nearly 8 in 10 Americans Believe These Ethereal Beings Are Real', 23 Dec. 2011, www.huffingtonpost.com
[89] Bytheway *et al.*, *Too Old*, pp. 6, 9.
[90] Bill Bytheway, *Unmasking Age: The Significance of Age for Social Research* (2011), p. 56.
[91] Bytheway *et al.*, *Too Old*, pp. 18, 32–33.
[92] Richard Ward and Bill Bytheway (eds.), *Researching Age and Multiple Discrimination* (2008), esp. pp. 1, 7, 20.

or ageist banter. In public policy, there are many age restrictions that are widely supported and approved – for example, concessions to older people (such as free or subsidised public transport), laws that protect the young, age-based school curricula, mandatory retirement ages for occupations where public safety may be at risk and so on. Again, opinion surveys that adopt a psychological perspective tend to define the problem as one of constructed stereotypes based upon inter-group processes. This perspective is then illegitimately applied to the labour market problems of older workers as an 'explanation'. In an extraordinary process of elision, the problem of inter-personal ageism is conflated with that of long-run economic forces.

This focus on ageist attitudes has contaminated the debate on age discrimination in employment, causing it to be viewed as essentially irrational and prejudice-driven. The tendency to view economic problems as attitudinal runs through much government-commissioned research. For example, Smeaton and Vegeris maintain that longer unemployment is experienced by those aged 50+ 'largely as a result of age discrimination in the recruitment behaviour of employers'.[93]

Fashioning discourses on ageism that focus on the 'irrational' prejudices of employers and the public at large, the 'discriminatory' barriers to working, attitudinal factors and human agency is superficially attractive, and the associated activation remedies can be presented with seductive plausibility as 'empowerment' or the achievement of 'cultural change'. As one New Labour publication put it, 'The cultural attitudes of individuals and organisations towards ageing need to change to get to the root of exclusion and inequality.'[94] It is also a perspective that accords with the very understandable tendency of jobless older people to attribute their plight to 'ageism in the workplace'. However, attitudinal factors are much less important than structural economic ones in explaining the labour market disadvantages of older workers. Only a few points need be made in substantiation, and briefly.

First, a focus on attitudinal factors would need to explain the historical spread of retirement in terms of increasing age discrimination. As shown in Chapter 5, the proportion of men aged 65+ who were gainfully occupied has fallen from 74 per cent in 1881 to 13 per cent today. The proportion who were jobless has thus risen three-and-a-half times. It is highly unlikely that employers' ageist hostility towards older workers should have increased by this amount. As has been shown in Chapter 5, retirement was driven mainly by long-run economic imperatives and not

[93] Smeaton and Vegeris, *Older People*, p. 15.
[94] Office of the Deputy Prime Minister, *A Sure Start*, p. 97.

Figure 7.1 Average age of withdrawal from the labour market: by sex, 1984–2012.
Source: Office for National Statistics, *Pension Trends – Chapter 4*, p. 20.

by employer hostility. Second, that there have been historical variations in the employment rates of late middle-aged men: a fall in the 1920s and 1930s; a rise during the Second World War; a stabilisation to the early 1970s and then a rapid fall; a similar rise and fall in the late 1980s and early 1990s; finally, a slow rise from the early 1990s. This can be illustrated by using the average age of permanent withdrawal from the labour market for men and women (an accurate indication of their labour market fortunes) since 1984 for men and women (see Figure 7.1). A 'discrimination' explanation would have to account for these attitudinal swings over time: why, for example, would age discrimination in employment apparently intensify in the early 1990s and then diminish from the late 1990s onwards?

Third, there are different age profiles in different sectors of the economy. Older workers have the highest employment rates in long-established sectors, such as 'agriculture and fishing', 'manufacturing', 'transport and communications' and 'public administration, education and health', and the lowest in newly established, technology-intensive sectors. Fourth, as shown in Chapter 5, there are pronounced regional variations in older people's employment rates in the UK, whereby their job prospects are worst in areas of deindustrialisation.[95] Dealing with these last three points together, it is implausible that temporal, sectoral and regional variations in older people's employment rates reflect variations in levels of discrimination.

Fifth, mandatory retirement (when it existed in the UK) was often seen as an egregious example of age discrimination since it amounted to a denial of the right to work. However, this overestimates its extent and is a misinterpretation of its historical origins.[96] Mandatory retirement ages were most often state pension ages and, as shown in Chapter 2, state pension ages have had little influence on actual ages of retirement. Today, only about 10 per cent of men (though half of women) leave work exactly at state pension age.

Sixth, there is the slightly flippant but telling point that, if 'discrimination' is a major causal factor, it must be *sex* discrimination against older men, since their economic activity rates have fallen since the 1970s while those of older women have risen slightly. Finally, an analysis emphasising the alleged 'irrational' prejudices of employers is deficient, in that it is confined to personnel policies at the level of the individual firm: the implication is that the 'attitudes' of human resource managers play a major part in determining the employment opportunities of older workers. This analysis ignores the complex supply–demand mismatches of age, gender, skill, region, sector and so on that have always characterised modern economies, but which have intensified since the 1970s and have resulted in the disappearance of work for older men. Once again, economic change is simplistically reduced to attitudinal factors and human agency.

Conclusion

To conclude, therefore: ageism is a complex phenomenon with diverse meanings. The recognition of ageism in many areas of social life, and the various legislative steps that have been taken to combat it, represent on the face of it a long-overdue and laudable recognition of the disadvantages suffered by citizens on grounds of age. However, anti-ageism is a double-edged sword. In the UK, the attack on employment discrimination has

---

[95] Macnicol, 'Older Men', pp. 587–588.
[96] Richard V. Burkhauser and Joseph F. Quinn, 'Is Mandatory Retirement Overrated? Evidence from the 1970s', *Journal of Human Resources*, 18, 3, Summer 1983, pp. 337–358.

been used to justify a neoliberal strategy of more intensive labour market activation and a raising of state pension ages. There has operated a three-stage process. The starting-point is the contentious proposition that age discrimination (particularly in the form of mandatory retirement) has been the major cause of the employment problems of older workers. It is a proposition that confuses inter-personal ageism (quantified by method-ologically suspect opinion surveys) with long-run labour market changes. Alas, many gerontologists have been too ready to accept this simplistic and inaccurate analysis. The second stage is legislative action against age discrimination in employment and an ending of the default retire-ment age, purporting to remove the discriminatory 'barriers' that face older people. The final stage is to argue that, because age discrimination and mandatory retirement have apparently been abolished by legislation, older workers will henceforth experience no difficulty remaining in jobs until they are aged in their late sixties. As *Fuller Working Lives* (2014) puts it, 'the removal of the default retirement age means the vast majority of people now have a choice about when to retire'.[97] State pension ages can therefore be raised, and the right to retirement undermined. An appar-ent enhancement of employment rights has thus been accompanied by a significant diminution of welfare rights. In the final analysis, forcing people to work later in life, when there are no jobs for them, may be the ultimate form of ageism.

---

[97] DWP, *Fuller Working Lives – A Framework for Action*, p. 5.

8   Conclusion

Since the 1970s, the old age agenda has slowly but surely changed, driven by both neoliberalism as an ideology and the associated labour market restructuring that has placed the expansion of labour supply at the centre of macro-economic policy. The process of change has been slow and incremental, with every stage presented as purely evidence-driven, inevitable and apolitical – a key feature of all aspects of the neoliberal revolution. This creates interpretative difficulties – one is challenging a powerful consensus. Many who read this book will disagree with its analysis. They may prefer to take a technocratic approach, examining the dysfunctional complexity that has become a feature of the UK state pension system, notionally as a consequence of its piecemeal development since 1908, and argue that the seemingly persuasive case articulated by recent UK governments represents a 'sensible' compromise between difficult options. Again, they may argue that the post-2008 economic situation makes painful public expenditure constraints inevitable, or that the demographic pressures are very 'real', and that some other European countries are also raising their state pension ages – though at the time of writing the number is very small.[1] Finally, they may point out that many model occupational schemes that have been run responsibly and prudently (like the John Lewis Partnership scheme in the UK) are now under fiscal and demographic pressure, and are having to reduce accrual rates.[2]

The interpretative problem is that the demographic and pension-funding factors are both technically challenging to research and riddled with uncertainties – regarding future fertility, mortality, health, labour supply, performance of the economy and so on – which by no means present an unequivocal case for raising state pension ages; and then these

---

[1] According to the website www.68istoolate.org.uk, by 2050 only four other countries in Europe will have a state pension age of 68.

[2] Graham Ruddick, 'John Lewis to Cut Back Gold-Plated Pension Scheme', *Telegraph*, 30 Jan. 2014, www.telegraph.co.uk

uncertainties are mediated through the distorting lens of neoliberalism and thereby transformed into inevitabilities, producing highly pessimistic conclusions that justify what amounts to a major cutback in the most expensive item of the welfare state budget. However, it is clear that the largely uncritical debate in political and academic circles does not reflect popular opinion: according to a YouGov poll in May 2012, 77 per cent of UK citizens think it is unfair that state pension ages are being raised, and 62 per cent believe the policy will hit hardest at the poorest pensioners.[3]

The new old age agenda need not have emerged like this. A crucial event was the Thatcher government's attack on state pensions in the 1980s, the results of which are still very much with us.[4] At other key points (such as New Labour's accession to government in May 1997) a very different agenda could have been fashioned – one that encouraged and assisted those who wish to work later in life while at the same time protecting retirement as a social right for those displaced from the labour force prematurely, and addressing the very real and continuing problem of pensioner poverty (especially among women). Before judging the 'sustainability' of the UK's state pension scheme it should always be borne in mind that the UK is the sixth-richest nation in the world, yet has one of the worst state pensions, as measured by replacement rates – and we are now living in a more income- and wealth-unequal society since the 1930s. The wealthiest 1 per cent of the UK population now owns as much wealth as the poorest 55 per cent, and the Gini Coefficient of income inequality has risen from c. 25 per cent in 1961 to c. 35 per cent in 2006/7 – higher than most other industrialised societies.[5] This must be borne in mind when judging the validity of Chancellor of the Exchequer George Osborne's assertion that the UK's state pension scheme faces 'collapse' unless eligibility ages are raised.[6]

However, the political changes that have taken place have led to a very different agenda. As this study has shown, it is an agenda that has a long lineage: raising state pension ages has been a neoliberal cause for decades, as has reducing the state pension to a residual system of income support for only the very poorest. Both have their roots in nineteenth-century neoclassical views of old age, and there is an extraordinary continuity between the conceptualisation of old age offered by the

---

[3] David Woods, 'Three-quarters of Employees Think a Delay in UK State Pension Age is Unfair, Reveals YouGov', 8 May 2012, www.hrmagazine.co.uk
[4] Neil Clark, 'Britain's Pensioners Aren't Being Served by Policy Changes that Date from 1979', Guardian, 1 Dec. 2013, www.theguardian.com
[5] Hills et al., An Anatomy of Economic Inequality, pp. 39, 53.
[6] 'Osborne: "System Would Have Collapsed Without My Pension Age Rise"', 6 Dec. 2013, Telegraph, www.telegraph.co.uk

late-nineteenth-century Charity Organisation Society and that of neoliberalism today. The apparent inevitability of today's demographic and fiscal pressures must be placed in that context.

It is likely that state pension ages for men and women in the UK will be raised to 70 by the middle of the century – and possibly, if there continues to be little organised opposition, by the 2030s. Eligibility ages may rise above 70 thereafter, and it is not beyond the realm of possibility that the state pension could be privatised. The justification is that fiscal and demographic pressures mean that citizens must work for at least another five years. What are the specific obstacles in the way of extending working lives by this amount? The key questions – never answered or even asked in official reports – are: exactly how many jobs will be required, exactly where will they come from, and what other obstacles stand in the way of a significant extension of working lives? The whole debate has been characterised by a marked reluctance on the part of those advocating higher state pension ages to provide clear answers to these crucial questions. Governments have been very willing to offer robust demographic projections, but curiously reticent when it comes to the number of jobs that will be needed in the future.

First, there will be major problems of **job creation**. In the long-run, joblessness at later ages has been mainly caused by demand-side factors, and this is where the answer must lie (despite the fact that the few solutions that are discussed tend to be exclusively supply-side ones, which assume that more supply of labour will automatically create more demand for it). It is unclear whether the strategy will be to create new jobs at the top of the age range, or to add them to the UK labour market at every age. Whichever it is, the number of new jobs required will be formidable.

It is instructive to examine this problem with regard to the population now aged 50–69, imagining that state pension ages have just been raised to 69. This may be an artificial exercise, because much can change in the future: most notably, there is disagreement among economists over whether there will be labour shortages in the future (as the government contends) or whether we are on the verge of a new industrial revolution in which new electronic technology will destroy many existing jobs. Economic forecasting is inherently hazardous: few economists in 1970 would have predicted accurately what the UK labour market would be like today. However, it is instructive to consider what would need to happen in the context of today's labour market.

There are currently in the UK 11,417,000 people aged 50–64, of which 7,693,000 are in employment, and 3,385,000 aged 65–69, of which 689,000 are in employment. Applying a highly optimistic overall target employment rate of 81 per cent (the employment rate for the

25–49 age group) to the 50–69 age group, then c. 3,508,000 new jobs would be needed. If, on the other hand, one applies a more realistic target employment rate of 73 per cent (the overall rate for the 18–64 age group) to the 50–69 age group, then c. 2,423,000 new jobs would be needed. Even if one scales these expectations right down, and applies to the 65–69 age group the current employment rate of the 50–64 age group (67 per cent), it is still the case that c. 1,579,000 new jobs would be the basic minimum for this policy to succeed. Formal unemployment in the UK is currently c. 1,860,000 – but, as mentioned in Chapter 4, many consider that, if one adds in the 'hidden unemployed', including both the de facto jobless and the under-employed, the total could be at least 5,000,000. (Recent official estimates are that some 3,000,000 workers are classified as under-employed, in that they want to work more hours; this could well be on the conservative side.[7]) Those who support raising state pension ages therefore need to provide a clear answer to the question: exactly where will the jobs come from? Supply-side sloganising is not enough.

Related to this is the issue of **intergenerational equity**. Although the justifying arguments for a generational misallocation of resources are unconvincing, this could be a major political obstacle, given the concern across Europe about high unemployment among 16 to 24 year-olds. As was shown in Chapter 5, **caring responsibilities** affect between one-fifth and one-quarter of 45–64 year-olds and inhibit their labour market participation, in full or in part. **Ill-health** is, on the face of it, the main reason for early exit, but here the problem is more work-disability – a self-definition that is profoundly affected by labour market demand.[8] Reducing levels of work-disability will only be achieved by stimulating labour market demand. More straightforwardly, the future of **healthy life expectancy** is uncertain and the health-damaging factors outlined in Chapter 4 may prevail in the future. **Burn-out** and a **retirement expectation** are important factors: as argued in this book, retirement may in the long run have been caused primarily by demand-side factors and economic restructuring, but it has also (as a natural consequence) been elevated into a social right. As was shown in Chapter 5, a majority of people aged 50–69 express a desire to work past state pension age, but only a tiny fraction want a fulltime job (see below). There is also a predominance of **part-time working** and **self-employment** at later ages: of those aged 65–69 still working, 63 per cent work part-time and 32 per cent are self-employed. Self-employment and/or part-time working

[7] Office for National Statistics, *Underemployment and Overemployment in the UK, 2014* (2014).
[8] Macnicol, 'History of Work-Disability'.

do not constitute a viable platform for adequate incomes in later life –
unless supplemented by some kind of **basic income** or **citizen's income**
scheme to replace existing social security benefits for all aged 60+.

There are marked **regional inequalities** in older people's employment rates, with the lowest rates to be found – unsurprisingly – in areas
of deindustrialisation (the worst casualties of the economic restructuring
of the 1980s). The litmus test of policies to encourage later-life working
will be whether they can work in such chronically deindustrialised areas.
Another major obstacle is that there are pronounced **sectoral differences** in older people's employment: if the required new jobs are to be
added to the top of the age range, are they to come from those sectors that
have traditionally employed older workers (agriculture, manufacturing,
transport, communications), or from new, developing sectors (notably,
low-grade, poorly paid service jobs)? Tellingly, half of economically inactive older men previously worked in one of only four labour market
sectors – manufacturing, construction, transport and wholesale/retail.[9]
These sectors will continue to shed labour, in response to technological
improvements, and so one must assume that the latter sectors will provide the jobs – indeed, that the justification for raising state pension ages
is really to supply the bottom end of the labour market with cheap labour.
Class unfairness has been somewhat discussed: those who retire earliest do so for involuntary reasons and are working class, least skilled and
with the worst health, lowest savings and poorest pension provision – in
other words, those least able to exercise choice. For example, of people
aged between 50 and state pension age, 81 per cent with a degree are
still in employment, compared with 52 per cent with no qualifications.
The seven-year difference in life expectancy at birth between the top
and bottom social classes means that, if state pension ages are raised,
more working-class people will not survive to claim the state pension
and will claim it for an even shorter time. There are some moderately
reformist suggestions that could alleviate this problem, such as different
state pension ages for different occupations (hard to enforce), or paying a
state pension as of right after forty years of working and paying National
Insurance contributions: someone who entered a manual occupation at
age 16 could thereby claim a pension at age 56. Less often discussed
is **cohort unfairness**: since the future demographic problem is one of
cohort size rather than 'people living longer', those born in the small
birth cohort 1950s and 1970s should feel unfairly treated. As this study
has shown, losing one's job when aged in one's fifties and sixties can
be traced back to **early life origins** (being born into an income-poor

---

[9] DWP, *Fuller Working Lives – A Framework for Action*, p. 9.

home, leaving school at the minimum age, living in rented accommodation, working in hard manual jobs, being of ethnic minority status and so on). Social-class inequalities are so repeatedly reinforced across the lifecourse that policies to extend working lives applied in later life are too little, too late. Again, many surveys (for example, the McKinsey & Co. study cited in Chapter 5) have shown that, in later life, the best-laid plans can be brutally disrupted by **the unexpected** – a sudden, catastrophic illness, the death of one's partner, redundancy and so on. Finally, in Chapter 5 it was argued that, viewed in the long term, **job insecurity at later ages** was a feature of working-class life in the past (though admittedly not as much as it is now). In the UK, very high employment rates among late middle-aged men were an unusual feature of the period of full-employment 'fordist' capitalism (1945–1975). Governments should acknowledge this, and desist from pursuing unrealistic ambitions.

Interestingly, those who have recently researched retirement and have engaged with ordinary people tend to be sceptical about the prospects of extending working lives. As two experienced researchers have put it, 'Based on the available research evidence, extending working life is probably only realistic at present for a select number of groups.'[10] Another recent investigation found that, among those interviewed, there was 'only limited appetite for extending working lives' and a resistance to being forced to do so. Respondents displayed a 'widespread cynicism' of the government's motives; most thought that the state pension age should be lowered to 60 and there was 'virtually no support' for the idea of deferring the state pension.[11] Interestingly, another survey sponsored by the DWP, examining why people left work, concluded that 'Currently most respondents expected to retire at SPA [State Pension Age] and believed that they had earned the right to retire. Many people in this group had fixed views about working and retirement and were unlikely to be influenced by policies and initiatives to encourage them to work longer.'[12] From one authoritative survey in the USA comes the sobering verdict that 'it would take nothing short of monumental advances on both the labor and health care fronts to reduce the incidence of forced retirement to levels that significantly lessen the nation's retirement savings gap'.[13]

While the desire to do some sort of work in later life *is* present, survey respondents tend to be understandably choosy about remuneration, working conditions, hours of work and likely pressures. For example, one

[10] Phillipson and Smith, *Extending Working Life*, p. 62.
[11] Vickerstaff *et al.*, *Encouraging Labour Market Activity*, pp. 103, 117, 119.
[12] Pat Irving, Jennifer Steels and Nicola Hall, *Factors Affecting the Labour Market Participation of Older Workers: Qualitative Research* (2005), p. 137.
[13] McKinsey & Company, *Cracking*, p. 9.

recent UK survey of people aged between 50 and 69 found that, while over half of the sample expressed a desire to work past state pension age, only 6 per cent wanted fulltime work.[14] The fact that this paradox has been known since at least the 1950s[15] should moderate claims that extending working lives will be easy.

If, therefore, these powerful factors prevent a significant expansion of employment taking place, the likely consequences for older people will be higher unemployment, a depletion of their savings, massive reliance on means-tested benefits and more financial and personal hardship. Being forced to work later in life, when an individual's health status does not permit it, will cause a deterioration in health; alternatively, more years of enforced, benefit-supported idleness towards the end of a life may exacerbate any mental health problems. Both of these scenarios will increase National Health Service expenditure. More will have to be paid out in social security benefits for the jobless.

Yet claiming benefits will not be easy. In order to qualify for means-tested, income-based Job Seeker's Allowance (or its successor, Universal Credit),[16] an individual's savings must be below £6,000. Between that and £16,000 benefit income is reduced at the rate of £1 a week per £250 in savings. Savings above £16,000 render an individual completely ineligible for the benefit (currently, £72 per week – under half the value of maximum Pension Credit). In order to qualify for benefit income, therefore, any significant savings will have to be used up. Thus one arm of government is telling citizens to save more for their retirement, but another arm of government is doing everything it can to deplete such savings. The distinct possibility is that this policy will end up costing the taxpayer *more*. In essence, the taxpayer will be subsidising employers, who will be the only ones to benefit from an enlarged pool of unemployed labour (just as occupational/private pensions systems will gain from paying out benefits later). Finally, a very real ethical and political conundrum is how far strict benefit sanctions should be brought to bear against those aged in their sixties who have worked all their lives but have now been made redundant and cannot find work, therefore having to rely on benefits. Older job-seekers are currently treated more leniently than younger ones, but that may well change as conditionality is intensified: for example, in May 2014 it was announced that claimants of Job Seeker's Allowance face losing their benefits for three months or more if

---

[14] Cited in Loretto *et al.*, *Older Workers*, p. 37.
[15] See, for example, Shenfield, *Social Policies*, p. 63.
[16] At the time of writing, most of the details regarding how Universal Credit will actually operate have yet to be clarified.

they refuse to take jobs with zero-hours contracts.[17] Already, the threat of three months' benefit suspension applies to those ex-claimants who leave a new job without good cause, or existing claimants who fail to provide evidence of daily job search. Will it be acceptable to see older citizens treated the same way?

Policy solutions

There are, however, some policies that could help older workers. Of those still working in the UK after state pension age, 62.7 per cent have been with their employer for more than ten years, and 17.5 per cent between five and ten years. That means that fully 80.2 per cent had been with their existing employer from more than five years.[18] A somewhat negative conclusion to draw from this is that activation policies directed at jobless sixty-somethings will only have very limited success – so limited, indeed, that they should not be applied. The scale of the problem can be illustrated by the statistic that the proportion of economically inactive people aged 65+ who are 'interested in work' is only 2 per cent in the case of men and 1 per cent in the case of women.[19] More positively, retention in an existing job is therefore the key: it has long been known, from both anecdotal and systematic evidence, that it is enormously difficult to regain good employment once one has been made jobless in later life. Those who wish to work later could be assisted – to an extent – by human capital policies to improve occupational health and employability (as pioneered in the Finnish concept of 'workability'). These would include flexible working hours, job sharing, redeployment within a firm to more suitable tasks, workplace adjustments and job modifications, flexible or phased retirement, allowance for caring responsibilities, sabbaticals and so on.[20] However, such supply-side solutions do nothing to stimulate labour market demand – the crucial factor. Related to this are broader 'age management' policies in the workplace, to achieve a better fit between specific jobs and employees as they age. The problem here is that this solution operates at the level of the individual firm, where the problem is really one of differential demand between various industrial sectors. Again, later-life working in the same job could perhaps be encouraged by more generous financial incentives to defer claiming

[17] Rowena Mason, 'Jobseekers Told They Must Take Zero-Hours Jobs', *Guardian*, 6 May 2014, www.theguardian.com
[18] Office for National Statistics, *Pension Trends. Chapter 4*, p. 16.
[19] DWP, *Older Workers 2013*, p. 17.
[20] Tony Maltby, 'The Employability of Older Workers: What Works?', in Loretto *et al.*, *The Future*; Loretto *et al.*, *Older Workers*, pp. 63–71.

the state pension – though this does nothing to counter involuntary early retirement (the major problem) and might end up merely rewarding those who were going to work later anyway.

Demand-side solutions could be tried. These would involve public investment in projects that would boost blue-collar employment (for example, improving the public transport infrastructure, or new 'green' projects – such as extending solar energy). A difficulty would of course be engaging employees of the right age and nationality. There could be more state help with the caring responsibilities borne by older people. Most radical of all would be age-based employment quotas for older people and/or employment subsidies. If working later in life is really so important to the physical and mental well-being of older people, as governments have been arguing, then they should be accorded special status via affirmative action in hiring and retention. Such a policy could founder on the issue of intergenerational equity, adding ammunition to the charges that older people have been over-favoured by governments. Nevertheless, the key question is: should sub-optimal productivity be a protected characteristic, such as to justify positive discrimination? It is in the case of disability: should this be extended to age? Finally, there are alternative fiscal incentives to later-life working, of which the most interesting has been mentioned – a basic income or citizen's income for all aged 60+, with income from employment topping this up.

The key issue that has emerged in recent years and remains unresolved is: how we can reconcile, on the one hand, the right to retirement for those who wish to retire and need to retire when aged in their sixties (notably, manual workers, those in repetitive, boring or stressful jobs, those with poor health, those with caring responsibilities, those with shorter life expectancy and so on) with, on the other hand, the right to work later in life for those who wish to do so and need to do so (involving strategies to combat age discrimination in employment and provide special help to older workers). Neoliberalism shows no interest in resolving this dilemma humanely: instead, its only concern is to flood the labour market with job-seekers. Governments today pay lip-service to choice, yet there has been little in the way of policy innovation to reconcile these two options. No positive incentives to 'nudge' people gently into working a few years later have been offered. Instead, the very opposite has taken place: people are to be forced to work later in life (if they can find work) by a withdrawal of benefits – a policy based upon the erroneous proposition (backed by dubious research and much assertion) that retirement has been caused by the incentive effect of state and private/occupational pensions. Since the requisite number of jobs will not be forthcoming, the only logical conclusion to draw is that this is essentially about creating a large reserve army of unemployed labour in order to depress wages, weaken the power of organised labour and worsen working conditions. This hard-nosed macro-economic strategy has been accompanied by soothing neoliberal mood music relating to the enhancement of rights, choice, opportunity and empowerment. What appears to be an inevitability, forced upon governments by naturalistic demographic and fiscal pressures, is actually the next chapter in the slow neoliberalisation of old age.

Bibliography

Aaron, H. J. 'Introduction', in H. J. Aaron (ed.), *Behavioral Dimensions of Retirement Economics* (Washington, D.C., 1999).

'Retirement, Retirement Research, and Retirement Policy', in H. J. Aaron (ed.), *Behavioral Dimensions of Retirement Economics* (Washington, D.C., 1999).

Aaron, H. J. and Burtless, G. 'Introduction and Summary', in H. J. Aaron and G. Burtless (eds.), *Retirement and Economic Behaviour* (Washington, D.C., 1984).

Aaron, H. J. and Callan, J .M. *Who Retires Early?* (Chestnut Hill, MA, 2011).

Abrams, D. and Houston, D. M. *Equality, Diversity and Prejudice in Britain: Results from the 2005 National Survey* (Canterbury, 2006).

Abrams, D., Russell, P. S., Vauclair, C. M. and Swift, H. *Ageism in Europe: Findings from the European Social Survey* (London, 2011).

Abrams, M. 'Changes in the Life-styles of the Elderly, 1959–1982', in UK Central Statistical Office, *Social Trends No.14 1984 Edition* (London, 1984).

Ackerman, B. A. *Social Justice in the Liberal State* (New Haven, CT, 1980).

Acton Society Trust, *Retirement: A Study of Current Attitudes and Practices* (London, 1960).

'Age-Analysis of Employed Persons', *Ministry of Labour Gazette*, LIX, 6, June 1951, p. 224.

Age Concern, *Age of Equality? Outlawing Age Discrimination Beyond the Workplace* (London, 2007).

Age Concern England, *How Ageist is Britain?* (London, 2005).

Age Concern and Help the Aged, *Insurance and Age: Exploring Behaviour, Attitudes and Discrimination* (London, 2007).

Age Scotland, *What is Ageism?* n.d., www.ageuk.org.uk/scotland

Age UK, *A Snapshot of Ageism in the UK and Across Europe* (London, 2011).

Later Life in the United Kingdom (London, 2014).

Agiesta, J. 'Angels: Nearly 8 in 10 Americans Believe These Ethereal Beings Are Real', 23 Dec. 2011, www.huffingtonpost.com

'Alan Milburn Says Child Poverty "No Longer Problem of the Workless and Work-shy"', BBC News, 17 Oct. 2013, www.bbc.co.uk

Alford, B. W. E. *Britain in the World Economy Since 1880* (New York, 1996).

'America's Aging Workforce', AARP Brief No. 3, March 1991, p. 9 (Washington, D.C., 1991).

Americans for Generational Equity, 'Mission Statement and Plan of Action', c. 2007, www.americanbenefitscouncil.org

'An Increase in Earlier Retirement for Men', *Employment Gazette*, April 1980, pp. 366–369.

Arthur, S. *Money, Choice and Control: The Financial Circumstances of Early Retirement* (Bristol, 2003).

Article 1, *The Universal Declaration of Human Rights*, 1948, www.un.org./en/documents/udhr

Atchley, R. C. *The Sociology of Retirement* (New York, NY, 1976).

Atkinson, A. B. *State Pensions for Today and Tomorrow* (London, 1994).

Atkinson, W. 'Anthony Giddens as Adversary of Class Analysis', *Sociology*, 41, 3, Jun. 2007, pp. 533–549.

Atkisson, A. 'Equity Between Generations. An Interview with Sam Preston', *Caring for Families*, Spring 1989, pp. 26–31, www.context.org

Bagilhole, B. *Understanding Equal Opportunities and Diversity: The Social Differentiations and Intersections of Inequality* (Bristol, 2009).

Banfield, E. *The Moral Basis of a Backward Society* (Glencoe, IL, 1958).

Banton, M. P. *Discrimination* (Buckingham, 1994).

Bardasi, E., Jenkins, S. P. and Rigg, J. A. 'Retirement and the Income of Older People: A British Perspective', *Ageing and Society*, 22, 2, March 2002, pp. 131–159.

Barker, D. J. P. *Mothers, Babies and Health in Later Life* (London, 1994).

Barnard, H. and Turner, C. *Poverty and Ethnicity: A Review of the Evidence* (York, 2011).

Barnes, H. and Parry, J. 'Renegotiating Identity and Relationships: Men and Women's Adjustments to Retirement', *Ageing and Society*, 24, 2, March 2004, pp. 213–233.

Barnes, H. and Taylor, R. *Work, Saving and Retirement Among Ethnic Minorities: A Qualitative Study*, Department for Work and Pensions Research Report No. 396 (London, 2006).

Barr, N. 'Pensions: Challenges and Choices: What Next: The First Report of the Pensions Commission', London, 17 Jan. 2005, www.econ.lse.ac.uk/staff

'Retirement Age – a Good News Story', British Politics and Policy at LSE, 12 Mar. 2010, blogs.lse.ac.uk

Barrell, R., Kirby, S. and Orazgani, A. *The Macroeconomic Impact from Extending Working Lives*, Department for Work and Pensions Research Report No. 95 (London, 2011).

Barrow, B. 'Only 46% of Women Get Full Basic State Pension', *Daily Mail*, 11 Dec. 2013, www.dailymail.co.uk

Barry, N. 'Pensions and Policy-Making in Great Britain', in A. Peacock and N. Barry, *The Political Economy of Pension Provision* (Glencorse, 1986).

BBC Today Programme, 8 Apr. 2010, www.bbc.co.uk

Beatty, C., Fothergill, S. and Gore, T. *The Real Level of Unemployment 2012* (Sheffield, 2012).

Beaumont, J. 'Population', in Office for National Statistics, *Social Trends 41 2011 Edition* (London, 2011).

Becker, G. S. *The Economics of Discrimination* (Chicago, IL, 1957).

'Discrimination, Economic', in D. L. Sills (ed.), *International Encyclopedia of the Social Sciences, Vol. IV* (New York, 1968).

Becker, H. S. 'Introduction', in H. S. Becker (ed.), *Social Problems: A Modern Approach* (New York, 1966).

Beckett, F. *What Did the Baby Boomers Ever Do for Us?* (London, 2010).

Bengtson, V. L. 'Generation and Family Effects in Value Socialisation', *American Sociological Review*, 40, 3, June 1975, pp. 358–371.

'Will "Generational Accounting" Doom the Welfare State?', *The Gerontologist*, 33, 6, 1993, pp. 812–816.

'Is the "Contract Across Generations" Changing? Effects of Population Aging on Obligations and Expectations Across Age Groups', in V. L. Bengtson and W. A. Achenbaum (eds.), *The Changing Contract Across Generations* (Hawthorne, NY, 1993).

Bengtson, V. L., Furlong, M. J. and Laufer, R. S. 'Time, Aging and the Continuity of the Social Structure: Themes and Issues in Generational Analysis', *Journal of Social Issues*, 30, 2, Spring 1974, pp. 1–30.

Berger, B. M. 'How Long Is a Generation?', *British Journal of Sociology*, 11, 1, March 1960, pp. 10–23.

Berry, C. *The Future of Retirement*, International Longevity Centre-UK Discussion Paper (London, 2010).

Bevin, E. *My Plan for 2,000,000 Workless* (London, 1933).

Biggs, S. *The Mature Imagination: Dynamics of Identity in Midlife and Beyond* (Buckingham, 1999).

Bingham, J. 'Scientology is a Religion, Rules Supreme Court', *Telegraph*, 11 Dec. 2013, www.telegraph.co.uk

Binstock, R. H. 'From Compassionate Ageism to Intergenerational Conflict?', *The Gerontologist*, 50, 5, October 2010, pp. 574–585.

Black, C. *Working for a Healthier Tomorrow* (London, 2008).

Blackburn, R. *Banking on Death* (London, 2002).

Blackley, W. L. 'National Insurance: A Cheap, Practical, and Popular Means of Abolishing Poor Rates', *Nineteenth Century*, 4, November 1878, pp. 834–857.

'Blackstone Group', 2014, www.sourcewatch.org

Blaikie, A. 'The Emerging Political Power of the Elderly in Britain 1908–1948', *Ageing and Society*, 10, 1, March 1990, pp. 17–39.

Blair, T. 'Speech to Labour Party Conference', 1 Oct. 1999, www.bbc.co.uk

Blekesaune, M., Bryan, M. and Taylor, M. *Life-course Events and Later-life Employment*, Department for Work and Pensions Research Report No. 502 (London, 2008).

Blondal, S. and Scarpetta, S. *The Retirement Decision in OECD Countries* (Paris, 1999).

Blundell, R. and Johnson, P. 'Pensions and Retirement in the United Kingdom', in J. Gruber and D. Wise (eds.), *Social Security and Retirement Around the World* (Chicago, IL, 1999).

Blundell, R., Meghir, C. and Smith, S. 'Pension Incentives and the Pattern of Early Retirement', *Economic Journal*, 112, 478, March 2002, pp. C153–C170.

Blyth, M. *Great Transformations. Economic Ideas and Institutional Change in the Twentieth Century* (Cambridge, 2002).

Bone, J. and Mercer, S. *Flexible Retirement* (London, 2000).

Bone, M., Gregory, J., Gill, J. and Lader, D. *Retirement and Retirement Plans: A Survey Carried Out by the Social Survey Division of OPCS on Behalf of the Department of Social Security* (London, 1992).

Booth, C. *Old Age Pensions and the Aged Poor: A Proposal* (New York, 1899).

Bosanquet, H. *The Strength of the People: A Study in Social Economics* (London, 1902).

Boskin, M. J. 'Social Security and Retirement Decisions', *Economic Inquiry*, XV, 1, Jan. 1977, pp. 1–25.

Bourdieu, P. and Wacquant, L. 'NewLiberalSpeak: Notes on the New Planetary Vulgate', *Radical Philosophy*, 105, Jan/Feb. 2001, pp. 2–5.

Bowcott, O. 'Conservatives Pledge Powers to Ignore European Court of Human Rights Rulings', *Guardian*, 3 Oct. 2014, www.theguardian.com

Brabrook, E. 'Old-Age Pensions', in J. St. L. Strachey (ed.), *The Manufacture of Paupers: A Protest and a Policy* (London, 1907).

Burkhauser, R. V. and Quinn, J. F. 'Is Mandatory Retirement Overrated? Evidence from the 1970s', *Journal of Human Resources*, 18, 3, Summer 1983, pp. 337–358.

Burnett, J. *Generations: The Time Machine in Theory and Practice* (Farnham, 2010).

Burtless, G. 'An Economic View of Retirement', in H. J. Aaron (ed.), *Behavioral Dimensions of Retirement Economics* (Washington, D.C., 1999).

'Introduction and Summary', in G. Burtless (ed.), *Work, Health, and Income Among the Elderly* (Washington, D.C., 1987).

Bury, M. 'Arguments About Ageing: Long Life and its Consequences', in N. Wells and C. Freer (eds.), *The Ageing Population: Burden or Challenge?* (London, 1988).

Butler, R. N. 'Age-Ism: Another Form of Bigotry', *The Gerontologist*, 9, 4, 1, Winter 1969, pp. 243–246.

Butricia, B. A., Murphy, D. P. and Zedlewski, S. R. 'How Many Struggle to Get By in Retirement?', *The Gerontologist*, 50, 4, August 2010, pp. 482–494.

Butterworth, M. 'Plans to Raise State Pension Age Not Radical Enough, Says Lord Turner', *Telegraph*, 3 July 2009, www.telegraph.co.uk

Bytheway, B., *Ageism* (Buckingham, 1995).

Unmasking Age: The Significance of Age for Social Research (Bristol, 2011).

Bytheway, B., Ward, R., Holland, C. and Peace, S. *Too Old: Older People's Accounts of Discrimination, Exclusion and Rejection* (London, 2007).

Cabinet Office. Performance and Innovation Unit, *Winning the Generation Game: Improving Opportunities for People Aged 50–65 in Work and Community Activity* (London, 2000).

Cahill, D., Edwards, L. and Stilwell, F. (eds.), *Neoliberalism: Beyond the Free Market* (Cheltenham, 2012).

Callinicos, A. *Equality* (Cambridge, 2000).

Capaldi, N. 'Affirmative Action: Con', in A. G. Mosley and N. Capaldi, *Affirmative Action: Social Justice or Unfair Preference?* (Lanham, MD, 1996).

Cardarelli, R., Sefton, J. and Kotlikoff, L. J. 'Generational Accounting in the UK', *Economic Journal*, 110, 467, Nov. 2000, pp. 547–574.

Carr-Saunders, A. M., Jones, D. C. and Moser, C. A. *A Survey of Social Conditions in England and Wales as Illustrated by Statistics* (London, 1958 edn.).

Carstairs, V. 'Our Elders', in R. F. A. Shegog (ed.), *The Impending Crisis of Old Age: A Challenge to Ingenuity* (Oxford, 1981).

Castella, T. D. 'Have Young People Never Had it So Bad?', *BBC News Magazine*, 5 Feb. 2013, www.bbc.co.uk

Central Statistical Office, *Annual Abstract of Statistics No. 99 1962* (London, 1962).

Annual Abstract of Statistics No. 109 1972 (London, 1972).

Social Trends No. 3 1972 (London, 1972).

Chamberlain, Neville to Duncan C. Fraser, 20 May 1924, National Archives TNA PIN 1/4.

Chang, H. J. *23 Things They Don't Tell You about Capitalism* (London, 2010).

Chapman, J. 'Millions More to Wait Until 68 for Pension', *Daily Mail*, 19 July 2010, www.dailymail.co.uk

'"People Are Living Longer So it's Time to Pay Up": Government Remains Defiant in Face of Strike Over Pension Reforms', *Daily Mail*, 18 June 2011, www.dailymail.co.uk

Charles, E. *The Twilight of Parenthood: A Biological Study of the Decline of Population Growth* (London, 1934).

Chorley, M. 'Today's Tots Could "Live to be 120"', *Independent*, 31 July 2011, www.independent.co.uk

Clark, F. Le Gros *Pensioners in Search of a Job* (London, 1969).

Clark, F. Le Gros and Dunne, A. C. *Ageing in Industry* (London, 1955).

Clark, N. 'Britain's Pensioners Aren't Being Served by Policy Changes that Date from 1979', *Guardian*, 1 Dec. 2013, www.theguardian.com

Clarke, L. *Discrimination* (London, 1995).

Cockett, R. *Thinking the Unthinkable: Think Tanks and the Economic Counter-Revolution, 1931–1983* (London, 1994).

Cole, T. R. *The Journey of Life: A Cultural History of Aging in America* (Cambridge, 1992).

'Generational Equity in America: A Cultural Historian's Perspective', *Social Science and Medicine*, 29, 3, 1989, pp. 377–383.

Commission on Social Justice, *Social Justice: Strategies for National Renewal. The Report of the Commission on Social Justice* (London, 1994).

Connor, S. 'Ageism "Bigger Problem Than Racism or Sexism"', *Independent*, 7 Sept. 2005, www.independent.co.uk

Cordery, S. *British Friendly Societies, 1750–1914* (Basingstoke, 2003).

Costa, D. L. *The Evolution of Retirement: An American Economic History, 1880–1990* (Chicago, IL, 1998).

Craig, F. W. S. *British General Election Manifestos 1900–1974* (London, 1975).

Conservative and Labour Party Conference Decisions 1945–1981 (Chichester, 1982).

Cribier, F. 'Changes in Life Course and Retirement in Recent Years: The Example of Two Cohorts of Parisians', in P. Johnson, C. Conrad and D. Thomson (eds.), *Workers Versus Pensioners: Intergenerational Justice in an Ageing World* (Manchester, 1989).

Crimmins, E. M., Hayward, M. D. and Saito, Y. 'Changing Mortality and Morbidity Rates and the Health Status and Life Expectancy of the Older Population', *Demography*, 31, 1, Feb. 1994, pp. 159–175.

Crouch, C. *Post-Democracy* (Cambridge, 2004).

The Strange Non-Death of Neoliberalism (Cambridge, 2011).

Crouch, K. A. 'Late Life Job Displacement', *The Gerontologist*, 38, 1, 1998, pp. 7–17.

Crystal, S. *America's Old Age Crisis: Public Policy and the Two Worlds of Aging* (New York, 1982).

Cumming, E. and Henry, W. E. *Growing Old: The Process of Disengagement* (New York, 1961).

Daguerre, A. 'New Corporate Elites and the Erosion of the Keynesian Social Compact', *Work, Employment and Society*, 28, 2, Apr. 2014, pp. 323–334.

Daniels, N. 'Justice and Transfers Between Generations', in P. Johnson, C. Conrad and D. Thomson (eds.), *Workers Versus Pensioners: Intergenerational Justice in an Ageing World* (Manchester, 1989).

'David Cameron Suggests Cutting Benefits for under-25s', BBC News, 2 Oct. 2013, www.bbc.co.uk

Dean, M. 'Free Economy, Strong State', in D. Cahill, L. Edwards and F. Stilwell (eds.), *Neoliberalism: Beyond the Free Market* (Cheltenham, 2012).

Department for Work and Pensions, *Simplicity, Security and Choice: Working and Saving for Retirement*, Cm. 5677 (London, 2002).

A New Deal for Welfare: Empowering People to Work, Cm. 6730 (London, 2006).

Building a Society for All Ages, Cm. 7655 (London, 2009).

Older Workers Statistical Information Booklet. Quarter Two 2010 (London, 2010).

'20-year-olds Three Times More Likely to Reach 100 than their Grandparents', DWP Press Release, 4 August 2011, www.dwp.gov.uk

Older Workers Statistical Information Booklet 2013 (London, 2013).

Households Below Average Income: An Analysis of the Income Distribution 1994/5–2012/13 (London, 2014).

Fuller Working Lives – A Framework for Action (London, 2014).

Fuller Working Lives – Background Evidence (London, 2014).

The Pensioners' Incomes Series: United Kingdom, 2012/13 (London, 2014).

Department of Employment and Productivity, *British Labour Statistics Historical Abstract 1886–1968* (London, 1971).

Department of Health and Social Security, *A Happier Old Age: A Discussion Document on Elderly People in Our Society* (London, 1978).

Growing Older, Cmnd. 8173 (London, 1981).

Reform of Social Security, Vol. I, Cmnd. 9517 (London, 1985).

Social Security Statistics, 1986 (London, 1986).

Department of Trade and Industry, *Age Legislation Fact Sheet No. 1* (London, 2006).

Dickens, L. 'The Road is Long: Thirty Years of Equality Legislation in Britain', *British Journal of Industrial Relations*, 45, 3, Sept. 2007, pp. 463–494.

Disney, R., Grundy, E. and Johnson, P. (eds.), *The Dynamics of Retirement: Analyses of the Retirement Surveys* (London, 1997).

Dryzek, J. S., Honig, B. and Phillips, A. (eds.), *The Oxford Handbook of Political Theory* (Oxford, 2006).

Dublin, L. I. *Health and Wealth: A Survey of the Economics of World Health* (New York, 1928).

Dumenil, G. and Levy, D. 'The Crisis of Neoliberalism as a Stepwise Process: From the Great Contraction to the Crisis of Sovereign Debts', in D. Cahill, L. Edwards and F. Stilwell (eds.), *Neoliberalism: Beyond the Free Market* (Cheltenham, 2012).

Duncan, C. 'The Dangers and Limitations of Equality Agendas as a Means for Tackling Old-Age Prejudice', *Ageing and Society*, 28, 8, Nov. 2008, pp. 1133–1158.

Dworkin, R. *Taking Rights Seriously* (London, 1977).

Easterlin, R. A., Macunovich, D. J. and Crimmins, E. M. 'Economic Status of the Young and Old in the Working-Age Population, 1964 and 1987', in V. L. Bengtson and W. A. Achenbaum (eds.), *The Changing Contract Across Generations* (Hawthorne, NY, 1993).

Ekerdt, D. J. and Hackney, J. K. 'Workers' Ignorance of Retirement Benefits', *The Gerontologist*, 42, 4, 2002, pp. 543–551.

'The End of Retirement', *Economist*, 27 June–3 July 2009.

Epstein, R. *Forbidden Grounds: The Case Against Employment Discrimination Laws* (Cambridge, MA, 1992).

Equality and Human Rights Commission, 'Commission Welcomes Outlawing of Age Discrimination', 2008, www.equalityhumanrights.com

Equal Opportunities Commission, *Equalising the Pension Age* (London, 1978).

Estes, C. L. *The Aging Enterprise* (San Francisco, CA, 1979).

Estes, C. L., Biggs, S. and Phillipson, C. *Social Theory, Social Policy and Ageing* (Maidenhead, 2003).

Eurostat news release, 'EU27 Population is Expected to Peak by around 2040', 8 June 2011, ec.europa.eu/eurostat

Evandrou, M. 'Introduction', in M. Evandrou (ed.), *Baby Boomers: Ageing in the 21st Century* (London, 1997).

Evandrou, M. and Glaser, K. 'Combining Work and Family Life: The Pension Penalty of Caring', *Ageing and Society*, 23, 5, Sept. 2003, pp. 583–602.

Falkingham, J. 'Dependency and Ageing in Britain: A Re-Examination of the Evidence', *Journal of Social Policy*, 18, 2, Apr. 1989, pp. 211–33.

'Who Are the Baby Boomers? A Demographic Profile', in M. Evandrou (ed.), *Baby Boomers: Ageing in the 21st Century* (London, 1997).

Feldman, G. and Gartenberg, M. (eds.), *Protest: The Beat Generation and the Angry Young Men* (London, 1958).

Feldstein, M. 'The Economics of the New Unemployment', *The Public Interest*, 33, Fall 1973, pp. 3–42.

'Social Security, Induced Retirement, and Aggregate Capital Accumulation', *Journal of Political Economy*, 82, 5, Sep./Oct. 1974, pp. 905–926.

'Toward a Reform of Social Security', *The Public Interest*, 40, Summer 1975, pp. 75–95.

'Facing the Social Security Crisis', *The Public Interest*, 47, Spring 1977, pp. 88–100.

'The Social Security Explosion', *The Public Interest*, 81, Fall 1985, pp. 94–106.

(ed.), *Privatizing Social Security* (Chicago, IL, 1998).

Ferguson, N. 'The Rule of Law and its Enemies', The Reith Lectures, BBC Radio 4, broadcast 19 June 2012, www.bbc.co.uk

Field, F. and Owen, M. *Private Pensions for All: Squaring the Circle* (London, 1993).

Fleming, S. 'Pensioners "Better off than Most" as Working Parents Take Brunt of Cuts', *The Times*, 23 Mar. 2012, www.thetimes.co.uk

Fogarty, M. P. *Retirement Age and Retirement Costs* (London, 1980).

Foner, A. 'Age Integration or Age Conflict as Society Ages?', *The Gerontologist*, 40, 3, 2000, pp. 272–276.

Foner, N. *Ages in Conflict: A Cross-Cultural Perspective on Inequality Between Old and Young* (New York, 1984).

'When the Contract Fails: Care for the Elderly in Nonindustrial Cultures', in V. L. Bengtson and W. A. Achenbaum (eds.), *The Changing Contract Across Generations* (Hawthorne, NY, 1993).

'Forbes 400', 2013, www.forbes.com

Foresight (Ageing Population Panel), *The Age Shift – Priorities for Action* (London, 2000).

Foster, L. 'Towards a Fairer Pension System for Women? Assessing the Impact of Recent Pension Changes on Women', in K. Farnsworth, Z. Irving and M. Fenger (eds.), *Social Policy Review 26: Analysis and Debate in Social Policy, 2014* (Bristol, 2014).

Francis, D. R. 'Social Security Causes Earlier Retirement', National Bureau of Economic Research Press Release, 24 Feb. 2014, www.nber.org

Friedman, M. *Capitalism and Freedom* (Chicago, IL, 1962).

Fries, J. F. 'Aging, Natural Death and the Compression of Morbidity', *New England Journal of Medicine*, 303, 3, 17 July 1980, pp. 130–135.

'The Compression of Morbidity', *Milbank Memorial Fund Quarterly/Health and Society*, 61, 3, Summer 1983, pp. 397–419.

Fries, J. F., Bruce, B. and Chakravarty, E. 'Compression of Morbidity 1980–2011: A Focused Review of Paradigms and Progress', *Journal of Aging Research*, 2011, 10 pages.

Fullinwider, R. K. *The Reverse Discrimination Controversy: A Moral and Legal Analysis* (Totowa, NJ, 1980).

Galbraith, J. K., Wray, L. R. and Mosler, W. *The Case Against Intergenerational Accounting: The Accounting Campaign Against Social Security and Medicare* (Annandale-on-Hudson, NY, 2009).

George, S. 'How to Win the War of Ideas: Lessons from the Gramscian Right', *Dissent*, 44, 3, Summer 1997, pp. 47–53.

George, V. *Wealth, Poverty and Starvation: A World Perspective* (Brighton, 1988).

Giddens, A. *Modernity and Self-Identity* (Cambridge, 1991).

In Defence of Sociology: Essays, Interpretations and Rejoinders (Cambridge, 1996).

The Third Way: The Renewal of Social Democracy (Oxford, 1998).

The Third Way and Its Critics (Oxford, 2000).

Gilligan, A. '"Poverty Barons" Who Make a Fortune from Taxpayer-Funded Aid Budget', *Telegraph*, 15 Sept. 2012, www.telegraph.co.uk

Goldman, P. *The Welfare State* (London, 1964).

Gomes, A. M. 'I Am an Immigrant', *The Listener*, 80, 2062, 3 Oct. 1968, pp. 425–427.

Goodley, S. 'Southern Cross Care Fiasco Sheds Light on Secretive World of Private Equity', *Guardian*, 3 June 2011, www.theguardian.com

Goodwin, J. and O'Connor, H. 'Notions of Fantasy and Reality in the Adjustment to Retirement', *Ageing and Society*, 34, 4, Apr. 2014, pp. 569–589.

Gordon, C. *The Myth of Family Care? The Elderly in the Early 1930s* (London, 1988).

Gough, O. and Adami, R. 'Saving for Retirement: A Review of Ethnic Minorities in the UK', *Social Policy and Society*, 12, 1, Jan. 2013, pp. 147–161.

Gough, O. and Hick, R. 'Ethnic Minorities, Retirement Planning and Personal Accounts', *International Journal of Sociology and Social Policy*, 29, 9, 2009, pp. 488–497.

Government Equalities Office, 'Policy Paper: Equality Strategy', 2010, www.gov.uk/government/publications/equality-strategy–7

'Government Says State Pension Age is Rising Too Slowly', BBC News, 11 Sept. 2011, www.bbc.co.uk

Grady, J. 'From Beveridge to Turner: Laissez-faire to Neoliberalism', *Capital and Class*, 34, 2, 2010, pp. 163–180.

'Trade Unions and the Pension Crisis: Defending Member Interests in a Neoliberal World', *Employee Relations*, 35, 3, 2013, pp. 294–308.

'Grandparents Will Pay More to Fund Grandchildren's University Education, Says New Study', *UCU News*, 9 Oct. 2013, www.ucu.org.uk

Grattan, P. 'Ageing and Employment: Looking Back, Looking Forward', in L. Bauld, K. Clarke and T. Maltby (eds.), *Social Policy Review 18: Analysis and Debate in Social Policy* (Bristol, 2006).

Gregory, R. F. *Age Discrimination in the American Workplace: Old at a Young Age* (New Brunswick, NJ, 2001).

Grice, A. 'Miliband: Young Jobseekers Must Train or Lose Their Benefits', *Independent*, 18 June 2014, www.independent.co.uk

Gruber, J. and Wise, D. 'Introduction and Summary', in J. Gruber and D. Wise (eds.), *Social Security and Retirement Around the World* (Chicago, IL, 1999).

Gruenberg, E. M. 'The Failures of Success', *Milbank Memorial Fund Quarterly/Health and Society*, 55, 1, 1977, pp. 3–24.

Haber, C. and Gratton, B. *Old Age and the Search for Security: An American Social History* (Bloomington, IN, 1994).

Hammarstrom, G. 'The Constructions of Generation and Cohort in Sociological Studies of Ageing: Theoretical Conceptualisations and Some Empirical Implications', in B. M. Oberg, A. L. Narvanen, E. Nasman and E. Olsson (eds.), *Changing Worlds and the Ageing Subject* (Aldershot, 2004).

Hannah, L. *Inventing Retirement: The Development of Occupational Pensions in Britain* (Cambridge, 1986).

Harding, T. *Rights at Risk: Older People and Human Rights* (London, 2005).

Harris, B., Gorsky, M., Guntupalli, A. and Hind, A. 'Sickness Insurance and Welfare Reform in England and Wales, 1870–1914', in B. Harris (ed.), *Welfare and Old Age in Europe and North America: The Development of Social Insurance* (London, 2012).

Harris, R. and Seldon, A. *Over-Ruled on Welfare* (London, 1979).

Harvey, D. *A Brief History of Neoliberalism* (Oxford, 2005).

Hausman, J. A. and Pacquette, L. 'Involuntary Early Retirement and Consumption', in G. Burtless (ed.), *Work, Health and Income Among the Elderly* (Washington, D.C., 1987).

Hawkes, A. 'Blackstone Denies Blame for Southern Cross's Plight', *Guardian*, 2 June 2011, www.theguardian.com

Helm, T. 'Osborne's Cuts Shape the Economy and the Future Role of the State Too', *Guardian*, 23 June 2013, www.theguardian.com

Hendrick, H. *Images of Youth: Age, Class and the Male Youth Problem, 1880–1920* (Oxford, 1990).

Hewitt, E. S. 'Industrial Retirement Plans As Viewed by Management', in G. B. Hurff (ed.), *Economic Problems of Retirement: A Report on the Fourth Annual Southern Conference on Gerontology held at the University of Florida January 1954* (Gainesville, FL, 1954).

Hills, J. 'Does Britain Have a Welfare Generation?', in A. Walker (ed.), *The New Generational Contract: Intergenerational Relations, Old Age and Welfare* (London, 1996).

Hills, J., Brewer, M., Jenkins, S., Lister, R., Lupton, R., Machin, S., Mills, C., Modood, T., Rees, T. and Riddell, S. *An Anatomy of Economic Inequality in the UK: Report of the National Equality Panel* (London, 2010).

Hirsch, D. *Crossroads After 50: Improving Choices in Work and Retirement* (York, 2003).

Hohman, H. F. *The Development of Social Insurance and Minimum Wage Legislation in Great Britain* (Boston, MA, 1933).

Hood, A. and Joyce, R. *The Economic Circumstances of Cohorts Born between the 1940s and the 1970s* (London, 2013).

Hotopp, U. 'The Ageing Workforce: A Health Issue?', *Economic and Labour Market Review*, 1, 2, Feb. 2007, pp. 30–35.

House of Commons Debates, 5s, 183, 28 April 1925, Cols. 77–79.

House of Commons Library, *National Insurance Contributions: An Introduction* (London, 2014).

House of Lords. Select Committee on Economic Affairs, *Aspects of the Economics of an Ageing Population: Vol. I – Report* (London, 2003).

Howe, G. *Conflict of Loyalty* (London, 1995).

Howker, E. and Malik, S. *Jilted Generation: How Britain Has Bankrupted Its Youth* (London, 2010).

Howse, K. 'Updating the Debate on Intergenerational Fairness in Pension Reform', *Social Policy and Administration*, 41, 1, 2007, pp. 50–64.

'Review of Longevity Trends to 2025 and Beyond', January 2009, *Beyond Current Horizons* (Department for Children, Schools and Families), www.beyondcurrenthorizonz.org.uk

Hudson, R. 'Preface', in R. B. Hudson (ed.), *Boomer Bust? Economic and Political Issues of the Graying Society, Volume II: The Boomers and Their Future* (Westport, CT, 2009).

Hughes, D. 'Thatcher's Work-to-70 Plan for the Old', *Sunday Times*, 29 Jan. 1989.

Hunt, E. H. 'Paupers and Pensioners: Past and Present', *Ageing and Society*, 9, 4, Dec. 1989, pp. 407–430.

'Income Tax Revenue Could be Lower than Expected, Finance Watchdog Says', *Guardian*, 13 Oct. 2014, www.theguardian.com

Inman, P. 'Retirements to Spike in 2012 Due to Postwar Passions', *Guardian*, 21 Sept. 2010, www.theguardian.com

'Debt and Housing Costs Make Young Worse Off than Past Generations', *Guardian*, 5 Aug. 2014, www.theguardian.com

'Intergenerational Foundation', 2014, www.intergenerational.org.uk

International Longevity Centre-UK, *Choosing Population Projections for Public Policy* (London, 2009).

Institute of Economic Affairs, *Work Longer, Live Healthier* (London, 2013).

Ipsos MORI, 'How Britain Voted in 2010', 2010, www.ipsos-mori.com

Iremonger, F. A. *William Temple. Archbishop of Canterbury. His Life and Letters* (Oxford, 1948).

Irving, P., Steels, J. and Hall, N. *Factors Affecting the Labour Market Participation of Older Workers: Qualitative Research* (Leeds, 2005).

Jacobs, A. L. *Pursuing Equal Opportunities: The Theory and Practice of Egalitarian Justice* (Cambridge, 2004).

Jagger, C., Matthews, R. and Lindesay, J. 'Compression of Disability? Morbidity and Disability in Older People to 2030', in New Dynamics of Ageing, *Modelling Needs and Resources of Older People to 2030* (London, 2010), www.lse.ac.uk/collections/MAP2030

Jamieson, A. 'State Pension Age Could Climb to 70', *Telegraph*, 8 Aug. 2009, www.telegraph.co.uk

Jerrome, D. 'Ties That Bind', in A. Walker (ed.), *The New Generational Contract: Intergenerational Relations, Old Age and Welfare* (London, 1996).

Johns, N. Book review, *Social Policy and Administration*, 44, 5, Oct. 2010, pp. 641–643.

Johnson, P. 'The Structured Dependency of the Elderly: A Critical Note', in M. Jefferys (ed.), *Growing Old in the Twentieth Century* (London, 1989).

'The Employment and Retirement of Older Men in England and Wales, 1881–1981', *Economic History Review*, XLVII, 1, 1994, pp. 106–128.

Johnson, P., Conrad, C. and Thomson, D. 'Introduction', in P. Johnson, C. Conrad and D. Thomson (eds.), *Workers Versus Pensioners: Intergenerational Justice in an Ageing World* (Manchester, 1989).

Johnson, P. *The Pensions Dilemma* (London, 1994).

Joseph Rowntree Foundation, *Tackling Poverty Across All Ethnicities in the UK* (York, 2014).

Judy, R. W. and D'Amico, C. *Workforce 2020: Work and Workers in the 21st Century* (Indianapolis, IN, 1997).

Kaye, T. S. 'Divided by a Common Language: Why the British Adoption of the American Anti-Discrimination Model Did Not Lead to an Identical Approach to Age Discrimination Law', *Journal of International Aging, Law and Policy*, 4, 2009, pp. 17–97.

Keynes, J. M. 'Economic Possibilities for Our Grandchildren' (1930), in J. M. Keynes, *Essays in Persuasion* (London, 1931).

Klare, M. T. *Blood and Oil: The Dangers and Consequences of America's Growing Petroleum Dependency* (New York, 2004).

Knoll, M. 'Behavioural and Psychological Aspects of the Retirement Decision', *Social Security Bulletin*, 71, 4, 2011, pp. 15–32, www.ssa.gov

Kohli, M. 'Ageing as a Challenge for Sociological Theory', *Ageing and Society*, 8, 4, Dec. 1988, pp. 367–394.

'Ageing and Justice', in R. H. Binstock and L. K. George (eds.), *Handbook of Aging and the Social Sciences*, 6th edn. (New York, 2006).

'Generational Equity: Concepts and Attitudes', in C. Arza and M. Kohli (eds.), *Pension Reform in Europe: Politics, Policies and Outcomes* (London, 2008).

Koppelman, A. *Antidiscrimination Law and Social Equality* (New Haven, CT, 1996).

Kotlikoff, L. J. *Generational Accounting: Knowing Who Pays, and When, for What We Spend* (New York, 1992).

Kotlikoff, L. and Sachs, J. 'Privatizing Social Security: It's High Time to Privatize', *The Brookings Review*, Summer 1997, pp. 16–22.

Kramer, M. S. 'The Rising Pandemic of Mental Disorders and Associated Chronic Diseases and Disabilities', *Acta Psychiatrica Scandinavia*, 62, 1980 (Suppl. 283), pp. 382–397.

Kymlicka, W. *Contemporary Political Philosophy: An Introduction* (2002).

Labour Party, *Security in Retirement* (London, 1996).

Laczko, F. and Phillipson, C. *Changing Work and Retirement: Social Policy and the Older Worker* (Buckingham, 1991).

Lamont, N. *In Office* (London, 1999).

Laslett, P. and Fishkin, J. S. 'Introduction: Processional Justice', in P. Laslett and J. S. Fishkin (eds.), *Justice Between Age Groups and Generations* (New Haven, CT, 1992).

Laws, D., Alexander, D. and Oakeshott, M. *Reforming UK Pensions: Liberal Democrat Proposals* (London, 2005).

Layard, R. *More Jobs, Less Inflation: The Case for a Counter-Inflation Tax* (London, 1982).

How to Reduce Unemployment by Changing National Insurance and Providing a Job-Guarantee (London, 1985).

How to Beat Unemployment (Oxford, 1986).

What Labour Can Do (London, 1997).

Layard, R. and Nickell, S. 'Unemployment in Britain', in C. R. Bean, P. R. G. Layard and S. J. Nickell (eds.), *The Rise in Unemployment* (Oxford, 1986).

Layard, R. and Philpott, J. *Stopping Unemployment* (London, 1991).

Layard, R., Nickell, S. and Jackman, R. *Unemployment, Macroeconomic Performance and the Labour Market* (Oxford, 1991).

Layard, R., Nickell, S. and Jackman, R. *The Unemployment Crisis* (Oxford, 1995 edn.).

Lazear, E. P. 'Why Is There Mandatory Retirement?', *Journal of Political Economy*, 87, 6, Dec. 1979, pp. 1261–1284.

'Comment', in G. Burtless (ed.), *Work, Health and Income Among the Elderly* (Washington, D.C., 1987).

Lemann, N. *The Promised Land: The Great Black Migration and How it Changed America* (New York, 1991).

Leonesio, M. V. 'Social Security and Older Americans', in O. S. Mitchell (ed.), *As the Workforce Ages: Costs, Benefits and Policy Challenges* (Ithaca, NY, 1993).

'The Economics of Retirement: A Nontechnical Guide', *Social Security Bulletin*, 59, 4, Winter 1996, pp. 29–50.

Levine, M. L. *Age Discrimination and the Mandatory Retirement Controversy* (Baltimore, MD, 1988).

Light, P. *Baby Boomers* (New York, 1988).

Littlewood, M. 'Work on Into Your 70s. It Will be Good for You', *The Times*, 16 May 2013.

Loch, C. S. 'Pauperism and Old-Age Pensions', in B. Bosanquet (ed.), *Aspects of the Social Problem* (London, 1895).

Lockhart, J. G. *Cosmo Gordon Lang* (London, 1949).

Longman, P. *Born to Pay: The New Politics of Aging in America* (Boston, MA, 1987).

'Justice Between Generations', *Atlantic Monthly*, June 1985, www.theatlantic. com

Lopatto, E. 'Life Expectancy in the US Drops for First Time Since 1993, Report Says', *Bloomberg*, 9 Dec. 2010, www.bloomberg.com.news

Loretto, W., Vickerstaff, S. and White, P. *Older Workers and Options for Flexible Work* (Manchester, 2005).

Lukes, S. *Power: A Radical View* (New York, 2005).

Lusardi, A. 'Information, Expectations and Savings for Retirement', in H. J. Aaron (ed.), *Behavioral Dimensions of Retirement Economics* (Washington, D.C., 1999).

Lyon, D. *Postmodernity* (Buckingham, 1994).

Mabbett, D. 'The Second Time as Tragedy? Welfare Reform under Thatcher and the Coalition', *Political Quarterly*, 84, 1, Jan.–Mar. 2013, pp. 43–52.

Macaulay, T. B. *Warren Hastings*, edited by A. D. Innes (Cambridge, 1916).

Mackay, T. 'National Pensions', *Charity Organisation Review*, 8, 88, Apr. 1892, pp. 125–133.

'Old Age Pensions and the State', *Charity Organisation Review*, 121, Feb. 1895, pp. 37–51.

Methods of Social Reform (London, 1896).

Macnicol, J. 'Old Age and Structured Dependency', in M. Bury and J. Macnicol (eds.), *Aspects of Ageing: Essays on Social Policy and Old Age* (Egham, 1990), ch. 3.

'Ageing and Justice', *Labour History Review*, 55, 1, Spring 1990, pp. 75–80.

The Politics of Retirement in Britain 1878–1948 (Cambridge, 1998).

'Introduction', in J. Macnicol (ed.), *Paying for the Old: Old Age and Social Welfare Provision, Vol. I: The 19th-century Origins* (Bristol, 2000).

'Retirement', in J. Mokyr (ed.), *Oxford Encyclopedia of Economic History, Vol. IV* (Oxford, 2003).

'Analysing Age Discrimination', in B. M. Oberg, A. L. Narvanen, E. Nasman and E. Olsson (eds.), *Changing Worlds and the Ageing Subjects* (Aldershot, 2004).

'The Age Discrimination Debate in Britain and the USA: From the 1930s to the Present', *Social Policy and Society*, 4, 3, July 2005, pp. 295–302.

'Retirement in an Ageing Society: The British Debate', *Progressive Politics*, 4, 2, Summer 2005, pp. 44–49.

'Age Discrimination in History', in L. Bauld, K. Clarke and T. Maltby (eds.), *Social Policy Review 18: Analysis and Debate in Social Policy 2006* (Bristol, 2006).

Age Discrimination: An Historical and Contemporary Analysis (Cambridge, 2006).

'The American Experience of Age Discrimination Legislation', in W. Loretto, S. Vickerstaff and P. White (eds.), *The Future for Older Workers: New Perspectives* (Bristol, 2007).

'Older Men and Work in the Twenty-first Century: What Can the History of Retirement Tell Us?', *Journal of Social Policy*, 37, 4, Oct. 2008, pp. 579–595.

'Differential Treatment by Age: Age Discrimination or Age Affirmation?', in R. B. Hudson (ed.), *Boomer Bust? Economic and Political Issues in the Graying Society, Vol. I: Perspectives on the Boomers* (Westport, CT, 2009).

'Ageism and Age Discrimination: Some Analytical Issues', 2010, www.ilcuk.org.uk

'Action Against Age Discrimination: USA and UK Comparisons', National Academy on an Aging Society, *Public Policy and Ageing Report*, 22, 3, Summer 2012, pp. 21–24.

'The History of Work-Disability', in C. Lindsay and D. Houston (eds.), *Disability Benefits, Welfare Reform and Employment Policy* (Basingstoke, 2013).

'Intergenerational Equity: Historical Reconstructions', in C. Torp (ed.), *Challenges of Aging: Retirement, Pensions, and Intergenerational Justice* (Houndmills, 2015).

Mainous III, A. G., Tanner, R. J., Baker, R., Zayas, C. E. and Harle, C. A. 'Prevalence of Prediabetes in England from 2003 to 2011: Population-based, Cross-sectional Study', *BMJ Open*, 9, June 2014, bmjopen.bmj.com

Malik, S. 'The Dependent Generation: Half Young European Adults Live With Their Parents', *Guardian*, 24 March 2014, www.theguardian.com

Maltby, T. 'The Employability of Older Workers: What Works?', in W. Loretto, S. Vickerstaff and P. White (eds.), *The Future for Older Workers: New Perspectives* (Bristol, 2007).

Mann, K. *Approaching Retirement: Social Divisions, Welfare and Exclusion* (Bristol, 2001).

'Activation, Retirement Planning and Restraining the "Third Age"', *Social Policy and Society*, 6, 3, July 2007, pp. 279–292.

Mannheim, K. 'The Problem of Generations', in K. Mannheim, *Essays on the Sociology of Knowledge. Collected Works Volume Five*, edited by P. Kecskemeti (London, 1957).

Manton, K. G. 'Changing Concepts of Morbidity and Mortality in the Elderly Population', *Milbank Memorial Fund Quarterly*, 60, 2, Spring 1982, pp. 183–244.

'The Dynamics of Population Aging: Demography and Policy Analysis', *Milbank Quarterly*, 69, 2, Spring 1991, pp. 309–338.

Manton, K. G. and Soldo, B. J. 'Dynamics of Health Changes in the Oldest Old', *Milbank Memorial Fund Quarterly*, 63, 2, Spring 1985, pp. 206–285.

Marshall, T. H. 'Citizenship and Social Class', in T. H. Marshall, *Sociology at the Crossroads and Other Essays* (London, 1963).

Mason, A. *Levelling the Playing Field: The Idea of Equal Opportunity and its Place in Egalitarian Thought* (Oxford, 2006).

Mason, R. 'Jobseekers Told They Must Take Zero-Hours Jobs', *Guardian*, 6 May 2014, www.theguardian.com

McConnell, S. R. 'Age Discrimination in Employment', in H. S. Parnes (ed.), *Policy Issues in Work and Retirement* (Kalamazoo, MI, 1983).

McKinsey & Company, *Cracking the Consumer Retirement Code* (New York, 2006).

Meadows, P. *Early Retirement and Income in Later Life* (Bristol, 2002).

Retirement Ages in the UK: A Review of the Literature (London, 2003).

Means, R. and Smith, R. *The Development of Welfare Services for Elderly People* (Beckenham, 1985).

Ministry of Labour and National Service, *Employment of Older Men and Women* (London, 1952).

Minkler, M. 'Scapegoating the Elderly: New Voices, Old Theme', *Journal of Public Health Policy*, 18, 1, 1997, pp. 8–12.

Moffitt, R. A. 'Life-cycle Labour Supply and Social Security: A Time-series Analysis', in G. Burtless (ed.), *Work, Health, and Income Among the Elderly* (Washington, D.C., 1987).

Morris, N. 'Lord Freud: Tory Welfare Minister Apologises after Saying Disabled People are "Not Worth" the Minimum Wage', *Independent*, 15 Oct. 2014, www.independent.co.uk

Morrison, M. H. and Barocas, V. S. 'The Aging Work Force – Human Resource Implications', in The Ageing Society Project, *Human Resource Implications of an Ageing Work Force* (New York, 1984).

Moynihan, D. P. *Family and Nation* (San Diego, CA, 1986).

Mullan, P. *The Imaginary Time Bomb: Why an Ageing Population is Not a Social Problem* (London, 2000).

Murphy, M. 'The "Golden Generations" in Historical Context', *British Actuarial Journal*, 15, Supplement, 2009, pp. 151–184.

Murray, C. *Losing Ground: American Social Policy, 1950–1980* (New York, 1984).

'Does Welfare Bring More Babies?', *The Public Interest*, 115, Spring 1994, pp. 17–30.

Myles, J. 'Postwar Capitalism and the Extension of Social Security into a Retirement Wage', in M. Weir, A. S. Orloff and T. Skocpol (eds.), *The Politics of Social Policy in the United States* (Princeton, NJ, 1988).

National Advisory Committee on the Employment of Older Men and Women. First Report, Cmd. 8963 (London, 1953).

Second Report, Cmd. 9628, (London, 1955).

National Association of Pension Funds, *Towards Equality in Retirement Ages* (London, 1977).

Towards a Citizen's Pension (London, 2005).

National Bureau of Economic Research, 'About the NBER', 2014, www.nber. org

'National Bureau of Economic Research', 2010, www.sourcewatch.org

National Center for Health Statistics, *Health, United States, 2012: With Special Feature on Emergency Care* (Hyattsville, MD, 2013).

National Pensioners Convention Briefing, *Single Tier State Pension* (London, 2013).

Nelson T. (ed.), *Ageism: Stereotyping and Prejudice Against Older Persons* (Cambridge, MA, 2002).

Nesbitt, S. M. *British Pensions Policy Making in the 1980s: The Rise and Fall of a Policy Community* (Aldershot, 1995).

Neugarten, B. L. 'Age Distinctions and Their Social Functions', in D. A. Neugarten (ed.), *The Meanings of Age: Selected Papers of Bernice L. Neugarten* (Chicago, IL, 1996).

'The End of Gerontology?' in D. A. Neugarten (ed.), *The Meanings of Age: Selected Papers of Bernice L. Neugarten* (Chicago, IL, 1996).

'The Young-old and the Age-irrelevant Society' (1979), in D. A. Neugarten (ed.), *The Meanings of Age: Selected Papers of Bernice L. Neugarten* (Chicago, IL, 1996).

Neugarten, B. L., Moore, J. W. and Lowe, J. C. 'Age Norms, Age Constraints, and Adult Socialisation', in D. A. Neugarten (ed.), *The Meanings of Age: Selected Papers of Bernice L. Neugarten* (Chicago, IL, 1996).

Neville, S. '£1bn Gamble of the Care Home Sharks Revealed: Southern Cross Predators Sold Off Almost 300 Homes to RBS', *Daily Mail*, 4 June 2011, www.dailymail.co.uk

Nuffield Foundation, *Old People: Report of a Survey Committee on the Problems of Ageing and the Care of Old People Under the Chairmanship of B. Seebohm Rowntree* (London, 1947).

Oeppen, J. and Vaupel, J. W. 'Broken Limits to Life Expectancy', *Science*, 296, 10 May 2002, pp. 1029–1031.

Office for National Statistics, *Social Focus on Older People* (London, 1999).

National Population Projections 1996-based (London, 1999).

Social Trends No. 37, 2007 Edition (London, 2007).

Social Trends No. 41, 2011 Edition (London, 2011).

UK Interim Life Tables 1980–2 to 2008–10 (London, 2011).

Pension Trends. Chapter 2: Population Change (London, 2012).

Pension Trends. Chapter 4: The Labour Market and Retirement, 2013 Edition (London, 2013).

Pension Trends. Chapter 5: State Pensions, 2013 Edition (London, 2013).

Pension Trends. Chapter 7: Private Pension Scheme Membership, 2013 Edition (London, 2013).

Life Expectancy at Birth and at Age 65 for Local Areas in England and Wales,
2010–12 (London, 2013).
'2011 Census', 7 Feb. 2014, www.ons.gov.uk
The Effects of Taxes and Benefits on Household Income, 2012/13 (London, 2014).
National Life Tables, United Kingdom, 2010–2012 (London, 2014).
Underemployment and Overemployment in the UK, 2014 (London, 2014).
Office of the Deputy Prime Minister. Social Exclusion Unit, *A Sure Start to Later Life. Ending Inequalities for Older People: A Social Exclusion Unit Final Report* (London, 2006).
Olshansky, S. J. and Ault, A. B. 'The Fourth Stage of the Epidemiologic Transition: The Age of Delayed Degenerative Diseases', *Milbank Quarterly*, 64, 3, 1986, pp. 355–391.
Olshansky, S. J., Passaro, D. J., Hershow, R. C., Layden, J., Carnes, B. A., Brody, J., Hayflick, L., Butler, R. N., Allison, D. B., and Ludwig, D. S., 'A Potential Decline in Life Expectancy in the United States in the 21st Century', *New England Journal of Medicine*, 325, 11, 17 March 2005, pp. 1138–1145.
O'Neill, G. 'The Baby Boom Age Wave: Population Success or Tsunami?' in R. B. Hudson (ed.), *Boomer Bust? Economic and Political Issues of the Graying Society, Vol. I: Perspectives on the Boomers* (Westport, CT, 2009).
Organisation for Economic Co-operation and Development, 'Gross and Net Pension Replacement Rates', in OECD, *Pensions at a Glance 2013: OECD and G20 Indicators* (2013), www.oecd-library.org
Pensions at a Glance 2011: Retirement-income Systems in OECD and G20 Countries (2010), www.oecd-library.org
Pensions at a Glance 2013: OECD and G20 Indicators (2013), www.oecd-library.org
'Osborne: "System Would Have Collapsed Without My Pension Age Rise"', *Telegraph*, 6 Dec. 2013, www.telegraph.co.uk
Padilla, E. 'Intergenerational Equity and Sustainability', *Ecological Economics*, 41, 2002, pp. 69–83.
Palmore, E. B. *Ageism: Negative and Positive* (New York, 1990).
'Compulsory Versus Flexible Retirement: Issues and Facts', *The Gerontologist*, 12, 4, Winter 1972, pp. 343–348.
'Is Age Discrimination Bad?', *The Gerontologist*, 46, 6, 2006, pp. 848–850.
Palmore, E. B. and Manton, K. 'Ageism Compared to Racism and Sexism', *Journal of Gerontology*, 28, 3, 1973, pp. 363–369.
Park, A., Clery, E., Curtice, J., Phillips, M. and Utting, D. *British Social Attitudes: The 29th Report. 2012 Edition* (London, 2012).
Parnes, H. S. 'The Retirement Decision', in M. E. Borus, H. S. Parnes, S. H. Sandell and B. Seidman (eds.), *The Older Worker* (Madison, WI, 1988).
Paterson, G. 'The Caring for the Old that Leaves Me Cold', *Sunday Telegraph*, 10 Jan. 1988.
Pearson, M. 'The Transition from Work to Retirement (1)', *Occupational Psychology*, 31, 2, Apr. 1957, pp. 80–88.
'The Transition from Work to Retirement (2)', *Occupational Psychology*, 31, 3, July 1957, pp. 139–149.
Pelling, H. *Winston Churchill* (London, 1974).

Pemberton, H. 'Politics and Pensions in Post-war Britain', in H. Pemberton, P. Thane and N. Whiteside (eds.), *Britain's Pensions Crisis: History and Policy* (London, 2006).

'Pension Age Could Rise to 68 Quicker Under Cameron', *Daily Mail*, 23 Sept. 2009, www.dailymail.co.uk

Pensions Commission, *Pensions. Challenges and Choices: The First Report of the Pensions Commission* (London, 2004), www.pensionscommission.org.uk

A New Pension Settlement for the Twenty-First Century: The Second Report of the Pensions Commission (London, 2005), www.pensionscommission.org.uk

Implementing an Integrated Package of Pension Reforms: The Final Report of the Pensions Commission (London, 2006), www.pensionscommission.org.uk

Peterson, P. G. 'The Morning After', *The Atlantic Monthly*, Oct. 1987, www.theatlantic.com

Peter G. Peterson Foundation, 'Peter G. Peterson', 2014, pgpf.org/board/peter-g-peterson

Phillipson, C. *Ageing* (Cambridge, 2013).

Phillipson, C. and Smith, A. *Extending Working Life: A Review of the Research Literature* (London, 2005).

Piachaud, D. 'Social Justice and Public Policy: A Social Policy Perspective', in G. Craig, T. Burchardt and D. Gordon (eds.), *Social Justice and Public Policy: Seeking Fairness in Diverse Societies* (Bristol, 2008).

Piachaud, D., Macnicol, J. and Lewis, J. *A Think Piece on Intergenerational Equity* (London, 2009).

Pickering, A. *Pensions Policy: How Government Can Get Us Saving Again* (London, 2004).

Pierson, C. 'The Welfare State: From Beveridge to Borrie', in H. Fawcett and R. Lowe (eds.), *Welfare Policy in Britain: The Road from 1945* (London, 1999).

Pilcher, J. 'Mannheim's Sociology of Generations: An Undervalued Legacy', *British Journal of Sociology*, 45, 3, Sept. 1994, pp. 481–495.

Piven, F. F. and Cloward, R. A. *The New Class War: Reagan's Attack on the Welfare State and its Consequences* (New York, 1982).

Platt, L. *Inequality Within Ethnic Groups* (York, 2011).

Political and Economic Planning, *The Exit from Industry* (London, 1935).

Employment Group Memorandum, 'A Retirement Policy for Industry', London, 21 Jan. 1935, Political and Economic Planning Archives, British Library of Political and Economic Science WG 3/5.

Pollock, I. 'Autumn Statement: Wait Longer for Your State Pension', BBC News, 5 Dec. 2013, www.bbc.co.uk

Press Association, 'Women's Pensions "a National Scandal"', *Guardian*, 20 Oct. 2004, www.theguardian.com

Press cutting from *Yorkshire Evening Post*, 11 Feb. 1937, Beveridge Papers XII 15.

Preston, S. 'Children and the Elderly: Divergent Paths for America's Dependents', *Demography*, 21, 4, Nov. 1984, pp. 435–457.

Price, D. 'Closing the Gender Gap in Retirement Income: What Difference Will Recent UK Pension Reforms Make?', *Journal of Social Policy*, 36, 4, Oct. 2007, pp. 561–583.

'Towards a New Pension Settlement? Recent Pension Reform in the UK', in T. Maltby, P. Kennett and K. Rummery (eds.), *Social Policy Review 20: Analysis and Debate in Social Policy, 2008* (Bristol, 2008).

Price, D. and Livsey, L. 'Financing Later Life: Pensions, Care, Housing Equity and the New Politics of Old Age', in G. Ramia, K. Farnsworth and Z. Irving (eds.), *Social Policy Review 25. Analysis and Debate in Social Policy, 2013* (Bristol, 2013).

Prudential Press Release, 'Expected Retirement Incomes Hit Five-Year Low', 11 Jan. 2012, www.prudential.co.uk

'2 in 5 Retirees Support Their Families Financially', Apr. 2013, www. prudential.co.uk

Prynn, J. '£100,000 Deposit to Buy a First Home', *Evening Standard*, 24 Jan. 2013.

Quadagno, J. 'Generational Equity and the Politics of the Welfare State', *Politics and Society*, 17, 3, Sept. 1989, pp. 353–376.

Quinn, J. F. 'Work and Retirement: How and Why Older Americans Leave the Labor Force', Boston College Working Paper 743 (Chestnut Hill, MA, 2010).

Quinn, J. F. and Burkhauser, R. V. 'Work and Retirement', in R. H. Binstock and L. K. George (eds.), *Handbook of Aging and the Social Sciences*, 3rd edn. (San Diego, CA, 1990).

Quinn, J. F. and Kozy, M. 'The Role of Bridge Jobs in the Retirement Transition: Gender, Race and Ethnicity', *The Gerontologist*, 36, 3, 1996, pp. 363–372.

Rawls, J. *A Theory of Justice* (Cambridge, MA, 1971).

Ray, S., Sharp, E. and Abrams, D. *Ageism: A Benchmark of Public Attitudes in Britain* (London, 2006).

Report of the Committee on the Economic and Financial Problems of the Provision for Old Age, Cmd. 9333 (London, 1954).

Report of the Royal Commission on Population, Cmd. 7695 (London, 1949).

Report of the Unemployment Assistance Board for the Year Ended 31st December 1937, Cmd. 5752 (London, 1938).

The Retirement Income Inquiry, *Pensions: 2000 and Beyond, Vol. 1* (London, 1996).

Rice, D. P. and Feldman, J. J. 'Living Longer in the United States: Demographic Changes and Health Needs of the Elderly', *Milbank Memorial Fund Quarterly*, 61, 3, Summer 1983, pp. 362–396.

Richardson, I. M. *Age and Need: A Study of Older People in North-East Scotland* (Edinburgh, 1964).

Robbins, L. *The Great Depression* (London, 1934).

Roberts, N. *Our Future Selves* (London, 1970).

Robson, W. A. 'Introduction: Present Principles', in W. A. Robson (ed.), *Social Security* (London, 1943).

Rogers, S. and Sedghi, A. 'UK GDP since 1955', *Guardian*, 25 Oct. 2013, www. theguardian.com

Rones, P. L. 'Using the CPS to Track Retirement Among Older Men', *Monthly Labor Review*, 108, Feb. 1985, pp. 46–49.

Rowntree, B. S. *Poverty and Progress: A Second Social Survey of York* (London, 1941).

Ruddick, G. 'John Lewis to Cut Back Gold-Plated Pension Scheme', *Telegraph*, 30 Jan. 2014, www.telegraph.co.uk

Runciman, W. G. *Relative Deprivation and Social Justice* (London, 1972).

Sahlgren, G. H. *Income from Work – the Fourth Pillar of Income Provision in Old Age. IEA Discussion Paper No. 52* (London, 2014).

Samuelson, P. *Economics: An Introductory Analysis* (New York, 1958).

Sandell, S. H. 'Introduction', in S. H. Sandell (ed.), *The Problem Isn't Age: Work and Older Americans* (New York, 1987).

Sargeant, M. (ed.), *Age Discrimination and Diversity* (Cambridge, 2011).

Saunders, P. *The Rise of the Equalities Industry* (London, 2011).

Scales, J. and Scase, R. *Fit and Fifty?* (Swindon, 2000).

Scottish Widows UK Ninth Annual Pensions Report, *Retirement Savings Across the Nation* (Edinburgh, 2013).

Shenfield, B. E. *Social Policies for Old Age: A Review of Social Provision for Old Age in Great Britain* (London, 1957).

Sheppard, H. L. 'Work Continuity Versus Retirement: Reasons for Continuing Work', in R. Morris and S. A. Bass (eds.), *Retirement Reconsidered: Economic and Social Roles for Older People* (New York, 1988).

Sheppard, H. L. and Rix, S. E. *The Graying of America: The Coming Crisis in Retirement-Age Policy* (New York, 1977).

Shildrick, T., MacDonald, R., Furlong, A., Roden, J. and Crow, R. *Are 'Cultures of Worklessness' Passed Down the Generations?* (York, 2012).

Shock, N. W. *Trends in Gerontology* (Stanford, CA, 1951).

Smeaton, D. and Vegeris, S. *Older People Inside and Outside the Labour Market: A Review* (Manchester, 2009).

Smeaton, D., Vegeris, S. and Sahin-Dikmen, M. *Older Workers: Employment Preferences, Barriers and Solutions* (Manchester, 2009).

Smith, A. *The Theory of Moral Sentiments* (London, 1759).

The Wealth of Nations, edited by Edwin Cannan (London, 1961).

Social Insurance and Allied Services, Cmd. 6404 (London, 1942).

Solow, R. M. 'On the Intergenerational Allocation of Natural Resources', *Scandinavian Journal of Economics*, 88, 1986, pp. 141–149.

Sontag, S. 'The Double Standard of Aging', in V. Carver and P. Liddiard (eds.), *An Ageing Population: A Reader and Sourcebook* (Sevenoaks, 1978).

Sowell, T. *Markets and Minorities* (New York, 1981).

Spijker, J. and MacInnes, J. 'Population Ageing: the Timebomb That Isn't?', *British Medical Journal*, 347, f6598, 12 Nov. 2013, www.bmj.com

Spitzer, A. B. 'The Historical Problem of Generations', *American Historical Review*, 78, 1973, pp. 1353–1385.

Squires, J. 'Equality and Difference' in J. S. Dryzek, B. Honig, and A. Phillips (eds.), *The Oxford Handbook of Political Theory* (Oxford, 2008).

Steventon, A. and Sanchez, C. *The Under-pensioned: Disabled People and People from Ethnic Minorities* (London, 2008).

Taylor, P. and Walker, A. 'Intergenerational Relations in the Labour Market: the Attitudes of Employers and Older Workers', in A. Walker (ed.), *The*

New Generational Contract: Intergenerational Relations, Old Age and Welfare (London, 1996).

Thane, P. *Old Age in English History: Past Experiences, Present Issues* (Oxford, 2000).

'Social Histories of Old Age and Ageing', *Journal of Social History*, 37, 1, Fall 2003, pp. 93–111.

Thatcher, M. 'Speech to Conservative Party Conference', Brighton, 1980, www.margaretthatcher.org

Thompson, P., Itzin, C. and Abendstern, M. *I Don't Feel Old: The Experience of Later Life* (Oxford, 1990).

Thomson, D. *Selfish Generations? How Welfare States Grow Old* (Cambridge, 1996).

'The Decline of Social Welfare: Falling State Support for the Elderly since Early Victorian Times', *Ageing and Society*, 4, 4, Dec. 1984, pp. 451–482.

'The Welfare State and Generation Conflict: Winners and Losers', in P. Johnson, C. Conrad and D. Thomson (eds.), *Workers Versus Pensioners: Intergenerational Justice in an Ageing World* (Manchester, 1989).

'A Lifetime of Privilege? Aging and Generations at Century's End', in V. L. Bengtson and W. A. Achenbaum (eds.), *The Changing Contract Across Generations* (New York, 1993).

Thurow, L. 'The Birth of a Revolutionary Class', *New York Times Magazine*, 19 May 1996.

Titmuss, R. M. *Problems of Social Policy* (London, 1950).

'Social Administration in a Changing Society', in R. M. Titmuss, *Essays on 'The Welfare State'* (London, 1958).

'Pension Systems and Population Change', in R. M. Titmuss, *Essays on 'The Welfare State'* (London, 1958).

Titmuss, R. M. and Titmuss, K. *Parents Revolt* (London, 1942).

Townsend, P. 'The Structured Dependency of the Elderly: A Creation of Social Policy in the Twentieth Century', *Ageing and Society*, 1, 1, March 1981, pp. 5–28.

'Persuasion and Conformity: An Assessment of the Borrie Report on Social Justice', *New Left Review*, 213, Sept.–Oct. 1995, pp. 137–150.

Townsend, P. and Walker, A. *The Future of Pensions: Revitalising National Insurance* (London, 1995).

Trades Union Congress, *Pensions Watch 2013: A TUC Report on Directors' Pensions in the UK's Top Companies* (London, 2013).

Travis, A. 'Margaret Thatcher's Role in Plan to Dismantle Welfare State Revealed', *Guardian*, 28 Dec. 2012, www.theguardian.com

Tuckman, J. and Lorge, I. 'Attitudes Toward Old People', *Journal of Social Psychology*, 37, May 1953, pp. 249–260.

Turgeon, L. *State and Discrimination: The Other Side of the Cold War* (Armonk, NY, 1989).

United Nations Development Programme, *Human Development Index* (2014), hdr.undp.org

U.S. Bureau of the Census, *Statistical Abstract of the United States: 1986* (Washington, D.C., 1985).

De Vaus, V., Wells, Y., Kendig, H. and Quine, S. 'Does Gradual Retirement Have Better Outcomes than Abrupt Retirement? Results from an Australian Panel Study', *Ageing and Society*, 267, 5, Sept. 2007, pp. 667–682.

Verbrugge, L. M. 'Longer Life But Worsening Health? Trends in Health and Mortality of Middle-aged and Older Persons', *Milbank Memorial Fund Quarterly*, 62, 3, Summer 1984, pp. 475–519.

'Recent, Present, and Future Health of American Adults', *Annual Review of Public Health*, 10, 1989, pp. 333–361.

Vickerstaff, S., Baldock, J., Cox, J. and Keen, L. *Happy Retirement? The Impact of Employers' Policies and Practice on the Process of Retirement* (Bristol, 2004).

Vickerstaff, S., Loretto, W., Billings, J., Brown, P., Mitton, L., Parkin, T. and White, P. *Encouraging Labour Market Activity Among 60–64 Year Olds* (London, 2008).

Victor, C. R. *Health and Health Care in Later Life* (Milton Keynes, 1991).

Ageing, Health and Care (Bristol, 2010).

Wacquant, L. *Punishing the Poor: The Neoliberal Government of Social Insecurity* (Durham, NC, 2009).

Waddell, G. and Burton, A. K. *Is Work Good for Your Health and Well-being?* (London, 2006).

Waine, B. 'Paying for Pensions', in H. Jones and S. MacGregor (eds.), *Social Issues and Party Politics* (London, 1998).

Walker, A. 'Towards a Political Economy of Old Age', *Ageing and Society*, 1, 1, March 1981, pp. 73–94.

'The Politics of Ageing in Britain', in C. Phillipson, M. Bernard and P. Strang (eds.), *Dependency and Interdependency in Old Age: Theoretical Perspectives and Policy Alternatives* (London, 1986).

'Intergenerational Relations and the Provision of Welfare', in A. Walker (ed.), *The New Generational Contract: Intergenerational Relations, Old Age and Welfare* (London, 1996).

Walker, P. 'Half of UK Men Could be Obese by 2030', *Guardian*, 26 Aug. 2011, www.theguardian.com

Wall, R. 'Intergenerational Relationships Past and Present', in A. Walker (ed.), *The New Generational Contract: Intergenerational Relations, Old Age and Welfare* (London, 1996).

Warnes, A. M. 'The Ageing of Populations', in A. M. Warnes (ed.), *Human Ageing and Later Life: Multidisciplinary Perspectives* (London, 1989).

Ward, R. and Bytheway, B. (eds.), *Researching Age and Multiple Discrimination* (London, 2008).

Wearden, G. 'Brown Vows to Keep Inflation Under Control', *Guardian*, 6 July 2007, www.theguardian.com

West, A. and Pennell, H. *Underachievement in Schools* (London, 2003).

White, S. *Equality* (Cambridge, 2007).

Whiting, E. 'The Labour Market Participation of Older People', *Labour Market Trends*, 112, 6, July 2005, pp. 285–296.

Willetts, D. *The Age of Entitlement* (London, 1993).

The Pinch: How the Baby Boomers Took Their Children's Future – and Why They Should Give it Back (London, 2010).

Williamson, J. B. and Watts-Roy, D. M. 'Framing the Generational Equity Debate', in J. B. Williamson, D. M. Watts-Roy and E. R. Kingson (eds.), *The Generational Equity Debate* (New York, 1999).

Winnett, R. 'State Pension Age to be Lifted to 67 a Decade Earlier Than Planned', *Telegraph*, 12 Sept. 2011, www.telegraph.co.uk

Wise, D. A. 'Retirement Against the Demographic Trend: More Older People Living Longer, Working Less, and Saving Less', *Demography*, 34, 1, Feb. 1997, pp. 83–95.

Woods, D. 'Three-quarters of Employees Think a Delay in UK State Pension Age is Unfair, Reveals YouGov', 8 May 2012, www.hrmagazine.co.uk

World Bank, *Averting the Old Age Crisis: Policies to Protect the Old and Promote Growth* (New York, 1994).

 How Far Are We from Ensuring Opportunities for All? The Human Opportunity Index, 2012, www.worldbank.org

 Inequality of Opportunity Hampers Development, 28 June 2012, www.worldbank. org

Young, M. and Schuller, T. *Life After Work: The Arrival of the Ageless Society* (London, 1991).

Zame, W. R. 'Can Intergenerational Equity be Operationalised?', *Theoretical Economics*, 2, 2007, pp. 187–202.

Index